PIKES PEAK

&

SOUTH PARK REGION

by

ZOLTAN MALOCSAY

2325 E. Platte Ave.
Colorado Springs, Colo. 80909

Copyright, 1983
by
Zoltan Malocsay

ISBN 0-937080-11-X

ABOUT THE AUTHOR

Zoltan Malocsay is a Phi Beta Kappa graduate of the University of Oklahoma School of Journalism and Professional Writing. While traveling as a magazine correspondent, Zoltan and his wife backpacked in Canada, the United States and Mexico, following the seasons and virtually living in a mountain tent for three years. His fiction stories appear frequently in BOY'S LIFE magazine and are reprinted in eight textbooks. His first novel, GALLOPING WIND, is a wild horse adventure published by Putnam. Zoltan and his wife reside in Colorado Springs, where they design and make fine jewelry of gold, platinum and precious gems.

ACKNOWLEDGEMENTS

The author wishes to thank the National Forest Service for all of its cooperation and the Pikes Peak Area Council of Governments for making the first edition possible. Special thanks go to Roland Gow, former executive director of the PPACG, and to all the PPACG personnel who helped out: Pat Skinner, who edited and coordinated the publication of the first draft; Dave Salamon, who prepared the final copies of maps and compiled the index; Bill Gosnell, who supervised graphics and the printing of the original edition; Dave Bamberger, who coordinated the project; Manuel Fresquez and Rodney Martinez, printers, and Patricia Denham, consultant. Thanks also to personnel of the Solar Trails Center, the El Paso County Parks Department, the City of Colorado Springs Park and Recreation Department and the Colorado State Department of Health. Local guides Robert Ormes and Monte Barrett did what they could to keep the author from getting lost, and Carl Wiese of Fountain provided horseback transport.

TABLE OF CONTENTS

TABLE OF CONTENTS

TABLE OF CONTENTS

TABLE OF CONTENTS

TABLE OF CONTENTS

TABLE OF CONTENTS

LET'S GO HIKING

LET US SHOW YOU

The hiking and horseback trails of the Pikes Peak region exist for everyones enjoyment, so the purpose of this guide is to help you enjoy them as much as possible -- with comfort and safety. We'll try to show you all the little things that a walking, talking human guide would show you, including tips on what to take along and why, what to do and what to avoid, where to go and what you'll find when you get there. We'll show you where to camp and fish, tell you a little about the plants and wildlife, about the history and geology, and we'll recommend other books that give more details. We'll also show you how to preserve and protect these delicate areas so that you and your family and friends can enjoy them -- as they are -- for years to come.

Our guide covers virtually all the trails in the three-county (El Paso, Park and Teller) region that are maintained, marked and closed to motorized vehicles. It would take another such guide to describe the routes open to motorcyclists and four-wheelers. There are many other hiking trails that we could not mention because they have become so eroded and obscure that no written guide could lead you safely there.

WHAT YOU CAN DO - - AND WHY

We'll show you where you can hike and ride horseback, picnic, daycamp or camp overnight, fish the lakes and streams (with a valid Colorado State license), explore the rocks, camp in one spot for ten days if you like, and best of all, there are no entry fees. Not all of these activities are allowed everywhere, of course, so you have to know what is allowed in which areas.

Areas that receive the heaviest use, such as park nature trails, cannot permit overnight camping, and often there are specific rules about pets, rock climbing, fires and so forth. But for those who wish to walk or ride a ways, the National Forest trails offer camping and fishing and all the other freedoms and responsibilities of backcountry. Indeed, the vast majority of our trails are in the Pike National

Forest, trails that range from one-half mile to thirty-seven miles or more in length.

Some of the most popular trails have niceties, such as bridges over streams, but backcountry hikers will be lucky to find logs across many of the streams. In these wild areas, the Forest Service offers virtually no facilities, only paths and very few signs. In the backcountry you are on your own. Your safety and your comfort are your own responsibility.

But there are other responsibilities, also. The Forest Service could never clean up after all those who use the trails, so hikers and horseriders themselves must watch over the land and protect it by careful use. This even extends to trail maintenance. If you find a rock or log on the trail, move it out of the way, if you can, to prevent a new trail from developing around the object. That's how you pay your way in the wilds.

We'll try to show you how to practice the art of "minimum impact," how to enjoy the mountains without changing anything, without ruining anything. But don't be afraid to do more than your share. If someone in your party is not behaving, then clean up after them; they might catch on. And if you see other visitors abusing YOUR forest, be cordial but don't be shy about correcting them. Many greenhorns just don't know any better or don't believe that anyone cares.

Right now there are only a few rules for those trails marked with a Forest Service trail number. You may not pick or dig up wildflowers or other plants, may not carve or paint on rocks, may not cut on living trees or plants; may not remove moss or take souvenirs. You are welcome to look and touch and smell and take photographs, but you are asked to leave everything in its place, to treat the forest as a living museum.

HIKING WITH OUR GUIDE

Our guide offers every kind of trail, so plan your expedition around the weakest member of your party. Try not to take friends and loved ones on a hike that is so difficult that they will never want to go hiking or riding with you again.

We present our trails in order of location to keep from repeating the same road directions for different trails in the same area. Each section begins with road directions to the trailheads, then is followed by descriptions of the individual trails.

Our maps cannot show every dip and bump, of course, so a series of switchbacks may be symbolized by a single switchback, and this points up the problem of estimating trail lengths. The Forest Service is only now beginning to measure its trails as they exist on the ground, so many of the trail lengths in our guide and on the signs you find in the woods are only map estimates, which means that they are somewhat inaccurate one way or the other. Rosalie Trail is probably longer than its given length, but Barr Trail proved to be a mile shorter when measured with a trailwheel (12 instead of 13 miles).

This compounds the problem of calculating hiking time, especially since individuals differ greatly in speed and purpose. As a rule of thumb, realize that many hikers figure on making only one mile per hour packing uphill. Check your own speed against this, and you will be able to estimate your own travel time better than we can.

Always tell someone where you are going, and when you expect to return. Of course, sign all trail registers and take along the equipment we recommend because your comfort and safety depend on it.

TRAILRIDING WITH OUR GUIDE

Visitors to our area should consider using local horses rather than bringing horses from lower altitudes because mounts have to be conditioned for the high country, just as people do. Even mounts raised at 6,000 feet will find the air thin at 11,000 feet, so take it easy and rest your mount with the head pointing downhill to help circulation. An anxious horse can expend so much energy in the first hour that it may never be able to recover for the rest of the day, so it is especially important to hold back for the first hour or so. Horses allowed to travel at their own pace may collapse and die.

CAMPING IN THE NATIONAL FOREST

With few exceptions, you may camp along any of the National Forest trails, but the Forest Service would like you to camp with ecology in mind. Camping at the edge of water, for example, may pollute the water as well as expose you to the danger of flashflood. Above timberline you can damage plantlife by simply walking around, so try to avoid making camp above timberline. You'll find more protection in the trees anyway.

Cutting green boughs for bedding is illegal, it damages the forest and it makes a lumpy bed for your effort. Light foam pads will serve both you and the forest better.

Trenching your tent may be necessary in other parts of the country, but Colorado soil is so porous that water tends to sink straight down instead of gathering around your tent. Trenching makes ugly scars that encourage erosion.

And all camp cleaning can be done with biodegradable soaps. The same soap will wash you and your clothes and the dishes, but even biodegradable soap should not be used near streams or lakes. Nobody likes to drink your wash water.

There are other things you should know about campfires and sanitation and drinking water, and we'll cover these items in detail, but the point of all this is to enjoy the forest without leaving a mark, without changing the beauty you came to admire.

BUILDING CAMPFIRES

Campfires are an outdoor tradition that may be going the way of the buffalo robe. They are becoming illegal in more and more areas and are banned in other areas when fire danger becomes high. They scar the land, encourage vandals to cut living trees when deadwood becomes scarce; they burn up wood used for homes and food by wildlife -- and sometimes they burn down the whole forest.

If you want to sit around a roaring campfire, it would be best to visit a facility with concrete and iron firegrates. (But you might bring some wood, too, for the Forest Service cannot keep everyone supplied.)

If you wish to cook in backcountry, better get used to carrying a lightweight backpacker stove. Once you have tried one on a wet and cold morning, you won't begrudge carrying the extra 18 ounces or so. They are clean, fast, efficient and they work when open fires won't. But most of all, they protect the forest, and that is why they are becoming required in more and more areas.

FISHING

You are welcome to fish along many of the trails in our guide, unless otherwise posted, so long as you carry a valid Colorado State fishing permit and observe the laws of Colorado. Indeed, the state has stocked some of our remote mountain lakes just for the enjoyment of backpackers and trailriders, but there are some reminders:

Always wet your hands before handling fish that are to be released. Dry hands remove some of the fish's protective coating, thus opening the way for fungal growths that will kill the fish.

Never throw fish cleanings back into the water. Colorado's cold water tends to delay decomposition, thus causing pollution.

TRAIL ETIQUETTE

A great many people can share a wilderness with a sense of privacy, if everyone shows a little consideration. Good manners are essential to the kindly and relaxed atmosphere that hikers and horse riders are seeking. Try to keep your party from becoming a loud party. Loud radios and shouting are not appreciated by other hikers, and shouting may be taken as a signal for help.

Always share information with anyone who asks, and if you are being overtaken by faster hikers, step aside and let them pass. If you should meet horses on the trail, remember that they always have the right-of-way. When meeting horses on the trail, move off to the side, preferably downhill, and talk among yourselves in order to make sure that the horses know that you are there and won't be startled by a sudden encounter.

Never allow members of your party to roll or throw rocks from the trail, even if you believe that nobody is below. The fact is that you cannot be certain, for well-mannered hikers don't make much noise and may easily be killed by a rock from above. If it should happen that a rock or log or any other object falls away toward a switchback below, yell the word "Rock!" -- even if it is not a rock. This word is used because it can be yelled faster than "Look Out!" and is meant to warn that some kind of object is falling.

In some places, barriers have been erected to keep hikers from shortcutting switchbacks and slopes, but never allow anyone in your party to short-cut whether barriers exist or not. It may not seem to do much damage at the time, but the first hard rainstorm will start making a gully out of your short-cut. This kind of erosion has erased hundreds of miles of interesting trails in our region, for the soil is very young, consisting mostly of crushed granite, and the shallow-rooted plants that hold this soil together are easily damaged. Remember this whenever you leave the trail for any reason; pick the gentlest route and tread carefully.

And please pack out your garbage. Anything that you try to hide or bury will only be dug up by animals and scattered around, so please carry out your garbage and as much of anyone else's garbage that you can. Unfortunately, disposable diapers must also be carried out for the same reason; animals dig them up and then rains wash them into streams, their contents held together and somewhat preserved by the plastic. Which leads us to an essential subject, sanitation.

SANITATION

All nature requires is a little cooperation. There are no restrooms on most of these trails. So, select an area at least 50 to 100 feet from any open water or spring. With your heel, scrape out a hole no deeper than several inches. That's because the first several inches -- the biological layer -- contains a system of disposers that will break down the wastes. If you go deeper, you spoil this effect.

If there is any sod, try to keep it intact and replace it after covering the hole with dirt. Nature does the rest.

MEETING CATTLE

Parts of the National Forest are leased to ranchers as pasture, so you are bound to encounter herds of cattle on some of our trails. Cattle rarely hassle hikers who know how to handle them, but bulls or cows with calves can be very protective, so don't assume that such powerful animals will always run away from you. Even a cow may charge if she feels that you are endangering her calf.

Cattle will usually be found directly in your path because it is really their path; in such areas cattle make more trails than the Forest Service does, and you will have to navigate carefully. The best thing to do is to keep your distance and hike quietly around them. If you climb high enough and keep enough distance, they will probably be too lazy to move, and you can pass them.

Carrying a large stick may make you feel more secure, but you must be careful not to spook cattle. If you do, they will start off along the trail ahead of you. They will not be anxious to leave their trail or to climb uphill, so they will continue to block your way, stopping when you stop, moving when you move, and you could be left following in their dust for miles.

Don't assume that you can scatter them because cattle have a herding instinct that makes them tend to huddle together when frightened. And the rancher won't appreciate your running precious pounds off his cattle. So the best thing to do is leave them where you find them, and try to pass at a distance.

USING MAP AND COMPASS

If you don't know how to use a USGS topographic map, visit the Solar Trails Center on 26th Street and compare a topographic map with their large model of Pikes Peak and the Rampart Range. This will help you learn to "see" the lines on the map as peaks and valleys. The elevation lines on the map are made like layers on a cake. That is, a line is drawn at one elevation along a mountainside until the line wraps around a peak and joins itself again. Lines drawn at different elevations (usually 40 feet apart) stack up to show topography. A series of lines very close together means a steep change in altitude, whereas lines spaced farther apart mean gentler slopes. By keeping track of the elevation, you can see that V-shaped lines pointing downhill mean a ridge, and V-shaped lines pointing uphill mean a gulley. The maps will not show small features such as small cliffs and don't show whether the vegetation is open meadow or brush or forest. Learning to read topographic maps is a basic skill for serious backpacking.

Trail hikers generally find it easy to keep their bearings by following their progress along the trail on a topographic map, even without a compass. Especially important is keeping track of which drainage you are in. If you are hiking up a trail that follows a stream, you only have to follow the same stream back again to know that you aren't lost, and you know that you cannot change streams unless you hike up and over a ridge that leads to a whole new drainage.

When you use a compass, remember that in the Pikes Peak region the needle does not point to true north, but instead points to magnetic north, which is about 14 degrees east of true north. Your maps are oriented to true north, the North Pole, not to the magnetic north shown on your compass. There is a diagram at the bottom of USGS maps showing the difference between the two. If you have measured a bearing on your map of say 75 degrees, to get a compass bearing you must add about 14 degrees to get a compass bearing of 89 degrees. If you measure a bearing of 89 degrees with your compass you must subtract about 14 degrees to convert the equivalent bearing to your map. Read a book on map and compass if you're confused; go out and practice.

If you know your position, but want to find out where something else is, all you have to do is find how many degrees from true north the point is and relate that to the terrain. To find your own position, you have to sight two features on the terrain such as two mountain tops. You then transfer those sightings to the map. This mountain top is so many degrees, from true north and that one is so many degrees, so a pair of lines drawn on the map at those angles intersects right where you are. Be aware, however, that this kind of sight reference is more difficult in the mountains than on the flats, for it can be hard to tell which peak is which. The closer peaks may appear taller, even if the farther peaks are much higher in elevation.

WHAT TO TAKE ALONG -- AND WHY

Having fun in the woods is largely a matter of being prepared because an inexpensive item can make the difference between misery and joy, between safety and danger. On the other hand, the hiker who carries too much will soon be suffering under the weight, so you must pack carefully to avoid either problem. To help you do this, we have prepared a checklist of useful items for day trips and a separate list of things to be added for overnighters. Some of these items may seem odd, so we'll explain as we go.

DAYHIKER CLOTHING

Waterproofed boots or sturdy shoes with heavy lug soles are all you need for dayhikes with light equipment. Avoid sneakers, street shoes or any other type of footwear without lug soles, however, for these may cause you to slip on steep trails lubricated with fine gravel. Never wear new boots on the trail. Break them in first.

Socks. To help prevent blisters, wear two pairs, a lightweight inner sock made of soft wool, and a heavy outer pair of wool blend. Only wool continues to insulate when wet. Always wear the same types of socks when you buy the boots and each time that you wear the boots. Carry extras in a plastic bag in case the others get wet.

Poncho. Extremely important to prevent hypothermia. An inexpensive poncho may also serve as emergency tent, ground sheet, etc. Do not go without one for each member of the party.

Rain chaps. These inexpensive tubes of waterproofed nylon prevent pantlegs from becoming wet as you walk in the drizzle or as you travel through wet brush after a rain.

Trousers. In sunny weather you may want to start your hike in shorts, but take along sturdy trousers in case it gets cool.

Shirts. Multiple layers of light clothing provide more warmth and versatility than a single heavy garment, so many hikers wear a knit T-shirt in the sun and carry a long-sleeved cotton shirt for use later on.

Jacket or vest. Summer exists only in the sunshine. Overcast may send you looking for something warmer than a shirt. Down-filled items are light and warm and compress to small size.

Bandana. Can be used as washcloth, handkerchief, bandage, sling, even as a sun hat by tying knots in all four corners.

Stocking cap and gloves. For high altitudes or cool weather hiking. Optional elsewhere in summer.

DAYHIKER EQUIPMENT

Daypack. Since you will be carrying little weight, almost any sort of daypack will do.

Sunglasses and sun lotion. There is more harmful ultraviolet light at high altitude. Use a sunscreen lotion.

Lip balm with sunscreen.

Knife.

Lightweight flashlight, with fresh batteries, is necessary for dayhiking because any kind of delay might trap you on a dark trail at nightfall. Check the batteries and tape down the switch so it won't come on in the pack.

Wristwatch. Very important to pace your hike so you know when to start back.

Water purification tablets or kit. Essential to prevent parasitic infestations or other diseases.

Canteen with fresh water.

Insect repellant in small plastic bottle.

Compass. But learn how to use it.

Map or guide. Our guide has the maps you need.

Sierra cup and one instant soup mix. Building a tiny fire to make hot soup in the Sierra cup is a pleasant way to sit out a storm or a faster way to help relieve hypothermia victims.

Whistle as emergency signal.

Ice axe. Useless on many trails, essential on others. Some high altitude trails require an ice axe in spring or early summer, but you must know how to use it. If you encounter icy conditions and do not have an ice axe for each member of the party, turn back. There are plenty of safer trails.

Extra plastic bag for carrying out your trash.

Toilet paper, unrolled from tube and packed flat in plastic.

Emergency kit. You can make your own, using a plastic soap bar box or pocket-sized tackle box as a container. Take only enough of each product to last for the trip -- only four tablets of aspirin, for example, wrapped in a piece of foil with a label made by writing on adhesive tape. Things such as tweezers, scissors and a surgical blade that are often mentioned in such kits may already exist on your Swiss Army knife. The kit should include:

- Several bandaids. Take no small ones.
- Adhesive tape, rewrapped onto tiny pencil stub or pill bottle.
- Antiseptic cream in small tube.
- Aspirin for headache or muscle pain.
- Three fishhooks are usually included in case you get lost and need to seek more food.
- Dental floss to clean teeth and for use as string or emergency fishing line.
- Safety pins, three of assorted sizes.
- One gauze dressing, sealed.
- Emergency matches sealed against moisture.
- Moleskin, very important for blister protection. If your foot feels hot or tender, stop at once and apply moleskin to the area. If blister has already started, do not apply moleskin to the blister itself! Instead, cut a hole in the mole-skin about the same size and shape as the blister, then apply moleskin so the blister lies within this protective hole.

DAYHIKER FOODS

Roaming the mountains burns up energy so fast that the best way to maintain strength is to eat and eat as you go.

Indians and mountainmen relied almost entirely on jerked meat, and hikers still find that to be an excellent source of slow burning protein. Candy or sugar foods are known for quick energy, but that energy quickly fades. Nibble sugar foods slowly and constantly to keep your blood sugar level constant.

Since dayhikers aren't burdened with tents and sleeping bags and other heavy equipment, the menu may include heavy foods such as fruit, sandwiches or tinned meats.

OVERNIGHTER CLOTHING AND EQUIPMENT

Take everything listed for dayhikes. There will be only one major change in your wardrobe. If you carry a heavy backpack, you need heavy hiking boots to protect your feet and to help you carry that load. Up to a point, the more weight you carry, the stiffer must be the sole of your boot. That's why they look so clumsy and heavy, but why they work so well. Be careful to buy a pair that fits well, break them in carefully before hitting the trail, and be sure to waterproof them several times. Also take all the equipment listed for dayhikes, with the addition of a warm sleeping bag with a foam pad, a tent and a larger pack to carry it all.

Fiber-filled sleeping bags are less expensive than down and they have the advantage of drying out quickly if they get wet, but they are heavier for the warmth they supply. Down is the lightest and most compressible for the warmth provided, but you must be very careful not to let it get wet. If your down sleeping bag gets wet, you may as well start for home.

A tent is recommended because it rains a lot in summer. Many other types of shelters are available, but they usually fail in the kind of windy storm that you would most likely be sheltered from and they offer no protectin against mosquitos.

Your backpack must be chosen more carefully than a daypack because you will be hauling a lot more weight. They all feel comfortable when empty, so have the salesman load it with weight before trying it on. Be sure the frame is not too long or too short for your height. A padded hip belt will take much of the weight off the shoulder straps. And keep changing adjustments as you hike to make the pack sit differently on your body. You may never find an adjustment that feels great all the time, but the idea is to make it feel different from time to time. Do not trust your precious dry clothing to this "waterproof" backpack; use locking plastic storage bags to make sure that you have dry clothes to put on if you and that pack fall into a stream or are caught in a prolonged downpour.

All this extra weight -- tent, sleeping bag, pad, extra food -- means that you won't be able to hike as far each day, so plan your trip accordingly. Aside from sleeping bag, pad, tent and backpack, overnighter equipment should also include:

- Extra batteries for your lightweight flashlight.
- Short candle for light in tent.
- Cooking pot. Aluminum pot either one or one and one-half quart in size. Lid may serve as frying pan.
- Plastic plates. Better than aluminum for keeping your meal hot.
- Spoon for each person.
- Cup. Either Sierra cup or plastic cup.
- Scouring pad.
- Biodegradable soap. Will wash you and your pots and clothes, but do not use near steams or lakes, even though it is biodegradable.

OVERNIGHTER FOODS

The length of your stay may depend on the amount of food you can carry, so weight becomes even more important. Freeze dried foods are so much lighter that they may be well worth the price for longer trips. For example, fruit that is dried to a crisp weighs much less than the type that is dried to a leathery consistency.

Your supermarket probably carries many of the foods you need: instant soups, instant cocoa, crackers or rye crisps, nuts, raisins, candy, instant oatmeal, instant eggs made from soy, imitation bacon bits made from soy, etc. And backpacker stores offer freeze-dried meals such as Shrimp Creole and Beef Almondine that only need to be soaked in hot water, with no cooking required.

For more information on outdoor cooking, etc., see Freedom of the Hills, by the Seattle Mountaineers.

REAL DANGERS OF THE MOUNTAINS

There are some real dangers in the mountains, but not the ones you might imagine. You have little to fear from wild animals, poisonous snakes or Rocky Mountain spotted fever, but you have more chance of being stricken by hypothermia, heat prostration, altitude sickness, water parasites, or even lightning.

For example, no one has been killed by a bear in Colorado in the past 70 years or more. Rattlesnakes have been known to climb as high as timberline, but they prefer to remain below 6,000 feet and are so rare in the mountains that most experienced hikers have never seen one at higher altitudes. As for Rocky Mountain spotted fever, your chances of contracting this rare disease are much greater in flatland states such as the Carolinas, Virginia, Oklahoma, etc., where ticks are more common. The State Department of Health reports that Colorado averages only ONE case per year and that no deaths have resulted in recent years.

There is a different disease called simply "tick fever" which has symptoms about like the flu, so it is not considered as dangerous, and even more rare is a kind of tick paralysis that may occur when certain ticks remain attached to the body for more than 24 hours. This paralysis quickly fades once the tick is removed.

THE GREAT KILLER -- HYPOTHERMIA

Too many hikers don't realize that you can freeze to death in 50-degree weather, and that is why hypothermia has become such a common killer. Even worse, this condition affects the brain, so victims show poor judgement about saving themselves.

Hypothermia -- also called "exposure" -- begins when the body starts losing more heat than it generates, and two things contribute to this: inadequate food and lack of warm, dry clothing. The hiker who skips breakfast or who eats lightly on the trail soon loses the nourishment that it takes to produce heat, and after that, even sweat can dampen clothing enough to begin the chilling process. No blizzard is required. A little wind, a little overcast, especially with a sudden rain to dampen clothing, and conditions are right for another fatal mishap.

Warm sunny mornings fool many a greenhorn into believing that the Rockies are a paradise where all you need are a pair of sneakers and shorts and sunglasses, and that may be true for a while, but rain showers occur often and suddenly. The weatherman may say that no storm systems are moving into the area, but the mountains create their own local weather, and the summer forecast will still read: "Clear to partly cloudly with chance of isolated thunderstorms". And that is precisely what happens all too often: clear, then cloudy, then rainy, then clear again.

As heat radiates from hands and feet and elsewhere, the body tries to conserve warmth by concentrating circulation among the vital organs and by restricting circulation to the extremities, including the brain! Our victim may be shivering constantly, but may also insist that everything is all right. Coordination gets bad as well. When the shivers start coming in violent waves, the victim's thinking becomes even more confused, disoriented, apathetic. The victim may lose the sense or the will power to zip up a jacket, so you must watch your friends and yourself and be ready to help.

If you suspect that a friend is coming down with hypothermia, stop at once to change out of damp clothing and to eat. Make hot soup or cocoa, but do not let your friend out of your sight, even to answer a call from nature, because victims sometimes wander off into the bush and just keep going and going and never come back.

Near the end, the victim may become even more convinced that everything is all right, for the shivering STOPS, though arms and legs feel strangely stiff. Coordination is so bad that victims often stumble and hurt themselves; sometimes they walk off cliffs or just keep plodding along until the earth rushes up and hits them in the face. The victim faints, and without aid, never wakes up again.

All this may happen in as little as 30 minutes, though usually it takes longer, and recovery with hot soup and everything may take six or eight hours, so be prepared for a long wait.

Make the victim eat while changing out of wet clothing. If you have a sleeping bag along, prewarm it with someone else's body and have the victim climb in. Better yet, double up in the bag so the patient shares body heat with one or two healthy persons. You may actually rescue the rescuers this way, for other members of the party may be ready to come down with hypothermia as well.

Of course, dayhikers don't carry sleeping bags or much in the way of cooking gear, yet run the same risk of getting hypothermia, so prevention is the key. You must stay warm and dry and well nourished, which means that you must take along the minimal dayhiker gear that we recommend, even if the weather seems warm and sunny when you start, even if members of your party complain.

Hypothermia has also been known to strike the exhausted camper who climbs into a sleeping bag without eating and without changing out of sweaty underclothes. It can also strike motorists who are stranded on a cold night, even if clothing is dry, so be aware of this slow killer and take along the stuff you need to survive.

WATER PARASITES

No matter what you have read or heard, our mountain water is not safe to drink without careful treatment. No matter how beautiful it looks, no matter how cold, no matter how high the altitude, no matter how far it tumbles, wild water may carry cysts that spread giardia lamblia, a single-celled parasite that attacks both people and animals worldwide.

Giardia infests the intestinal tract, causing diarrhea, gas, vomiting, loss of appetite and loss of weight. Symptoms may come and go, returning with greater strength later, and some people contract the disease but never show symptoms, thus becoming carriers.

Other types of disease can also be contracted by drinking wild water, but giardia may be the most difficult to avoid because its cysts are so difficult to kill, and the State Heath Department warns that ALL surface water supplies must be suspected of containing giardia.

It's a good idea to carry water processed by municipal filtration plants, but since it is not possible to carry enough safe water for longer trips, backpackers must either boil or treat water with chemicals or use one of the new filter devices made for backpackers. At present, filter devices yield fairly small amounts of water and offer no protection against any virus that might be present.

Lab studies show that both virus and Giardia cysts die quickly in boiling water, but experiments have not been done at very high altitudes. Many guidebooks recommend boiling for 20 minutes, but most cook kits will boil dry in less time than that. Still, boiling seems to offer the best all-around protection against all sorts of critters, both viral and bacterial, and surely produces good tasting water. Be sure that your water achieves a rolling boil, however.

If you choose to use pills to treat water, beware that Giardia cysts are especially hard to kill in very cold water, so directions must be followed carefully. Notice, for example that TWO hydroperiodide tablets are required for each quart, if the water is to remain cold during the waiting time, but only ONE tablet is required if the water is warmed. The water will taste better, of course, if you warm it during the waiting time—so you can use less disinfectant—and then rechill the water for drinking after the waiting time is over. Be sure tablets are fresh. Both Halazone and hydroperiodide pills quickly lose strength when exposed to air, moisture or heat.

When using chemicals, be sure to wait the proper amount of time. Lemonade crystals, for example, may improve taste, but do not add any product until the waiting time is over; otherwise, the product may react with your disinfectant, nullifying its effect before the cysts are dead.

HEAT PROSTRATION AND HEAT STROKE

Weakness, dizziness, cramps and rapid pulse are signs of heat prostration, and the victim who is not helped at this stage may faint with heat stroke. This can be fatal, so get the victim out of direct sunlight, give plenty of water and apply moist cloth to face and back of neck.

You may prevent this from happening, however, by drinking plenty of water as you hike and by adjusting clothing to the rapid changes of temperature.

ALTITUDE SICKNESS

Hiking burns up so much oxygen that visitors from lower altitudes sometimes become ill from the thinner air at high altitude. Symptoms include headache, dizziness, weakness, poor appetite, nausea, impaired judgment and -- in extreme cases -- severe shortness of breath caused by pulmonary edema. The only real treatment is retreat to lower altitude.

LIGHTNING

Trees split and charred by lightning mark almost every ridge, so let these remind you to watch the clouds overhead, especially as you cross ridges or wide meadows. You will never be entirely safe, but lightning usually strikes the highest point or peak, lone trees, cliff edges, caves high in cliffs or simply the largest object in a flat area. Retreat from high or open ground if a storm threatens and wait until it passes. If you find yourself trapped in an exposed area, crouch down with your poncho forming a tent around you and wait it out.

GETTING LOST

If you stick to the trails we suggest, you should have little chance of getting lost, but just in case the worst happens, here's a lesson that might help you anywhere. Never strike out alone -- someone should always know where you are going and when you expect to be back -- and your party MUST stay together. Don't allow individuals to race ahead or straggle behind or stray off on other routes, planning to meet up later. And never ignore your own backtrail. Keep turning and looking back so you know what the trail looks like in reverse. The same piece of trail can look far different from another angle. Follow your progress on your map and use a compass to help orient yourself.

That's how you keep from getting lost, but suppose you get lost anyway. Suppose you have lost the trail entirely. The first thing to do is to sit down and think and relax. There is a great temptation to panic, to run, to wear yourself out in a frantic search, so beware of that and try to remember that your first responsibility is to take good care of yourself. Virtually all people who get lost are eventually found, either alive or dead, so the idea is to stay alive no matter how long you have to stay lost.

But think for now. Which way did you come? Getting lost in the mountains isn't like being lost in a flatland forest where you might wander any direction at all. In the mountains your routes are restricted by the lay of the land. Trails tend to follow water or ridges or hillsides, so what kind of trail was it? By looking around and by using process of elimination, you may be able to discover which way you came simply because there aren't that many choices.

But suppose that doesn't work. Well, you have to make some cool and logical decisions. How much time do you have? Estimate how long it has been since you left camp and realize that it will take even longer to get back. If the weather is turning sour or nightfall is coming on, you may not be able to make it, so use your precious daylight to prepare for night. Hole up somewhere in the most sheltered spot you can find. Collect firewood, but don't let your pack out of your sight; if you lose your pack, you're in much worse trouble. Build a tiny fire that won't use up all your firewood, the kind you can huddle over. Try to make yourself as safe and comfortable as possible.

Never try to travel at night or in the rain or in fog. Sit it out. The wilderness SOS consists of three signals of any kind repeated at regular intervals, three flashes of a mirror or shiny knife, three shouts, three whistles. Aside from noise pollution, one of the reasons why hikers are asked not to shout in the woods is to make it easier to distinguish between calls for help and general monkey business.

But let's suppose that you have enough daylight to climb to a high lookout and still can't fathom which way to turn. In that case, the best way to go is the safest way, for the only thing worse than being lost is being hurt and lost. Never start down into a canyon or gorge that seems to be at your feet; you may trap yourself in a treacherous spot. Instead, follow the gentlest route, no matter which way it leads. Follow a ridge down to the timber, then look for any kind of game trail that leads downhill. That will take you to water. Once you have found a stream, you have found a route to civilization, for virtually all the water that drains from these mountains is used by people below. You may wind up in a different town or a different ranch than you hoped, but you won't be lost.

The only exception to this in the area our guidebook covers is the Lost Creek Scenic Area, where Lost Creek disappears into box canyons, running under cliffs and reappearing from caves in rocks beyond. This is very unusual geology and is cause for extra caution when hiking the trails near Lost Creek.

If you are injured and lost, try to make it to a clear area or a promontory of some kind where you can build a signal fire in daylight with wood and green boughs. Above all, remember that YOU WILL BE FOUND, either alive or dead, so concentrate on staying alive, no matter how long you have to stay lost.

FINDING OUT ABOUT: WILDFLOWERS, TREES MUSHROOMS, BIRDS AND MAMMALS

WILDFLOWERS

The meadows of Jones Park in the Cheyenne Canyon area used to boast colorful stands of the orange wood lily and the white mariposa lily, but unfortunately these and other wildflower varieties have disappeared from the meadow, probably because of human misuse. That is why you are asked not to pick or dig up wildflowers anywhere along our trails; the law forbids it, too.

Lightweight field guides with color photos include: Alpine Wildflowers of the Rocky Mountains, by Bettie W. Willard and Chester O. Harris; Mountain Wildflowers of Colorado and Adjacent Areas, A Denver Museum pictorial by Rhoda Roberts and Ruth Ashton Nelson; and Colorado Wildflowers, a Denver Museum pictorial by Harold and Rhoda Roberts.

TREES

Part of the magic of altitude is the way that trees tend to change in layers as you move up the mountains. Gambel's oak, pinon pine and juniper dominate the foothills, but at 6,000 feet the ponderosa pine and Douglas fir begin. At 7,000 feet the forest includes blue spruce, which is the Colorado State Tree, along with fir and pine and aspen. At 9,000 feet you find Englemann spruce, aspen, bristlecone pine, limber pine and corkbark fir. Near 11,500 feet the hardiest of these grow dwarfed and stunted, and above that altitude, you reach "timberline," where no trees grow.

The altitude of timberline is lower as you progress northward, so it reaches sea level at the Arctic Circle. This explains why the tundra found above timberline on our high mountains is the same sort of tundra found at the Arctic Circle.

Handbooks on trees of the region include: Rocky Mountain Trees, by Richard J. Preston, Jr.; and Western Forest Trees, by James Berthold Barry.

MUSHROOMS

So many different kinds of colors of mushrooms appear alongside these trails that you may be curious to know more about them. Some are bright red or yellow; some are shaggy or sticky or smooth; some have sponge-like undersides instead of gills.

The Denver Museum of Natural History has published a paperback guide with full color photos. Its called Mushrooms of Colorado and Adjacent Areas, by Mary Hallock Wells and D. H. Mitchel.

BIRDS

If you should see a small gray bird at streamside peering intently into the water, stop and watch. That may be a "dipper" about to take a plunge. The dipper dives headfirst into streams and sometimes actually walks around underwater, hunting for food. This is only one of the fascinating birds that inhabit the region.

Field books include: Birds of Rocky Mountain National Park, by Allegra Collister, which is an inexpensive guide with black and white photos that covers most of the birds found in our region; A Field Guide to Western Birds, by Roger T. Peterson; and Field Guide to North American Birds of the Western Region, by Miklos D. F. Udvardy. Both of the latter guides are sponsored by the Audubon Society and have color photos.

MAMMALS

The animal that Americans identify as an elk is not a true elk at all, but is a wapiti, and the little fellow that many people call a chipmunk is really a ground squirrel. Chipmunks look very much like ground squirrels, but are much smaller, hardly bigger than a well fed mouse.

You can learn more about Colorado mammals by visiting the Solar Trails Center or Cheyenne Mountain Zoo in Colorado Springs, the Denver Zoo and Denver Museum of Natural History, or by consulting The Guide to Mammals of Colorado, Hugo G. Rodeck, published by the University of Colorado at Boulder, or Peterson's Field Guide to Mammals, by Burt and Rossenheider.

TRAIL DESCRIPTIONS

COLORADO SPRINGS AREA

Road directions to Parks with nature trails:

PALMER PARK
GARDEN OF THE GODS
WHITE HOUSE RANCH
SOLAR TRAILS CENTER

PALMER PARK is located in northeastern Colorado Springs and may be approached by Templeton Gap Road or Paseo Road. Nature trails lace the area.

The GARDEN OF THE GODS may be approached via several different routes from Highway 24 or from Interstate 25, but the major entrance is Gateway Road off 30th Street.

The WHITE HOUSE RANCH access is located on Gateway Road between 30th Street and the Garden of the Gods.

The SOLAR TRAILS CENTER is located on south 26th Street. Follow the signs south of Highway 24.

PALMER PARK TRAILS City of Colorado Springs Park and Recreation Department, four different trails up to two miles long; feature pleasant nature walks, horse rental at nearby stables.

PALMER PARK in northeast Colorado Springs is a sprawling mesa area with evergreens and sandstone formations, the kind of park that is large enough to offer many semi-secluded spots but too small to get seriously lost in. A maze of gravel and paved roads lead to picnic areas that are scattered through the rocks, some on overlooks with views of the City and mountains and plains.

Nature trails lace the area. You are asked to stay on the paths. These are short and gentle walks, well suited for those who might not think of themselves as hikers. Horses can be rented at nearby stables.

The area abounds with chipmunks, ground squirrels, rabbits and the like. Minerals and lichens color the rocks, and many of the boulders have been weathered into odd shapes, some resembling mushrooms.

The top of the mesa is a botanical reserve called the Yucca Area, where thousands of yuccas blossom each June.

The park is open from 5:00 a.m. to 11:00 p.m. No overnight camping is allowed except for youngsters at the Youth Camp where a permit is required. The Lazy Land and Council Grounds Picnic Areas are open by permit. Make a reservation with the Colorado Springs Park and Recreation Department. Fires are permitted only in established firepits and no alcoholic beverages are allowed.

GARDEN OF THE GODS City of Colorado Springs Park and Recreation Department, short nature trails, features strolls through rare and beautiful geologic formations.

Millions of years ago the Pikes Peak area was flat, overrun by ancient seas that came and went and left behind sediment layers that are now seen as red and gray and white sedimentary rock. Then, very slowly Pikes Peak and other great mountains rose from below, not as volcanoes, but as rock masses created by igneous activity deep in the earth and then thrust upward. Granite from deep in the earth now towered above rock which had formed on the ocean floor, and at the edge of this upheaval, giant sandstone slabs were broken and tilted up on end to form the Garden of the Gods.

Even today, after centuries of erosion by wind and water, the slabs stand on edge, the biggest some 300 feet high. This exotic garden was fully appreciated by Indians of both the mountains and plains. The Utes visited the Garden as part of their pilgrimage to the sacred springs at Manitou, and the Daughters of the American Revolution erected a stone to mark the plains Indian Trail that enters the Garden from the east. Today the City of Colorado Springs owns and takes care of the Garden, and El Paso County Park and Recreation Department furnishes naturalist guides. The Garden is designated as a Registered Natural Landmark by the National Park Service. This area receives such heavy use that today hiking and horse riding are encouraged only on designated trails in order to allow delicate plant life to recover. Horses are available from nearby stables. No camping is permitted, for the park is open only for day use, from 5:00 a.m. to 11:00 p.m. all year. Dogs must be kept on a leash and no alcoholic beverages are allowed.

Daily 30-minute nature hikes are led by naturalists throughout the summer, and the Visitors Center has information, publications, exhibits and slide programs to help acquaint you with the Garden. Special activities led by a naturalist are available for any group of 15 or larger.

Photographers will find the Garden most spectacular near sunrise or sunset when the colors are most vivid. In late winter or early spring, watch for bighorn sheep that come down from the Rampart Range area to graze on the hogback ridge immediately north of the Garden.

WHITE HOUSE RANCH City of Colorado Springs Park and Recreation Department, features short living history trail and nature trail designed to serve the blind and those confined to wheelchairs.

You can step back in time at the White House Ranch, where life still goes on much as it did in the late 1800s. The blacksmith, carpenter, gardener and homesteader not only dress in period costumes, but they play the parts so thoroughly that you may as well not ask them about the Denver Broncos or any other modern subject.

Indians, trappers and early explorers used to meet at the area now occupied by the Ranch, and the trail to this place was well worn before Columbus sailed. Walter C. Galloway first homesteaded the Ranch in the 1860s, and his cabin is now being rebuilt in the old ways, using square nails and fittings made by the resident blacksmith.

Robert Chambers operated his Rockledge Ranch here in 1876, growing vegetables for the plush Antlers Hotel. His asparagus now grows wild along the Living History Trail, and the Chambers garden is still being tilled by hand, though now the vegetables are sold to the public in the Ranch's general store.

Yet the Ranch is named after the elegant White House built in 1907 by General William Jackson Palmer, railroad magnate and founder of Colorado Springs. The house was built for Mrs. Palmer's half-sister and has known a series of owners through the years, but it is now the property of the City of Colorado Springs. At present the house is not open for public tours.

In the barn area you can see sheep and goats and you might even meet an old miner coming to the general store with his loaded burro. You might also watch out for Indians as you take the Living History Trail through the woods.

Another trail at the Ranch has been provided by the Junior League of Colorado Springs and features facilities for the blind and those confined to wheelchairs. Nature signs along the path are translated in Braille.

The Ranch offers guided and self-guided tours June through September from 9:00 a.m. to 6:00 p.m., Monday through Saturday and from 12:00 to 6:00 p.m. on Sundays.

SOLAR TRAILS CENTER El Paso County Parks Department, features visitor center and five nature trails plus horse trail linking the Equestrian Center and Bear Creek Canyon Trail.

There is so much to see and learn at the Solar Trails Center that the place is truly hard to describe. In addition to the five nature trails that range in length from 0.2 to 1.2 miles, the center offers exhibits and displays that show you live creatures, stuffed creatures, hides, horns and antlers, tells you about solar heating, about animal tracks, about insects, birds, and many other things to help you understand the workings of nature in our area, and there's more.

If you have a hard time getting used to topographic maps that are used so much by hikers, you might compare maps with the three-dimensional model of the Pikes Peak vicinity. This model shows the Peak and much of the Rampart Range in color, with trees and rocks and roads and trails all laid out from an eagle's eye view.

Naturalists are available by reservation to lead groups outdoors, and the center plans special hikes and activities for the general public.

The nature trails are well marked and have station signs describing flora and fauna. The one called Songbird, for example, features a gentle grade that offers access to all ages and abilities, including the physically handicapped. Though it is short (0.2 mile), it leads through a creekbottom forest where you are likely to see songbirds.

In addition to the nature trails, a path used by trailriders extends between the center and the El Paso County Equestrian Center at Penrose Stadium, where horses may be rented. A branch of this path, located one mile from the Solar Trails Center, leads southwest toward Bear Creek Road and Bear Creek Canyon Trail. Trailriders wishing to ride Bear Creek often park trailers at the Solar Center.

The center is open 10:00 a.m. to 6:00 p.m., every day, May through September, and 10:00 a.m. to 4:00 p.m., on weekdays and 12:00 noon to 4:00 p.m. weekends through the rest of the year.

CHEYENNE CANYON - HIGH DRIVE AREA

Road directions for:

COLUMBINE
MOUNT CUTLER
NORTH CHEYENNE CANYON
NORTH CHEYENNE CUTOFF
ST. MARY'S FALLS
ST. PETER'S DOME
BEAR CREEK
PALMER-REDROCK LOOP

If you follow the signs advertising Seven Falls, you will wind up on West Cheyenne Road at an intersection where you can turn left to enter South Cheyenne Canyon (where Seven Falls is located) or right to enter North Cheyenne Canyon. Take the right fork and drive along the city picnic grounds that line the creek. Signs along the way show technical rock climbers the best routes up canyon walls. We mention this because the canyon is a famous practice area for climbers with technical gear, but is very dangerous for visitors who want to scramble on rocks. Climbing is prohibited without full equipment.

One mile after you enter the canyon, you find COLUMBINE trailhead on your right. MOUNT CUTLER is 0.5 miles farther and is on your left. Helen Hunt Falls is another 1.2 miles distant, and there you find the short path leading up above Helen Hunt Falls to Silver Cascade Falls, a path so short that it needs no description. Take care, though, and stay off the steep slippery rocks at the top of the trail. Those rocks have been the scene of a number of serious accidents. The western end of COLUMBINE meets the road on a switchback above Helen Hunt Falls.

Continue up this road another 0.6 miles and you come to a large intersection where you join the Gold Camp road and the High Drive. To find trailheads for NORTH CHEYENNE CANYON, ST. MARY'S FALLS and ST. PETER'S DOME, turn left here and take the upper Gold Camp Road.

NORTH CHEYENNE CANYON trailhead is on your right 0.6 miles from this intersection. ST. MARY'S FALLS has two lower trailheads on either side of the first tunnel you pass, which is 1.2 miles from the intersection. ST. PETER'S DOME trail begins at an overlook point that is 8.7 miles from the intersection. If you continue on the Gold Camp Road past this point, you will pass the Wye Campground and then arrive at a point where Penrose-Rosemont Reservoir is on your left, or south, and immediately on your right is a turnoff that leads to the upper trailhead for ST. MARY'S FALLS at Frosty Park. This turnoff, called Forest Development Road #379, can be very rough for passenger cars. Frosty Park is located about one mile from the Gold Camp Road on this road.

To find the trailheads for BEAR CREEK and PALMER-REDROCK LOOP, start at the intersection above Helen Hunt Falls and take the one-way High Drive (closed in winter). One mile up you find the Mount Buckhorn trailhead, with parking on the right. This multiple use trail is open to motorcycles, so we do not describe it here, but we mention the trailhead location because some hikers and riders like to use this trail to make a loop with Bear Creek (see BEAR CREEK). BEAR CREEK is located on the left at a metal gate 2.4 miles from the start of the High Drive. Only roadside parking is available, so horses often use the Solar Trail Center parking lot on Bear Creek Road below. The Bear Creek caretaker's parking lot at the base of the High Drive has space for another 10 cars.

The main trailhead for PALMER-REDROCK is 2.7 miles from the High Drive start, roadside parking only. To find the lower trailhead, continue downhill on the paved portion known as Bear Creek road and turn left at its intersection with the Gold Camp Road. Proceed 0.2 miles and watch for it on your left. There are a couple of small off-road parking lots there.

COLUMBINE City of Colorado Springs trail, 2 miles one way; elevation gain 620 feet, loss 200 feet; trailhead #5; located on map Manitou Springs D; approximate hiking time 1.2 hours; features an overlook of canyon and Silver Cascade and Helen Hunt Falls.

This one doesn't look like much from the map, for it only seems to follow a slope above a road, but this is a pretty trail that snakes among evergreens and rock formations with rarely any glimpse of the road below. The first mile is steep, but that section can be eliminated to take advantage of the prettier and gentler last section that leads toward the falls.

Columbines are the Colorado State Flower and grow in the moist shade of evergreens near Columbine Spring. Look for them blooming in late June and early July. It is illegal to disturb them.

As you leave the main trailhead, the path opens into a picnic area, then continues up past a rock cabin. From there it switchbacks up a scree (loose gravel and rock) slope for 3/4 of a mile. This is a good winter hike because sunny exposure helps keep it clear of snow. Higher up you will find Columbine Spring flowing except in the driest times. The trail follows the slope, climbing to an overlook called Buena Vista that is only a few yards below the Gold Camp Road. From here you can see the Broadmoor area to the left, Mount Muscoco directly across canyon and other peaks up canyon.

This overlook can be used as an alternative trailhead to avoid the difficult lower part of the trail. To find the spot by the road, enter the Lower Gold Camp Road by turning right at the intersection above Helen Hunt Falls and stop at the second railroad cut after the first tunnel. Roadside parking here is limited, so you may want to have someone drop you off. Buena Vista overlook is behind the rocks at this cut.

Columbine Trail was built as part of a Civil Works Administration project in 1934, and the work was so difficult that a blacksmith labored under the evergreens, resharpening 100 picks a day.

The final mile is the most beautiful, with views of Silver Cascade and Helen Hunt Falls. Try this one by morning light, for the falls are shadowed in the afternoon. The trail ends on the road just above Helen Hunt Falls.

PALMER-REDROCK LOOP El Paso Parks Department, 4.7 miles one way (from winter trailhead, add 0.7 mile); elevation gain 620 feet, loss 1,140 feet; trailhead #11; located on map Manitou Springs B; approximate hiking time 2.7 hours; features forest walk through area of geologic interest.

This is not a true loop trail because it does not return to the same trailhead, but since the road does connect the two trailheads, it can be hiked as a loop by traveling part way on the road. Part of this route used to be called the Crystal Park Trail, but private property has now cut off the access to Crystal Park, so hikers are urged to stay on the route we show you in order to avoid trespassing.

Because the lower part of this trail is steep, most hikers begin at the higher trailhead and walk the lower part downhill. The trail is much more difficult if hiked the other way around.

Starting at the trailhead on the High Drive, you enter an aspen grove and soon find a place where the main trail doubles back to the right and begins climbing. If you continue in the meadow instead of climbing, you will find a chimney from an old Boy Scout Camp and a dead-end below Sentinel Rock. Return to main trail.

Your path gains altitude, snaking through evergreens, then curves west through a mossy forest, keeping high on the mountainside to maintain altitude. You cross an intermittent stream called Hunter's Run that drips off a large rock near the trail.

You climb very gently from here and find an intersection on a small saddle ridge. The left fork leads 0.3 mile up and around some rocks to a small natural overlook. From there you can see the Garden of the Gods, the Rampart Range, etc. Do not explore farther because soon you run into private property.

Return to the intersection and the main trail that now heads east along a ridge saddle. This trail soon begins to angle downward and then dives along an old four-wheel track to end on the Gold Camp Road.

MOUNT CUTLER City of Colorado Springs Park and Recreation Department, 0.8 mile one way, extra 0.2 mile for Broadmoor overlook; elevation gain 600 feet; trailhead #6; located on maps Manitou Springs D, Colorado Springs C; approximate hiking time 1.2 hours; features overlooks of Colorado Springs and Seven Falls.

This is one of the few trails that we recommend for a night walk because it is short and wide and has no confusing points -- and because if offers a view of Colorado Springs that looks like a carpet of jewels. In the summer time, Seven Falls is illuminated with colored lights as well, so this can be a fine place to hike with good flashlights. Keep your small children close at hand for the trail does climb the canyon rim and the overlooks have steep dropoffs.

Near the top, the trail forks. The right fork climbs Mount Muscoco for a view of the seven distinct cascades in South Cheyenne Canyon. Seven Falls is a private tourist attraction.

The left fork wraps around Mount Cutler itself, passes a white quartz outcropping and dead-ends at an overlook where the Broadmoor complex lies 900 feet below.

There is no water enroute.

NORTH CHEYENNE CANYON Forest Service #622, 2.5 miles one way; elevation gain 1,800 feet; trailhead #7; located on maps Manitou Springs D, C; approximate hiking time 1.3 hours; features streamside walk over numerous bridges, 25-foot cascade.

Nobody quite knows what to call this trail, for its name has changed so many times. It used to be called Lovely Corners after John Lovely, a Frenchman who lived in a tent in this Canyon and who homesteaded several acres there in 1902. Later it was called Six Bridges because of its many steam crossings, and then another bridge was added so it was called Seven Bridges for a while. Perhaps the current name will stick.

These bridges give you close range views of the creek as it pours and splashes over polished stones. In early spring and late fall you can watch the air bubbles moving under the ice fringes and in the summer wildflowers are everywhere.

Near what we call the end of this trail, the stream slides down a steep granite face for 25 feet or more, forming Undine Falls. As you climb the trail overlooking the cascade, however, beware of a dangerous spot where a slab lubricated with gravel slants toward a drop-off.

There are campsites farther up near a tributary that joins from the north. Your trail leaves the creek here and skirts the base of Kineo Mountain, heading up that tributary toward a trail called North Cheyenne Cutoff that links with Bear Creek at Jones Park. As you climb the tributary, however, you see another trail coming down to join the tributary from your left. A metal sign marks the junction.

That other trail leads back toward the headwaters of North Cheyenne Creek, but this is a multiple use trail open to motorcycles. It climbs a steep section called "the ladders" that used to have wooden steps leading toward Nelson's Camp. Nelson used to pan gold up there in the late 1800s, and his cabin remained intact with bunk beds and metal stove until vandals destroyed it in the early 1970s.

If you use two vehicles, you can make a long circuit by hiking up North Cheyenne to the Cheyenne Cutoff and take that to Bear Creek and down again. See North Cheyenne Cutoff.

NORTH CHEYENNE CUTOFF Forest Service #668, 0.5 mile; elevation gain 200 feet; trailheads #7 and #10; located on maps Manitou Springs D, C; approximate hiking time 0.2 hour; features saddle ridge walk linking North Cheyenne and Bear Creek Trails.

At the upper end of North Cheyenne Canyon Trail, you find a distinct path leaving the creek and climbing past the north slope of Kineo Mountain. The path follows a tributary that joins North Cheyenne from the north. A small waterfall is hidden from view here, but when the tributary is flowing strong, you can find it by listening and by hiking down away from the trail a few yards.

As you continue upwards, another trail comes down to parallel the brook on the other side, but keep to the Kineo side of the brook. The other trail leads to Nelson's Camp on a multiple use trail, though the sign says Rosemont.

Soon you find a grassy area with scattered evergreens. Look for a distinct path that cuts away to the right, leading away from the tributary and up into the trees. Now you are crossing the saddle between Kineo and the high ground to the west, dropping down into another watershed. This is the edge of Jones Park, a high grassy area dotted with evergreens and wildflowers. This area is designated for multiple use, which means that hikers and horse riders share this area with motorcycles. The trail soon finds Bear Creek, crosses it and begins to follow it down. See BEAR CREEK CANYON TRAIL.

ST. MARY'S FALLS Forest Service #624, 4.5 miles to Frosty Park, 1.6 miles to base of the falls; elevation gain 2,700 feet; trailhead #8; located on maps Manitou Springs D, Mount Big Chief B, A; approximate hiking time 2.5 hours; features large cascade and overlook of Broadmoor area.

St. Mary's Falls is a water slide that churns for about 40 feet down the side of Stove Mountain. The trail that leads there climbs 1,200 feet in 1.6 miles, but starts out fairly gently, so the last section to the falls is quite steep. The higher section leading to Frosty Park has been newly reworked.

Starting at the lower trailheads at the tunnel on the Gold Camp Road, the trail follows Buffalo Creek upstream. This is the most popular part of the trail, for it climbs gently among pine and blue spruce, the Colorado State Tree. Many kinds of mushrooms and wildflowers grow along the route, and higher up there are small campsites among the trees.

Eventually the trail leaves the creek and switchbacks up the north slope. It forks at a metal sign that says, "Base of Falls 500 feet", pointing left, and "Top of Falls 0.2 mile", pointing right.

Both the base and top of the falls share a common overlook of the pine and blue spruce valley that slants toward the Broadmoor area. Be especially careful of falling rock, for a rock dislodged from the top of the falls will hit just about where people stand to view the bottom of the falls.

The trail continues up Buffalo Creek, skirts the south side of Mount Rosa and then goes down to end at Frosty Park, just a mile off the Gold Camp Road on Forest Service Development Road #379.

ST. PETER'S DOME Forest Service #621, 0.7 mile one way; elevation gain 400 feet; trailhead #9; located on map Mt. Big Chief B; approximate hiking time 0.5 hour; features scenic overlook of Colorado Springs.

Future improvements will make this trail easy for everyone, but at the time of this writing, the steps at the top had been destroyed by vandals so that visitors must pick their way over rocks to reach the top.

The path begins at the St. Peter's Dome overlook on the Gold Camp Road and gently wraps around the wooded hillside before beginning the climb in earnest.

BEAR CREEK Forest Service #666, 3 miles one way from High Drive, but add one mile for winter trailhead below High Drive; elevation gain 1,980 feet; trailhead #10; located on maps Manitou Springs D, C; approximate hiking time 1.5 hours; features historic climb through a scenic canyon.

In 1873 the U.S. Army Signal Corps built the highest signal station in the world atop Pikes Peak, and the trail leading to the top led through Bear Creek Canyon. This trail began at Manitou and wound 17 miles up through Jones Park and the Seven Lakes Area, but much of that route is now only history. The popular Lake House Hotel at Lake Moraine burned down long ago, and vandals have only recently destroyed buildings that used to stand in Jones Park.

What remains is this spectacular trail up the canyon. As you leave the summer trailhead on the High Drive (winter users must hike up to this point from where the road is closed below), you follow the creek bottom for a short way, then begin climbing a steady path up the side of a ridge. Soon the creek is nothing but a sound below you. Raspberries, dog roses and juniper grow in the loose rock beside the trail.

Another trail on the opposite slope provides a side trip through the spruce and fir to the area just below Josephine Falls, where it is necessary to cross over to the main trail to continue.

As you climb, notice the huge rocks standing above the spruce and fir across the canyon. These are Tenny Crags, named after a past president of Colorado College.

All this climbing leads you to a high overlook where bluffs tower overhead and the falls roar below you -- barely in sight, unfortunately. From this high ledge you can see all the way to the Black Forest.

Now the canyon narrows and you return to streamside. You pass the remains of an old toll road bridge built in 1891 to carry wagons and workers on their way to build reservoirs in the Seven Lakes area. Higher up the Buckhorn-Jones Park Multiple Use Trail crosses the creek to join Bear Creek Trail, and from this point Bear Creek shares its path with motorcycles traveling up to Jones Park.

Still higher, you pass a mine tunnel immediately beside the trail. This tunnel used to be covered to discourage those who don't realize the danger of exploring old mines. All the supporting timbers have now rotted away.

Bear Creek Trail ends at Jones Park, but there it links with North Cheyenne Cutoff to North Cheyenne Creek.

Horses may be rented from the El Paso County Equestrian Center at 1045 West Rio Grande.

PIKES PEAK VICINITY

Road directions for Barr Trail System including:

BOTTOMLESS PIT
MOUNTAIN VIEW
MANITOU RESERVOIR
FREMONT EXPERIMENTAL FOREST
INCLINE
EAGLE'S NEST - MOUNT CREST CRAGS
ELK PARK
UTE INDIAN
WALDO CANYON

Pikes Peak is rare among high mountains for having such convenient access. A toll highway and a cog railway extend to the very top, allowing hikers a choice of an uphill or downhill adventure, and the Manitou Incline Railway boosts hikers past the grueling lower section of BARR TRAIL.

To reach the lower trailhead for BARR TRAIL, drive up Ruxton Avenue from its intersection in downtown Manitou Springs. The lower stations of the Manitou Incline and the Cog Railway are also located on this Avenue, and the Barr trailhead is just beyond.

ELK PARK trailhead is reached via the Pikes Peak Toll Road and is located at Elk Park Knoll, which is a shoulder of Pikes Peak just above timberline. As you drive the toll highway a mile past Glen Cove, you will see a metal gate used to close off the upper road in winter. The turnoff is located just before this gate, but it is not apparent as you approach because it dives off steeply. Ease over to the left side of the road and watch for it between iron posts. There are several such posts, so be sure you have the right pair! A metal sign marks the trailhead on your right as you enter the Elk Park Area. Overnight parking is not allowed on the Pikes Peak toll road or any of the roads off of it.

The summit trailhead for BARR TRAIL is located near the Cog Railway tracks and summit house on the peak. Many trails branch off of Barr Trail, and each will be described individually.

The southern trailhead for the UTE INDIAN trail is located immediately behind the lower station of the Manitou Incline. The northern trailhead is located on Highway 24, about one-half mile south of Cascade. A large metal gate marked "private" means that vehicles cannot enter, but hikers may climb over to use this trail. Please respect the rights of property owners who have allowed the public to use this historic path.

To find the trailhead for WALDO CANYON, drive three miles west of Manitou Springs on Highway 24 and watch for the stairs and trailhead parking on your right.

PIKES PEAK ITSELF

BARR TRAIL Forest Service #620, 12 miles one-way; elevation gain 7,258 feet; trailhead #12; located on maps Manitou Springs B, A, Pikes Peak B; approximate hiking time 8.0 hours; features famous scenery and greatest altitude gain of any trail in Colorado.

This is a famous and popular trail which can be hiked in many ways to make your expedition long or short, easy or very difficult. Those who want an easy hike can take advantage of the gentler midsection that leads toward Barr Camp by taking the Manitou Incline Railway; this bypasses three miles of steep switchbacks and 2,000 feet of elevation gain. And for those who want a grueling challenge, Barr Trail offers the greatest base-to-summit climb in the state, an altitude gain of over 7,000 feet. Yet unlike other trails that force you to climb, Barr can be hiked entirely downhill, which makes it suited for those who want to experience high mountain hiking in a somewhat easier manner. The catch is the word "somewhat", for the uppermost and lowest parts of this route are steep enough that they can be painfully difficult, even downhill.

The operators of Barr Camp, located halfway up the mountain, estimate that fully two-thirds of the people who start up Barr Trail for the first time, expecting to reach the summit, turn back when they realize what they have attempted. So let's begin the easier way, at the top.

At the summit trailhead, you look out over the prairies toward Kansas, with Colorado Springs spread out some 8,000 feet below. The altitude is 14,110 feet, the air is thin, and you had best move slowly if you don't want to contract altitude sickness.

You start by making your way down a steep series of switchbacks high above timberline. Snow may cover part of this trail until sometime in June, so inquire about conditions and the need for an ice axe in spring.

Bighorn sheep, yellow-bellied marmots and the grouse-like ptarmigan are often seen on this slope. Both the ptarmigan and the bighorns are rock-colored in summer; the ptarmigan is white in winter, and sometimes you spot their movement or shadow first.

This is the most dangerous part of the mountain, so you must take along the gear to weather a sudden storm. Remember that the ptarmigan is found only above timberline and at the Arctic Circle, and that even the plant life above timberline is the same sort of tundra found at the Arctic Circle. So what you have on Pikes Peak is a piece of the Arctic! It can be very warm in the summer sunshine and deadly cold if the weather changes.

Soon you pass a metal sign that directs you to the edge of The Crater, which is a deep cirque where a glacier formed and scooted down, carving a pit. Return to the main trail and try to stay on the trail, for this high tundra is easily damaged and takes many years to regrow.

Some 3,000 feet below the summit, the trail finds timberline, which is marked by dwarfed trees that may be very old. Right at treeline, you pass an A-frame shelter with springwater coming from a pipe driven into the mountainside.

Now the trail dips into a world of tall spruce and fir. Watch for a turquoise-like gem called amazonite that washes out of the granite near the trail (no digging please). When you reach Barr Camp at 10,200 feet, you will have hiked about six miles and descended about 4,000 feet.

Barr Camp, which is operated by permit from the U. S. Forest Service, offers overnight accommodations for a small fee. It has rustic log cabins with wooden floors, cold spring water, outhouse facilities and very little firewood closeby. The camp provides hot chocolate and bunk beds with foam pads at modest cost and a few supplies at higher cost because everything at Barr Camp must be packed in.

This camp makes a convenient base from which to explore other trails in the region, or it can serve as a destination for easier hikes from below. Side trails provide tent camping along Sheep and Cabin Creeks, at the unnamed creek below Barr Camp, at various streams that cross the Manitou Reservoir Trail, or in the Fremont Experimental Forest.

Perhaps the most beautiful part of this route is the gentler midsection that extends between Barr Camp and the Incline Trail. The distance is about four miles, but the altitude change is only 1,200 feet.

Here the trail wanders among granite formations decorated with aspens and douglas fir and ponderosa pine. Sometimes you catch a glimpse of the flats to the east, or find spectacular views of the Peak itself. Along this route you will find the last of the Army's telegraph poles that carried the first communications to the summit in the 1800s.

A metal sign marks the intersection with the upper Incline Trail, which leads to the Incline Railway's upper station, and the Fremont Experimental Forest Trail, which follows a small brook uphill. This brook is the last water before the bottom. The Incline summit station has a drinking fountain, restrooms, giftshop and snackbar. A few yards farther down on Barr Trail, another metal sign points the way to another junction with Incline Trail that leads to the summit station. The Incline sells one-way tickets to exhausted hikers who decide not to walk the rest of the way down.

Below this point, Barr Trail is very steep, but this makes a convenient short hike for people who ride the Incline up and walk down. The City is visible only part of the time and much of the trail plunges through stands of ponderosa pine, white fir and blue spruce, with views of Camerons Cone and Pikes Peak. At one point, you walk under a huge pair of boulders that tilt together to cover the trail. It's a good place to get out of the rain.

The only branch off this lower section leads to an overlook where you can watch the Incline Railway pass by.

And while you're congratulating yourself for conquering Barr Trail, you might remember Fred Barr, who shoved the rocks and moved the dirt to build the trail.

TRAILS THAT JOIN BARR TRAIL

BOTTOMLESS PIT Forest Service #632, 1.5 miles one way beginning at 10,500 feet and continuing upward;

elevation gain 760 feet; trailhead #12, located on map Pikes Peak B; approximate hiking time one hour; features treeline scenery with small waterfalls spouting from high granite cliffs.

About a mile uphill from Barr Camp, you find a metal sign that shows the way to the Bottomless Pit. This rugged climb begins with a switchback and never really levels out, for oddly enough, you must climb UP into the bottom of the Bottomless Pit.

The Pit is a deep cirque, a semi-circular scoop in the cliffs gouged out by glacial ice, and when you get there, you may agree that it has no bottom, for the land continues to fall away at a sharp angle.

This one should be saved until mid-June or later, for the trail skirts a shady ridge that keeps its snow a long time. Ice axe and gaiters are necessary for earlier attempts.

The trail crosses an area called "windfall" on the map because so many large trees were flattened here by a windstorm. From there it climbs to timberline and dead-ends in a pocket where granite walls rise up to 3,000 feet around you on three sides. Many rock wall and ice climbers try their skill here, and it is a spectacular, if somewhat forbidding landscape with many waterfalls spouting from the cliffs above. The waterfalls decrease in late summer.

Be sure to fill your canteen at the stream near the Bottomless Pit turnoff at Barr Trail, for there is no other reliable water until you reach the Pit itself.

MOUNTAIN VIEW TRAIL Forest Service #671, 1.5 miles one-way; elevation gain 220 feet; trailhead #12, located on maps Manitou Springs A, Pikes Peak B; approximate hiking time 0.6 hour; features campsites, old log cabins and view of Cog Railway.

This short and gentle trail provides access to many campsites along Cabin and Sheep Creeks. To find the trailhead, watch for a metal sign on Barr Trail about one-half mile below Barr Camp. This sign reads "Barr Trail, Elevation 9,800, Barr Camp 0.5, Pikes Peak Summit 6.5, Manitou Springs 6.5", and does not mention Mountain View Trail at all, but the trail is right there in front of the sign, leading off to the south (that would be to the left as you go up Barr Trail).

It first crosses Cabin Creek, where you will find a roofless log cabin, and then Sheep Creek near the Cog Railway tracks. The trail dead-ends there at the Cog Railway's Mountain View Station, and you may not cross the tracks into watershed country without a free permit from the City of Colorado Springs Department of Public Utilities.

MANITOU RESERVOIR Forest Service #638, over 2.5 miles; elevation gain 275 feet, loss 900 feet; trailhead #12; located on maps Manitou Springs A, Cascade C; approximate hiking time 1.3 hours; features scenic vistas and camping.

A metal sign marks the turnoff 1.5 miles below Barr Camp. This trail offers many beautiful campsites along the streams it crosses, but it is steep going. This trail climbs up and down a series of steep ridges. The first few yards will give you an idea, for this trail literally dives off Barr Trail toward South French Creek. There you find a meadow filled with large aspens and stream big enough to produce five or six-inch trout. Your trail switchbacks up the opposite ridge, then drops again toward another brook which has no name.

Up another ridge and down again and you find yourself headed toward Manitou Reservoir, which is closed to the public. A caretaker lives there to make sure.

Unfortunately, there is no public access to the reservoir end of this trail, so you must turn around and backtrack to Barr Trail.

FREMONT EXPERIMENTAL FOREST Forest Service #669, 0.5 mile; elevation gain 380 feet; trailhead #12; located on map Manitou Springs A; approximate hiking time 0.3 hours; features campsites and exotic evergreens.

A metal sign marks where this trail intersects Barr Trail and the Incline Trail. Fremont Trail follows a tiny brook into the Experimental Forest where exotic evergreens were once planted to see which varieties would do well in this area. Only the foundations of the station buildings remain now, but a few Siberian larch still survive.

When hiking Barr Trail from the bottom, this area offers the first good campsites, so this area receives a lot of use. Treat the water.

This trail has been used as a road to haul fencing for Barr Trail, so it is wide and leads far beyond the one-half mile listed as the length of this trail, but beyond a certain point it is closed to the public. Follow the trail up to the right as the water curves away to the left. You climb a short, steep section and arrive at a ridgetop where you have a lofty view. That is the designated end of Fremont Trail.

INCLINE Forest Service #623, one-half mile one-way; elevation gain 120 feet; trailhead #12; located on map Manitou Springs A; approximate hiking time 0.2 hour; features access to gentlest part of Barr Trail.

There are actually two Incline Trails, but since they parallel each other closely, they share a common trail number. Look for a sign on the hill above the Manitou Incline's summit station for the beginning.

The single trail climbs around to the left to a place where boulders form a natural overlook, and it splits there. The lower route is wider because it was used as a road to haul machinery for the Incline Railway. It joins Barr Trail just below the intersection with Fremont Trail. The upper path is narrow, but passes beneath a huge boulder that spans the trail, an excellent shelter on rainy days.

The Incline Railway was built in 1906 to haul men and equipment to build the Manitou pipeline, and it has been operating as a tourist attraction ever since. It has a perfect safety record. The summit station has a snack bar, restrooms, and well-developed picnic areas with lofty views of the surrounding country. This area can be enjoyed by folks who would not ordinarily hike any kind of trail.

EAGLES NEST AND MT. CREST CRAGS 0.1 mile to Eagles Nest and about 0.5 mile to Mt. Crest Crags; elevation gain 650 feet; trailhead #12; located on map Manitou Springs A; approximate hiking time 0.3 hour.

As you climb the path behind the Manitou Incline's upper station, you see signs pointing right toward Eagle's Nest and Mt. Crest Crags. The path heads north past picnic tables. A side trail soon branches off and heads uphill toward the clump of rocks that overlooks the station. This is called the Eagle's Nest. The main trail wraps around the mountain and begins a series of switchbacks to a higher set of rocks known as Mt. Crest Crags. From there you can see the white bluffs of Williams Canyon, the Rampart Range beyond, and even portions of the Ute Indian Trail that snakes along toward Cascade.

ELK PARK Forest Service #652, 6 miles one-way; elevation gain 200 feet, loss 1,680 feet; trailhead #14; located on maps Woodland Park C, Pikes Peak B; approximate hiking time 3.4 hours; features tiny ghost town, large spring that flows from mine tunnel, access to Barr Camp.

This is the back way, downhill to Barr Camp, and it leads through an area romantically called Ghost Town Hollow. The so-called ghost town was a tiny mining and lumber camp, something like a half dozen cabins. Just above is the Cincinnati mine, which never produced much gold, but which still produces part of the drinking water for Manitou Springs.

Starting at Elk Park (see road directions), you follow a trail that once was a road. This curves down from timberline through timber to Ghost Town Hollow. At the bottom, you find a fork with a sign pointing left, or down creek, toward Barr Camp (4 miles), and straight ahead toward the Oil Creek Tunnel (1/4 mile).

To see the mine, you walk up a gentle valley that is heavily forested. Soon you pass a few crumbling log cabins. The roofs are gone, the walls collapsing, and wildflowers bloom from the floor spaces. Visitors have carried away everything but the most uninteresting rusted tin garbage.

The mine is just above, and most of North French Creek flows from the tunnel. In the winter, this produces weird ice sculptures. All of the mine timbers have rotted away, so exploration would be very dangerous. A huge iron boiler stands outside.

Backtrack to the trail fork and take the trail that leads down creek toward Barr Camp. The trail climbs for a while, following a sunny ridge high above the creek, then dips down to a trail fork nearer the creek. The left fork is marked for Cascade, but that route (Severy Creek Trail) is closed except by permit from the Cascade Water Department.

You turn right, cross the creek, and then switchback up the opposite ridge. This climb is fairly gentle and soon the trail almost levels out, skirting the end of the ridge. Manitou Reservoir is visible below. You hike around the ridge, cross a high park meadow, then drop down into the South French Creek valley.

Your trail follows the creek downhill a short way, though the creek is just out of sight to your right, and then you find a shallow crossing. On the other side, you climb to the left and find yourself walking a ledge on a cliff's side with the creek roaring below. Your trail goes past a prospect hole, over a rise, then descends to the cabins of Barr Camp. You arrive just a few yards above the cabins themselves.

UTE INDIAN TRAIL. Ute Pass Historical Society Trail, 3.7 miles one-way; elevation gain 1,040 feet, loss 340 feet; trailhead #15; located on maps Manitou Springs B, A, Cascade C; approximate hiking time 2 hours; features foothill and mountain hike over historic trail.

The Ute Indians believed that the gods lived below the springs at Manitou, that their breathing caused the bubbles in those mineral waters. So the Utes made pilgrimages to these springs over an ancient trail that extended clear to Utah. This trail was used by trappers, by mountain men, and later it carried wagons toward the mining areas in the mountains.

Now -- thanks to the efforts of many organizations-- a piece of this historic trail has been preserved for hikers. Horses are no longer allowed.

Our description begins at the southern trailhead directly below the Manitou Incline station on Ruxton Avenue. You hike up and around the base of the mountain, following a road-like path up Rattlesnake Gulch. (Trail builders say they have never seen rattlesnakes here.)

Your trail washboards over a series of ridges where the land is somewhat arid at first, dominated by Gambel's oak and yucca, and then the evergreens close in and soon you are hiking in a forest.

A metal sign marks the point where the Ute Wagon Trail joined the Ute Indian Trail, and farther on you walk under a pipeline that crosses the trail on a steel trestle. Several utility lines follow this trail toward Cascade, and much of the right-of-way belongs to the City of Colorado Springs Utilities Department. As you walk by steel pipes that jut from ridges, listen for gurgling caused by pressure changes in the water pipelines.

You pass by the remains of Long's Ranch, one of the oldest ranches in the area. Only one building still stands. You will find a spring nearby, but it is sporadic and small, so we advise bringing your own water.

Your last downhill section takes you into the French Creek watershed and the trail ends beside Highway 24, one-half mile east of Cascade.

This trail was built through the efforts and cooperation of the Chipita Park-Cascade Bicentennial Association, the Ute Pass Historical Society, the National Hiking and Ski Touring Association, Boy Scout Troop 18 and Explorer Post 24, the

the Lions and Kiwanis Clubs, the Colorado Springs Utilities Department, the Fourth Infantry Division of Fort Carson, and of course, private land owners.

WALDO CANYON Forest Service #640, 7 miles round-trip, including 2 miles to beginning of 3-mile loop, then 2 miles return; elevation gain 1,280 feet; trailhead #17; located on maps Cascade C, D; approximate hiking time 3.4 hours; features scenic hike through wooded canyon.

According to trails researcher Gwen Pratt, Waldo Canyon used to be the site of Waldo Hog Ranch, and Waldo used to haul garbage from Manitou to feed his stock. The mortgage was owned by a man named Jones, and one day the two men had a falling out. Waldo demanded to see the mortgage document, but when Jones handed it to him, Waldo ATE IT!

Such is the history of this scenic canyon that now provides one of the area's easier hikes. The journey begins with a long flight of steep concrete stairs, but once you have negotiated that section, the trail becomes gentle.

After hiking for two miles past an area that is somewhat arid, you arrive at the three-mile loop trail that leads through the canyon. Here you find a spring and grove of ponderosa pine.

At the time of this writing, some of the Ponderosa have been killed by the pine beetle. Actually, the beetle itself does not kill trees, but it spreads a fungus that clogs the tree's plumbing system. This fungus causes the blue stain found inside "beetle kill" wood. Although much has to be learned about the beetle and its fungus, foresters now understand that only weakened trees seem to fall victim. Strong trees tend to produce enough sap to keep the beetles from burrowing under the bark, while trees that have suffered from drought, for instance, cannot produce enough sap for their own protection.

U.S. AIR FORCE ACADEMY AREA

Road directions for:

FALCON
STANLEY CANYON
WEST MONUMENT CREEK (See Rampart Reservoir)

Enter the south gate of the U.S. Air Force Academy. Proceed three miles, cross the railroad overpass and turn left onto Pine Drive.

To find the trailhead for FALCON, follow Pine Drive for 3.6 miles and turn right onto Community Drive. At the top of the hill, a distance of almost a mile, you turn right and find your way back to the Youth Center, Building #5132, which is the small building on the southwestern corner of the complex. The trailhead is located behind the building and a large blue sign marks the spot.

To find the STANLEY CANYON trailhead, follow Pine Drive another 1.4 miles past the Community Drive turnoff. The paved road will rise on a hill until it overlooks the Academy Hospital on the right. There, on the left, is a gravel turnoff that leads back 0.9 mile to the parking area for Stanley Canyon. Follow the markers. There is only enough parking for five or six vehicles at Stanley trailhead but more parking is available at the Academy Hospital nearby (0.9 mile). The Hospital lot is constantly patrolled and is considered safer for overnight parking.

Remember that the Academy gates open to the public at 6:30 a.m. and close at 7:00 p.m., though you may park overnight for camping high on Stanley Canyon and West Monument Creek. No camping is permitted on the Academy itself. You may leave the Academy at any time.

The new location for the trailhead for WEST MONUMENT CREEK is uncertain at the time of this writing, as are parking arrangements. Contact the Forest Service or the Academy for instructions on parking and access.

FALCON U.S. Air Force Academy Trail, 12 mile loop trail; elevation gain 880 feet; trailhead #18; located on maps Pikeview A, Cascade B, Palmer Lake D, Monument C; approximate hiking time 4.8 hours; features well marked nature hike with protected wildlife, restored settler's cabin, varied terrain.

Most trails offer only fleeting glimpses of animals such as mule deer, but wildlife is protected on the U.S. Air Force Academy. On the day of our visit, a doe and two fawns grazed fearlessly within a few yards of the trail.

This long and varied trail is maintained by the Boy Scouts, but is open to all hikers for day use. No horses, firearms or fires are permitted. Hikers no longer need to register, but the Academy warns hikers to stay on the trail to avoid dangerous military training and construction that may be in progress nearby. The trail is marked with signs showing a white falcon against a blue background.

FALCON TRAIL begins on a hill at the Community Center's Youth Center Building. It first descends the wooded hillside, crosses Pine Drive and enters grassland. It climbs behind an arid hill with Blodgett Peak towering to the west and crosses the gravel road that leads to the filtration plant. Here the trail enters the trees once more, crosses a stream on a wooden bridge, and soon joins another stream, the one that flows from Stanley Canyon.

In this area Scouts have built small dams to help prevent soil erosion and to provide shelters for aquatic life. Fourteen signs point out natural and man-made features along the way, and the Academy Visitor Center provides brochures to explain the points of interest.

Your path wanders through ponderosa pine and Gambel's oak. It crosses Academy and Interior Drives and then skirts a small marsh where cattails grow. After crossing another road, the path climbs again to follow a pine-covered ridge that overlooks Reservoir No. 2. Eventually the trail leads past a pioneer cabin.

This log cabin has been so well preserved and restored that it looks almost as if the pioneer family has locked it up to go visit friends. Wooden tombstones in the yard mark the graves of family members.

The trail ends where it began at the Youth Center.

CAUTION: Rattlesnakes are sometimes seen along Falcon Trail.

STANLEY CANYON Forest Service #707, 3 miles one-way; elevation gain 1,500 feet; trailhead #19; located on maps Cascade B, Palmer Lake D; approximate hiking time 2 hours; features treacherous climb through spectacular canyon.

Recent improvements by the Forest Service and Air Force Academy have made this trail much safer, but it still requires caution, especially when wet or icy. Parts of it require scrambling up slated rock ledges on a cliff's side.

Your trail begins on Air Force Academy property, but quickly climbs into National Forest, following the stream that pours down Stanley Canyon. Within 1/4 mile you reach a bend in the trail where the trees open up, revealing an overlook of the surrounding country.

Higher up, you must pick your way along the wet streambed where the canyon grows most narrow. You have a fine view of the distant prairies, then the canyon turns sharply, shutting off the view. The trail grows more gentle after that, leading through forest and meadows toward Stanley Canyon Reservoir.

At the time of this writing, Stanley Reservoir is open to fishing ONLY for Academy personnel, but the Colorado Division of Wildlife hopes to enter into a new agreement with the City of Colorado Springs, owner of the lake, to stock the lake at State expense and allow public fishing. In addition, a new section of the trail is planned to extend one mile from the reservoir to Forest Service Road #329, near Rampart Reservoir. However, only walk-in access is planned for the lake.

RAMPART RESERVOIR AREA

Road directions for:

RAINBOW GULCH
BPW NATURE TRAIL
NICHOLS
WEST MONUMENT CREEK
LAKE SHORE

Except for a portion of West Monument Creek Trail, the trails of the Rampart Reservoir Area are for day use only. Camping is not permitted and fires are allowed only in grates provided by the Forest Service. Indeed, if you wish to camp along West Monument Creek, you may not leave a vehicle at the Rampart Reservoir (you may at the Air Force Academy, however).

Since the lower end of the Rampart Range Road is so rough, the best access is from Woodland Park. The way is well marked.

To find RAINBOW GULCH, turn south on the Rampart Range Road from the Woodland Park access and drive two miles. Look for the sign on your left.

The other trailheads can be found by following markers for Rampart Reservoir on Forest Development Road #306. Drive two miles on this road and you find two steep switchbacks just past Promontory Picnic Ground. The trailhead for the BPW NATURE TRAIL is located on your right at the second switchback. The parking lot holds about 15 cars.

NICHOLS trailhead is located on the north end of the reservoir dam at Dikeside Overlook. There is parking for at least a dozen vehicles, with another parking area located near the boat ramp.

WEST MONUMENT CREEK TRAIL joins NICHOLS TRAIL 0.4 mile from the dam trailhead. See AIR FORCE ACADEMY AREA for directions to eastern trailhead.

LAKE SHORE follows the shore of Rampart Reservoir, so it may be approached from any of the picnic areas, but the official trailheads with the most parking are located at either ends of the dam.

The Rampart Reservoir Road is closed in winter, but trails may be used by those who wish to hike or ski into the area.

RAINBOW GULCH Forest Service #714, 1.2 miles one-way; elevation gain 140 feet, loss 120 feet; trailheads #20 and #21; located on maps Woodland Park B, Cascade A; approximate hiking time 0.5 hour; features ski trail.

After leaving the Rampart Range Road, Rainbow Gulch trail slopes gently downhill to join Lake Shore at the Rampart Reservoir. The trail soon leaves the ponderosa pine forest and follows a grassy meadow and tributary to the lake. A sign at roadside only mentions it as a ski trail, but it is open to hikers and trailriders. The area near the Reservoir is for day use only.

BPW NATURE TRAIL Forest Service #712, 0.3 miles in loop trail; elevation gain 40 feet; trailhead #22; located on map Cascade A; approximate hiking time 10 minutes; features easy nature trail designed to serve all hikers including the blind and persons confined to wheelchairs.

The BPW Nature Trail is sponsored by the Colorado Federation of Business and Professional Women's Clubs, Inc., and offers a wilderness experience with special facilities. The trail itself leads through three different kinds of ecosystems, including a willow bottomland, a ponderosa pine and spruce-fir area. It has bridges, benches, and a wooden observation deck that overlooks Castaway Gulch. The path is about four feet wide and has a firm but natural tread.

This is a self-guiding nature trail with 14 stations along it. The station signs are also translated into Braille. Restrooms suitable for use by the physically handicapped are also provided.

NICHOLS Forest Service #709, 2 miles overall; elevation gain 40 feet; trailheads #20 and #21; located on map Cascade A; approximate hiking time 0.8 hour; features lake shore walk overlooking Nichols Reservoir (fishing permitted).

Nichols Trail begins at the Dikeside Overlook on the north end of the Rampart Reservoir Dam Parking Area, and provides access to the shores of Nichols Reservoir, although it does not go all the way around the lake. It goes down through a ponderosa pine forest and follows a small drainage toward the Reservoir. The trail forks at the Reservoir, both forks following a road for a very short distance and then dipping to follow the lake shore. There is no trail on the east side of the lake.

The area is for day use only, and campfires are permitted only in grates provided by the Forest Service. Please do not explore or fish around Reservoir #1, which is located downstream to the east. Nichols Reservoir is also known as Reservoir #4.

WEST MONUMENT Forest Service #713, 6 miles one-way; elevation gain 2,000 feet, loss 60 feet; trailheads #21 and #20; located on maps Cascade B, A; approximate hiking time 3.4 hours; features varied scenery along old logging route.

There are some special regulations for this trail because one end is in a day-use area and the other end needs a new trailhead at the time of this writing. You may NOT leave your vehicle overnight at Rampart Reservoir, and parking and access arrangements are in doubt for the downstream end, due to new fencing at the CSDPU filtration plant. Contact the Forest Service or the Air Force Academy for instructions.

The western trailhead branches off of Nichols Trail 0.4 mile from the reservoir dam. This ancient logging route ambles north past the ruins of cabins and a two-seater outhouse. Then it climbs over a ridge and washboards over two drainage areas before climbing to a level section on high ground. Heading southeast, it crosses more tributaries as it winds through ponderosa pine and aspen. Finally, it joins West Monument Creek downstream from Reservoir #1 (the reservoir is closed to fishing) and follows that Creek down a steep canyon toward the Air Force Academy. Do not enter utility property at the mouth of the canyon.

LAKE SHORE Forest Service #700, 12 miles in loop trail; elevation gain 40 feet, loss 40 feet; trailhead #21; located on map Cascade A; approximate hiking time 4.8 hours; features access to shores of Rampart Reservoir (fishing permitted).

This is a very pretty trail when the reservoir is full, but because the lake is a domestic water supply for the City of Colorado Springs, it is subject to considerable drawdown in dry years. This can leave Lake Shore somewhat distant from the water.

No camping is permitted in this area and fires are permitted only in grates provided by the Forest Service. The lake is stocked with fish by the State of Colorado.

MONUMENT AREA

Road directions for:

MOUNT HERMAN

At the present there is only one trail in this area that is marked, maintained, and closed to motor vehicles, and to reach it you drive through the Town of Monument, cross the railroad tracks at Third Street and turn south on Mitchell Avenue. Go past the turnoff for Monument Lake itself, which is private, and turn right on Mount Herman Road. A big sign marks the point where you enter Pike National Forest, and note your odometer reading here. Drive 1.6 miles and turn left at the fork in the road. Drive another 2.7 miles up on the side of the mountain and watch for the trailhead on your right as you make a tight curve at a drainage area leading down toward Beaver Creek. The overall distance from the National Forest boundary is 4.3 miles.

MOUNT HERMAN Forest Service #715, 8.1 miles one-way; elevation gain 200 feet, loss 1,200 feet; trailhead #23; located on maps Palmer Lake B, A; approximate hiking time 4.6 hours; features varied scenery.

Mount Herman Trail leads through every kind of vegetation found in the Rampart Range area. Beginning at the southern trailhead, it wanders through oak brush that offers vivid colors in the fall. Then it climbs up Beaver Creek through ponderosa pine and blue spruce, finally leaving the creek and climbing a tributary to Mount Herman Road. North of this road, your trail shares a four-wheeler route for about a third of a mile and cuts northwest off the road as the road continues southwest. Now your trail narrows and wanders through aspen until it connects with Monument Creek in Limbaugh Canyon. It follows the creek through willow-brush meadows for about a mile and a half, but then it forks. The right fork continues downstream for 1.1 miles to the Forest Service boundary. Beyond this point is private development, so the trail dead-ends here. The left fork leaves the creek and climbs uphill to the Balanced Rock four-wheel drive road. There it ends.

CRIPPLE CREEK AREA

Road directions for:

THE CRAGS
HORSETHIEF PARK

Drive to the Town of Divide on Highway 24 and turn south on Highway 67 toward Cripple Creek. The turnoff toward THE CRAGS is located 4.2 miles from that intersection. Watch for a bridge on your left. The sign may say only "Rocky Mountain Camp", but this refers to the Mennonite Camp that is located along this road. Another 1.5 miles past the camp, you reach a National Forest auto campground with restroom facilities, etc. The trailhead is located at the campground itself. Plenty of parking.

If you continue on Highway 67, turning left toward Gillette, you come to an old railroad tunnel. Drive through and park on the other side of the tunnel on the right. There is enough parking for about 10 cars because this is a popular overlook. HORSETHIEF PARK trail leaves this overlook and loops back up over the tunnel to head east on the other side. HORSETHIEF PARK trail ends 2.9 miles south of the tunnel on the same road just above the point where Oil Creek crosses the road.

THE CRAGS Forest Service #664, 4.5 miles one-way; elevation gain 700 feet; trailhead #24; located on maps Pikes Peak A, Woodland Park C; approximate hiking time 2.3 hours; features overlook of distant mountains in 3/4 panorama.

This is a popular and gentle trail that leads to one of the area's finest overlooks, a 3/4 panorama that is limited only by Pikes Peak on one side. From the top of these eroded granite formations, you can see distant mountains to the north and west and the flatlands with the City of Colorado Springs to the east, as well as nearer features such as the reservoirs of the Pikes Peak watershed.

At first you hike beside the stream, but as the valley opens up, the trail goes away to the left so the stream becomes hidden by trees and brush. Cross-country skiers enjoy another trail that is located in the trees on the other side of the creek. Another path on the other side of the creek leads up one of the tributaries, towards Pikes Peak, and is a popular ski trail in winter.

Continue on the main trail until it curves to the left at a rock formation that looks like an A-frame with a niche in the bottom.

Follow the tributary that joins the stream there. You walk through a shady ravine where many kinds of mosses and wildflowers grow. Soon you arrive at the toughest part of this trail, a short, steep section that goes up through jumbled boulders.

At the top of this climb you find yourself on a ridge saddle where suddenly three reservoirs are in view below. If you have small children along, this would be a good place to quit, for this impressive overlook of lakes and forest and flatlands is a rewarding sight, but does require scrambling around on rocks where children might fall. From here a little-used path dips over the saddle and continues eastward into watershed country, but you need a free permit from the Colorado Springs Department of Utilities to explore that region.

Instead, take the path that you find leading to your left, up and along the ridge to the top of the Crags rock formations. The trail is not very steep and the view grows more impressive as you go. The top of this rock formation is broad and rolling and is guarded by old and wind-gnarled evergreens. It does not take a rock climber to enjoy this area but do wear proper footgear and beware of crumbly granite near edges.

HORSETHIEF PARK Forest Service #704, 4.5 miles one-way; elevation gain 1,400 feet, loss 900 feet; trailhead #25; located on maps Cripple Creek North B, Pikes Peak A, C; approximate hiking time 2.5 hours; features scenic trail that loops back to road.

Horsethief Park is a meadow area often used by cross-country skiers, but the trail above the park switchbacks and climbs to almost 11,100 feet. It starts near an overlook at an old railroad tunnel on the road to Cripple Creek. The trail loops up over the tunnel and heads east, following Horsethief Creek upstream to the meadow area. Another trail branches to the north to follow a tributary up the park, and skiers also use this section. The major trail keeps heading east and then leaves the valley to begin climbing the high ground to the south. Switchbacks lead through spruce-fir forest to high rocky areas where the trees are sparce. You pass Pancake Rocks, which are to the north overlooking the trail, and then wind down a steep path through the forest to rejoin the road just north of Oil Creek.

FLORISSANT AREA

SAWMILL Florissant Fossil Beds National Monument, 2.7 miles on circle trail; elevation gain 200 feet, loss 200 feet; trailhead #26; located on map Lake George D; approximate hiking time 1.5 hours; features abandoned sawmill and petrified sequoia redwood stumps.

This gentle trail forms a loop at the Florissant Fossil Beds Visitor Center off Highway 24, where visitors can see petrified stumps of ancient redwoods as well as shale deposits and other fossils, plus several views of Pikes Peak.

One petrified sequoia stump measures 10 feet in diameter and 11 feet high, a relic from the days when redwoods stood 300 feet tall at the edge of a vanished lake. Volcanic ash washed down from surrounding hills, burying the region, and minerals in the water gradually petrified the wood by replacing organic material with silica.

You may hike the loop in either direction, of course, but we will describe it from left to right. As you leave the visitor center, the trail passes the picnic area and goes through a gate. Please close all gates behind you, for livestock graze in the area. The trail climbs a fire road to a gravel road that is still being used, so watch for traffic here and follow the markers. They lead to an old sawmill that operated from the late 1800s to the 1930s. You have not quite completed the first mile of the trail. From here you follow the markers along old roads and paths.

When you are almost within quarter of a mile of the visitor center again, you have a choice of returning to the center along a mowed path or taking a side trip of 100 yards north to see a large petrified redwood stump. The trail ends behind the visitor center.

It is strictly forbidden, of course, to remove or disturb fossils, rocks, wildflowers, petrified wood (no matter how small the piece) or other natural or historical features. Pets must be restrained at all times and no camping is allowed. Cross-country skiing is permitted, but snowmobiles are prohibited.

TARRYALL AREA

Road directions for:

BROOKSIDE-McCURDY
UTE CREEK
HANKINS PASS (See LOST CREEK SCENIC AREA)

As you drive northwest on Highway 24, the Tarryall Road turnoff is located only 1.2 miles beyond Lake George.

Travel 14.7 miles on Tarryall Road and you find Twin Eagles Picnic Ground with the southern trailhead for BROOKSIDE-McCURDY. This is an approach to HANKINS PASS. Restroom facilities, a horse loading chute and ample parking are available at the picnic ground. For directions to the northern trailhead, see BAILEY AREA. For directions to the middle of BROOKSIDE-McCURDY, see JEFFERSON AREA.

To find the trailhead for UTE CREEK, travel another 5.5 miles past Twin Eagles and look for parking and footbridge on your right. The parking lot holds more than a dozen vehicles.

BROOKSIDE-McCURDY Forest Service #607, about 37 miles one-way; elevation gain 5,750 feet, loss 4,180 feet; trailheads #27 and #43; located on maps McCurdy Mt. C, A, Farnum Peak B, Topaz Mt. D, B, Shawnee D; approximate hiking time 24 hours; features spectacular and varied scenery.

Beginning at Twin Eagles Picnic Ground on Tarryall Road, the path climbs up to an old road, turns left onto the road and soon changes into a foot and horse path that snakes through evergreens and tall straight aspens. A ranch meadow is spread below. Soon you pass the sign where Hankins Pass Trail splits away to the right on a saddle ridge. You cross tiny tributaries of Hay Creek and then begin the grueling switchbacks that take you up through red granite crags similar to those in the Lost Creek Scenic Area ahead. Two of the crags have holes through them, and each switchback offers a loftier view of Pikes Peak and the Tarryall Valley.

Near 10,700 feet you find the junction where Lake Park Trail heads uphill to your right. Your trail has now become the boundary of the Lost Creek Scenic Area.

You climb a meadow valley and follow its stream up to the saddle ridge above its headwaters. From here you overlook the broad valley of McCurdy Park, where a Forest Service shelter is open on a first-come basis. This overlook is the beginning of McCurdy Park Trail, but your trail turns left and climbs up past McCurdy Mountain toward Bison Pass.

Here you climb through a ghost forest created by a fire around the turn of the century. The trees died upright and many remain that way, now weathered to look like driftwood. Changes in soil after the fire prevented new trees from replacing the old, so you find a grassy timberline environment just below the altitude where timberline usually begins. Your trail continues to climb toward the real timberline, however, and this is bighorn sheep country. Indeed, the Pikes Peak herd was reestablished with bighorns captured here.

Near Bison Pass you arrive at a grassy knoll at 11,900 feet where you can see across South Park to Antero Reservoir and the mountain ranges beyond. Your trail dives off that western slope, switchbacking down through loose gravel and through bristlecone pines that have reestablished themselves in this part of the forest. You arrive at a ridge saddle where Ute Creek Trail heads southwest toward Tarryall River. Your trail turns north and follows a gentle path through spruce and fir and past long meadows, following a creek down to Lost Park Campground.

From here you follow the meadow of the North Fork of Lost Creek north for two miles. Your path curves northwest and finds the remains of an old sawmill. Oddly enough, nearby is the rusted shell of a steel and concrete safe that was blasted apart many years ago.

Your trail crosses the creek on an iron culvert and joins Colorado Trail #1776. The two trails are one for another two miles as you travel northwest up another meadow valley. A sign marks the point where Brookside-McCurdy heads north again beside a tributary that is hidden in the trees. This steep and rocky path leads up to a ridge saddle, then down the other side to Craig Park, which is similar to the brushy and boggy valley that you just left.

Again your trail switchbacks uphill, leading north. You arrive at a ridge overlooking McArthur Gulch. This section was scheduled for rerouting at the time of this writing. The new route will avoid the old jeep road and will follow land contours, possibly down McArthur Gulch.

The trail ends at the main gravel road at Bailey. See BAILEY AREA for directions.

UTE CREEK Forest Service #629, about 3 miles one-way; elevation gain 400 feet; trailhead #28; located on map Farnum Peak B; approximate hiking time 2 hours.

This one is sometimes used to form a loop with Brookside-McCurdy for it joins that longer trail at the top of Bison Pass. Both trails end at Tarryall Road, but 5.5 miles apart, so a considerable part of the loop will be road travel.

Ute Creek Trail begins at a footbridge crossing Tarryall River, skirts private property where a beaver pond lies, then begins climbing beside Ute Creek. This area boasts very large ponderosa pines, as well as aspen and blue spruce.

After crossing near the fork of tributaries, however, the trail leaves the creekside and climbs steeply on a wooded hillside. There is no more water beyond this point.

The trail ends on a saddle ridge at nearly 11,300 feet, with a grand vista of the Tarryall Valley below. Signs mark its juncture with Brookside-McCurdy.

The total distance of the Ute Creek/Brookside-McCurdy loop, including road travel, is estimated at 20.5 miles.

LOST CREEK SCENIC TRAILS

Road directions for:

HANKINS PASS
LAKE PARK
BROOKSIDE-McCURDY (See TARRYALL AREA)
McCURDY PARK
GOOSE CREEK

The Lost Creek region has been set aside as a scenic area to protect its primitive nature. You can only see this wonderland by hiking or riding horseback, a hard journey either way, but if it weren't so beautiful, it wouldn't be designated as a scenic area. Some of the granite formations will remind you of those on Barr Trail, though in much grander scale. And then there is the "lost" creek that churns into box canyons, disappearing under cliffs and then reappearing from caves beyond.

If you want a very long expedition, you can approach the Lost Creek area by two long trails, but the most popular route is the shortest one, a 24-mile loop that begins and ends near Goose Creek Campground. Many parts of this loop are difficult and most hikers take two to four days to complete it, so make sure that you take along what you need. You will be a long way from help.

The loop can be hiked in either direction, of course, but we will describe it from left to right, beginning with HANKINS PASS and ending with GOOSE CREEK TRAIL.

To find the GOOSE CREEK trailhead, take the gravel road that joins Highway 126 just three miles west of Deckers. Follow the signs to Goose Creek Campground, a distance of 11 miles, then keep heading south past the campground for 3.5 miles, taking Trailhead Road to your right. Watch for horses that unload at a special parking area along this road. Both HANKINS PASS and GOOSE CREEK share a common trailhead at the auto parking lot.

HANKINS PASS Forest Service #630, 5.9 miles one-way; elevation gain 1,820 feet, loss 1,040 feet; trailhead #30; located on maps McCurdy Mt. D, C; approximate hiking time 2.9 hours; features streamside camping, beaver ponds, access to Lake Park and Brookside-McCurdy Trails.

Hankins Pass shares a trailhead with the Goose Creek Trail and from this single trailhead, the path dips into Hankins Gulch and crosses a stream at the bottom. Here it divides, the left fork leading to Hankins Pass and the right fork leading to Goose Creek.

Now you begin following the stream uphill through spruce and large aspens. There are no confusing side trails. About halfway to the pass itself, you find an aspen meadow with active beaver ponds, a nice place to camp and fish. Above this point, the path crosses the stream and follows the hillside above it. The trail eventually leads above the headwaters to a saddle ridge, and there you find an intersection with Lake Park Trail.

If you continue straight ahead on Hankins you will be going down the other side of this ridge, picking up another stream, and joining Brookside-McCurdy Trail. Hankins Pass Trail ends there at the intersection with Brookside-McCurdy. From there you can take Brookside-McCurdy north to McCurdy Park, then McCurdy Park Trail, Goose Creek Trail, making a circuit.

This route is the longest and certainly the most difficult because you lose more than 1,000 feet of altitude following that stream downhill and must make up that loss by climbing many switchbacks.

The shorter and more popular route is still pretty difficult: turn right off Hankins Pass onto Lake Park Trail at the saddle ridge. This also leads you to Brookside-McCurdy below McCurdy Park where you are back on the main track.

LAKE PARK Forest Service #639, 3 miles from Hankins Pass to Brookside-McCurdy Trails, one mile and a quarter to Lake Park itself; elevation gain 1,480 feet, loss 720 feet; trailhead #30; located on maps McCurdy Mt. D, B, A; approximate hiking time 2.0 hours; features grand vistas and camping at Lake Park.

As you stand atop Hankins Pass itself, the sign says "Lake Park Three Miles" and points uphill. Be sure to fill your canteens at the headwaters of Hankins Gulch, for the Lake Park Trail is a long, dry march over high country. It begins at 10,000 feet, climbs to almost 11,000 feet before descending to join Brookside-McCurdy Trail.

Lake Park is a high meadow surrounded by majestic rock formations and the silvery snags of a ghost forest. Unfortunately, this ghost forest also explains why the lakes have so quickly turned to swampland. All lakes eventually silt up, but the process is quickened if a forest fire denudes the mountainside and increases erosion. Today, the lakes are only shallow pools in the midst of bog.

Campers will find high, level and dry ground on the south side of the meadow, but to reach flowing water, you must bushwhack carefully across the bogs to the streams that come down creases in the north slope. Test the ground with care because some of these bogs are very deep.

The trail climbs out of the park on the west side and becomes once again rocky and steep. As you hike over the highest portion, watch for alpine columbine, a high-altitude miniature of the state flower. There is a pleasant flat area to the top of this ridge, but no water. From here the trail dives down to join Brookside-McCurdy.

At this T-junction with Brookside-McCurdy, signs say that Lake Park is two miles behind, that Tarryall Creek is 4 3/4 miles to the south and McCurdy Park is one mile north. That last mile to McCurdy Park climbs to the headwaters of a creek and up to saddle ridge that overlooks the park.

McCURDY PARK Forest Service #628, 5.3 miles one-way; elevation gain 1,080 feet, loss 400 feet; trailhead #27; located on maps McCurdy Mt. A, B; approximate hiking time 3 hours; features meadow camping at McCurdy Park, lake fishing north of park; McCurdy Park Trail links Brookside-McCurdy with Goose Creek for a Lost Creek circuit trip.

McCurdy Park is a high valley with a flowing stream and a Forest Service A-frame shelter that is available on a first-come basis. Many of the most beautiful rock formations in the Lost Creek area are located along this trail.

Since we are describing the scenic area circuit from left to right, we assume that you will be approaching McCurdy Park from the south, along Brookside-McCurdy Trail. Brookside-McCurdy is a long trail that leads to McCurdy Park and branches away to the west. McCurdy Park Trail begins at this intersection on a ridge overlooking McCurdy Park itself.

From this point you hike through the long grassy valley, following a stream north. There are many pleasant camping spots along this part. Some maps show the trail leaving the creek and making one long switchback, but that is meant to symbolize a long series of steep switchbacks that take you down the side of a canyon. At the bottom you find a deep lake that was built by beaver at a narrow part of the gorge. There are only a couple of campsites, so if you wish to stay here, try to arrive early.

From here the trail climbs up and over ridges and crosses a stream. The older USGS topographic map shows this stream to be the one draining from the beaver lake, which would mean that the water comes from your right as you cross it, but the map is mistaken. The water comes from your left and is another lost piece of Lost Creek. A few campsites are available here.

Up and over more steep ridges and you find another stream crossing marked Refrigerator Gulch. The USGS map shows you crossing at beaver ponds, but these ponds have now turned to swamp so you would hardly know you were in the right place without the sign.

As soon as you cross this stream, you find that the trail branches left and right, following the stream both ways. Both trails climb steeply away from the creek. To complete the circuit toward Goose Creek, you must take the left branch. The right branch looks very distinct, however, for it leads to a box canyon used by horse riders as a campsite and corral. Another piece of Lost Creek emerges in the box canyon, so horses have water but limited forage here.

The left branch leads up to a saddle ridge where McCurdy Park Trail ends at a junction with Goose Creek Trail. From this point Goose Creek Trail follows the ridge north toward Wigwam Park or descends the ridge to complete the scenic area circuit by winding up at Goose Creek Campground. A sign marks the intersection.

GOOSE CREEK Forest Service #612, 11.8 miles one-way; elevation gain 2,000 feet, loss 780 feet; trailhead #30;

located on maps McCurdy Mt. D, B, Windy Peak D; approximate hiking time 6.7 hours; features fishing, camping and majestic rock formations.

If you are hiking the Lost Creek Scenic Area circuit from left to right, you will join Goose Creek Trail at a ridgetop east of Refrigerator Gulch. But there is no use beginning our description in the middle of the trail, so let's start back at the main trailhead near Goose Creek Campground.

The early part of this trail is popular among day hikers and fishermen, so it is wide and easy and has a fine bridge crossing at Goose Creek. (Lost Creek becomes Goose Creek when it stops being lost.)

As you leave the auto parking lot, you descend a trail and cross a fairly small stream that flows from Hankins Gulch. These signs direct you to the left for Hankins Pass or to the right for Goose Creek. Your trail follows the tributary down toward Goose Creek, then crosses the creek and continues up on the east side.

The creek is wide and active, occasionally interrupted by the beaver corps of engineers. The campsites are in the meadow across the stream, so campers can be away from the day traffic. Farther upstream the trail grows more narrow, more steep, less developed in every way.

As you descend a ridge well away from Goose Creek itself, you find a trickle of water crossing your path and a clear trail branching away to the left. This leads to a fascinating and scenic area called the Shafthouse.

Follow this path and you will find several log cabins that you may use on a first-come basis. There is very little firewood close by. At the cabins, the trail goes left and right, left to dead-end at Goose Creek itself and right to the Shafthouse area.

Many years ago engineers tried to dam Reservoir Gulch by sinking a shaft and pumping concrete underground in an attempt to stop the flow of Lost Creek. Yet the creek only found new channels underground and the project was abandoned.

You will not find a shaft and you will not find a house at the "Shafthouse", but you will find some rusting equipment on a concrete slab and some very pretty scenery. Just a few yards before you reach the machinery, there is an opening in the rock on the left side of the trail where giant boulders have tumbled together to form a cave-like room of impressive size. The room has a concrete floor.

If you follow the Shafthouse trail farther up canyon, you come to a place where an old wooden ladder lies wedged in the cracks between large rocks. This ladder was quite dangerous at the time of our exploration, so bring a rope and use the convenient tree at the top of the ladder if you wish to see the ice caverns where Lost Creek disappears underground.

Return to the main trail and follow it north to find another charming area, the upper end of Reservoir Gulch. This area offers more campsites with a convenient stream. It's a steep climb out of this area to the saddle ridge where Goose Creek Trail joins McCurdy Park Trail, and from there Goose Creek Trail leads north, crossing over into another watershed and following a stream downhill past a balanced rock pinnacle toward Wigwam Trail. That's where Goose Creek Trail ends.

WELLINGTON LAKE AREA

Road directions for:

ROLLING CREEK
WIGWAM
COLORADO TRAIL #1776

Wellington Lake is located on a gravel road between Bailey and Buffalo Creek. The lake itself is private, but since all the small roads in this area have signs pointing toward Wellington Lake, that's a good place to start our directions.

ROLLING CREEK TRAIL no longer begins at the Bancroft Ranch near Wellington Lake, but has a new trailhead a couple of miles north that allows you to bypass private property in the region. Proceed northwest on the gravel road #543 that leads from Wellington Lake to Bailey. Soon you pass the little community of Sylvania of the Rockies, and only 0.7 mile later you find a turnoff to the left. This dirt road leads to trailheads for the ROLLING CREEK and COLORADO TRAIL 0.3 mile later.

At the time of this writing, only certain sections of Colorado Trail #1776 had been completed and the trailhead itself had to be hidden in the trees to keep motorcycle damage to a minimum. The trail begins about 100 yards from the road and to find it you must follow blaze marks through the woods. You will find blazes on trees to your right as you start up the road marked for Rolling Creek Trailhead. The Rolling Creek Trailhead is on your left.

WIGWAM #609; if you take the gravel road leading south toward Deckers from Wellington Lake, the turnoff to WIGWAM trailhead will be on your right after you have crossed Stoney Pass. The distance from Wellington Lake is five miles and the turnoff is marked. Since this can be a rather round-about way of getting there, however, we will describe another route from Deckers. Take Highway 126 west of Deckers and three miles later turn left onto the gravel road marked for Lost Valley Ranch, Cheesman Lake, etc. Travel 1.1 miles and turn right at fork marked JVL and Lost Valley Ranch. Travel another 1.1 miles and turn right at the fork marked Wellington Lake. Two and one-half miles later you will turn right again following a sign toward Wellington Lake. Only 2.6 miles later you find the WIGWAM TRAIL road marked on your left. This is a dirt road that gets worse as you travel the 1.4 miles to the parking area. The last section may be very poor, so explore ahead on foot before attempting it with a passenger car.

ROLLING CREEK Forest Service #663, 9 miles one-way; elevation gain 2,650 feet, loss 1,200 feet; trailhead #31; located on maps Windy Peak B, D; approximate hiking time 4.5 hours; features rolling forest walk, then steep climb through mossy canyon.

This trail has been lengthened to avoid private property such as the Bancroft Ranch, but this new section is a pleasant forest walk with no exceptionally steep parts. You cross small ridges and intermittent streams, hiking toward the huge rock formation known as The Castle. Near the foot of this landmark you cross Rolling Creek itself. At first you leave the creek and hike up into the woods to a place where the old route from Bancroft Ranch has been closed off with many fallen logs. Turn right and climb a little farther and you return to the creek once more.

Now you begin the most beautiful part of the climb, a steep section that takes you up through a narrow canyon where boulders have tumbled together in interesting ways. The forest is cool and mossy here, a charming place.

Finally, you leave the creek as you start up the ridge that separates this watershed from the Wigwam watershed beyond. Old maps show two routes here, both converging higher up, but at the time of this writing, one of the routes was entirely gone and the other fading among rocks and roots and fallen timber. This section was scheduled for trail repair. Then you go up and over the ridge and down to Wigwam Park, where a sign marks the southern intersection with Wigwam Trail.

WIGWAM Forest Service #609, 13.3 miles one-way; elevation gain 2,220 feet, loss 500 feet; trailheads #32 and #29; located on maps Cheesman Lake A, Green Mountain C, Windy Peak D, C, Topaz D; approximate hiking time 7 hours; features meadow and forest walk with fishing at creeks and beaver ponds.

Wigwam is a long and varied trail with only a few steep sections. Much of the trail skirts long valleys rich in wildlife such as grouse, beaver and deer. Many of the rock formations are similar to those found in the Lost Creek Scenic Area which is just to the south. Indeed, the Goose Creek Trail from the Scenic Area ends at Wigwam Park.

Beginning at the eastern trailhead, you walk down a washed out four-wheel track to a glade where you find Wigwam Creek and a small pond. Your trail follows Wigwam upstream, crossing and recrossing on simple log bridges. You pass through a rolling forest, then climb more steeply.

The creek beside you forms small waterfalls, and some of the deeper pools have native cutthroat trout of pan size.

At Wigwam Park itself, the creek meanders through a green grassland, often interrupted by beaver dams. Your trail stays on the northern edge of this valley, finally coming to a sign indicating that Goose Creek Trail is to your left, across the valley. From there you can see the tributary ravine that Goose Creek Trail follows, and framed within this notch is a rock formation with a thumblike projection that has a large balanced rock on its tip. Since Wigwam Creek itself is muddy here, the best water for campers is found a short distance up the Goose Creek Trail.

The largest beaver pond marked on your old topographic maps is now a flat field of grass that makes comfortable camping. You can still see remains of the huge dam which stood about six feet tall and over 200 feet long. This kind of beaver activity built much of the flatland seen in Wigwam Park.

As you follow the valley higher, you find a sign indicating that Rolling Creek Trail begins on your right. At the time of our exploration, the sign itself was about all that remained of this half of Rolling Creek Trail. The sign mentions Wellington Lake (seven miles), but Rolling Creek's new trailhead is now located several miles north of Wellington Lake.

Farther up the valley, you find a place where the original trail becomes faint and where a newer trail crosses Wigwam Creek. Take the new trail, cross the creek, and follow it up through the woods to a higher park.

At the entrance of this higher park, your trail is covered with water from a spring that flows from beneath a huge rock. That is the best source of water in this park. There is more beaver activity, more marsh, but the valley is surrounded by magnificant rock formations that jut above the trees.

The trail grows more faint as you climb past this point to the low saddle ridge (only 10,150 feet) that separates

Wigwam from the East Lost Creek watershed. Wigwam Trail continues down into East Lost Park, across Lost Creek and along an even wider valley to end at Lost Park Campground. (For road directions, see JEFFERSON AREA).

COLORADO TRAIL # 1776 About 47 miles in our area alone; elevation gain 6,110 feet, loss 4,250 feet; trailheads #33 and #47; located on maps Windy Peak B, A, C, Topaz Mt. D, B, A, Observatory Rock B, A, Mt. Logan B, A, D, C, Jefferson D, C, Boreas Pass D, B; approximate hiking time 30 hours; features link between Denver and Durango.

When completed, Colorado Trail #1776 will extend from Denver to Durango. This is not an old historic route, but since the project was begun to commemorate Colorado's centennial and the nation's bicentennial, it has a new claim to history.

At the time of this writing, only parts of the trail had been completed, and some trailheads were hidden to keep motorcycle damage to a minimum during construction. The trail enters our area near the Rolling Creek Trailhead, but you must follow blaze marks on trees to find the beginning of the constructed trail. No signs at present.

This new piece of trail angles through the woods to avoid a ranch, then joins an old four-wheel road that used to be called the Hooper Trail. This road climbs southwest past the southern trailhead of Craig Meadow, then becomes less of a road where it crosses the giant bog of Bluestem Draw, where the log corduroy used to extend for almost a quarter of a mile in the old days.

Later the trail follows a long valley that leads to other long valleys at Brookside-McCurdy Trail. The remains of an old sawmill can be seen at the intersection on the North Fork of Lost Creek. For two miles, #1776 and Brookside-McCurdy Trail are one, but then Brookside-McCurdy branches away to the north and #1776 continues northwest, avoiding Lost Park Road, then winding around Black Canyon and across Rock Creek to Kenosha Pass. Between Rock Creek and Kenosha Pass, this trail offers spectacular views of South Park and the high ranges to the west and southwest.

From Kenosha Pass, the trail continues northwest across Guernsey Gulch, past Jefferson Hill, crossing the Jefferson Lake Road above Aspen Campground. Then it winds through the forest, climbing to a point where it leaves our area at Georgia Pass. This section offers magnificant views of South Park, Jefferson Lake, Pikes Peak and the western slope country.

For those who want to take it in small bites, the Colorado Trail will have a number of road access points between its junction with Brookside-McCurdy and the top of Georgia Pass. Among these are accesses at the North Fork of Lost Creek (the Rock Creek Road, a short spur off the Lost Park Road); at Kenosha Pass; at the Guernsey Gulch Road (primitive); Deadman Gulch road (primitive); Jefferson Creek and at Georgia Pass.

DEER CREEK AREA

Road directions for:

MERIDIAN
ROSALIE
TANGLEWOOD

In the northeast corner of Park County, on Highway 285 between Pine Junction and Bailey, you find a prominent turnoff marked Deer Creek. Follow this paved road 6.5 miles west to a fork. The right fork, marked "Camp Rosalie", leads to MERIDIAN trailhead. The left fork, marked "Deer Creek Campground", leads to the ROSALIE-TANGLEWOOD trailhead.

MERIDIAN can be hard to find. For one thing, if you find Meridian Campground, you've taken a wrong turn. Follow the cross-markers toward Camp Rosalie. Soon the pavement ends and you are following a gravel road that leads to a gate with a National Forest sign. Instead of entering here, turn right on another good gravel road and follow it around to an intersection marked by a sign saying "Elk Creek Highlands". Turn left there and right at the next T-junction. From here on, the road is dirt but passable. You cross a stream with a pond on the right and drive around the edge of Camp Rosalie. At the Y marked Church Fork, turn right and soon you will spot a small bridge over the stream on your right and a horse corral on the left. Park here. Forest Service maps show the road dead-ending here, but it does continue for quite a ways, so watch for the trailhead signs.

For ROSALIE-TANGLEWOOD take the left fork on Deer Creek Road marked "Deer Creek Campground". The pavement ends a mile later and the road becomes gravel. Then you come to a Y with the Deer Creek Campground on the left. The right fork may not be marked, but dead-ends shortly at the ROSALIE-TANGLEWOOD trailhead. The last half mile of the road is very rocky and rough but passable for passenger cars. Only one path leaves the parking area: ROSALIE and TANGLEWOOD divide several hundred yards higher up.

MERIDIAN Forest Service #604, 3 miles one-way to Meridian Trail Campground; elevation gain 1,600 feet; trailhead #34; located on map Harris Park D; approximate hiking time 2.5 hours; features forest hike to campground where other trails connect.

Meridian connects to a larger system of trails in Arapahoe National Forest. It is a very clear and well-marked trail, but there is one point of confusion: it does not leave Meridian Campground, but it arrives at a place that is also called Meridian Campground.

Since the other two trails in the Deer Creek area carry warnings about safety for horses, it would be well to point out that Meridian is a good trail for inexperienced trailhorses. It begins on a gentle gravel path that climbs steadily, then grows rocky only at the top.

From the trailhead bridge, the path climbs a long ridge high above Elk Creek. There are no real creeks along this route, but small springs that cross the path higher up provide water. As you angle northeast, you hike through a grove of aspen that are unusually tall and straight.

At the top there is a small spring, an outhouse, and a pair of signs on the northern edge of the saddle. The sign pointing northwest says "Lost Creek 4, Truesdell Creek 6, Beartrack Lakes 7", and the one pointing northeast says "Lost Creek 6, Indian Creek Park 7, Brook Forest 12", so get a good rest. These trails are not in our area.

ROSALIE Forest Service #603, 12 miles one-way; elevation gain 3,560 feet, loss 1,120 feet; trailheads #35 and #36; located on maps Harris Park C, Mt. Evans D, B, A.

Rosalie is a long and rough trail that twice climbs to timberline yet even at its highest points you find yourself surrounded by bald giants, including Mount Evans. Our description begins at the bottom because the lower section is the most popular.

Trailriders will find convenient corrals at the parking area, but Rosalie is so rocky and rugged that it can only be recommended for the most experienced trailhorses. This is not a good training ground for inexperienced mounts. About a hundred yards from the trailhead, the Rosalie-Tanglewood path splits and Rosalie takes the high road to the left that climbs along and across Deer Creek. This path snakes up through forest and clearings where grouse, deer and beaver are often seen. There are campsites all along the route.

As you can see by the map, you take the left or southern fork at the headwaters of Deer Creek, but since the right fork is by far the larger stream, the left fork may appear as only a minor tributary or marshy ravine in late summer. The right fork swerves hard to the north at this point, so your compass can help assure you that you have found the right place. The trail grows more indistinct in this area.

Keep heading west up the green ravine. You are headed for a bald saddle ridge between two bald peaks known as Tahana on the north and Kataka on the south. At the top of the saddle there is another road-like trail coming from Kataka Mountain and joining your own. This is the destination of Threemile Trail.

The ridge saddle is that kind of timberline margin where trees grow only in scattered spots, all stunted and windswept. To the north you can see Mount Evans with its building on top and cars going up the switchbacks. Due west is Geneva Mountain, and to its right you see two green ravines where streams angle down to join Scott-Gomer Creek, which runs north-south below you at this point. Rosalie will follow that wide ravine on the right up to timberline and then beyond to Guanella Pass.

A wooden post marks the place where your faint path starts switchbacking down the mountainside to cross Scott-Gomer. This narrow path angles down through a ghost forest created by a fire long ago. At the bottom you cross Scott-Gomer, then link with Scott-Gomer Trail to Abyss Lake in the manner shown on the map. This area near the creek is a popular campground, but just up the tributary ravine on Rosalie you will find a Forest Service shelter that is open on a first-come basis.

Now your trail begins to make up the altitude lost in descending to Scott-Gomer. It's a long and steady climb to timberline and above, eventually intersecting a path that used to be a road. A post marks this intersection so that hikers coming downhill won't miss Rosalie and wind up hiking south along the wrong route. This closed road leads to a dead-end on the shoulder of Geneva Mountain at 12,179 feet.

Rosalie itself climbs to 11,800 feet before winding down to the trailhead at Guanella Pass. To find the upper trailhead by road, see GUANELLA PASS AREA.

TANGLEWOOD Forest Service #636, 5 miles one-way; elevation gain 2,680 feet, loss 160 feet; trailhead #35; located on map Harris Park C; approximate hiking time 3.3 hours; features charming streamside hike, rugged climb above timberline to lakes.

If you want to fish Roosevelt Lakes, you'll certainly have to earn the opportunity for Tanglewood is a high and rocky route. The lower section is gentle and popular among dayhikers, but the higher you go, the rougher it gets.

There are convenient horse corrals at the trailhead and along Tanglewood itself, but trailriders are warned that it is not suitable for training horses unaccustomed to climbing in the rocks, (Meridian Trail would be better).

As you leave the trailhead, Tanglewood shares its route with Rosalie, but the two soon divide. You take the right fork, cross the creek on a culvert bridge, then follow up along a path that used to be a road. You cross and re-cross this tumbling creek, climbing through forest and small clearings. High up, the trail leaves the creek and climbs up above timberline. Here the trail fades in the rocks, so head toward a wooden post erected on the ridge saddle. There's not much of a trail there, either, but this marks the place where you're supposed to cross over.

From here you have a spectacular view and can see for miles, but oddly enough, you cannot see Roosevelt Lakes that lie directly below. The lakes are in the bottom of a glacial depression and you must hike some distance on this gentle incline before you see them.

A trail from Beartrack Lakes connects with Tanglewood at Roosevelt Lakes, but that's out of our area.

BAILEY AREA

Road directions for:

CRAIG MEADOW
BROOKSIDE-McCURDY (See TARRYALL AREA)
BEN TYLER
CRAIG PARK

Bailey is located in northeastern Park County on Highway 285. Turn south off this highway at Moore Lumber and Hardware in Bailey and follow a paved road until it curves back toward the highway. At the beginning of that curve is a gravel road that leads straight ahead toward the trailheads for CRAIG MEADOW and BROOKSIDE-McCURDY.

Proceed 1.4 miles on gravel and look for a gate on your left. This turnoff leads up Payne Gulch to CRAIG MEADOW trailhead, some 1.7 miles from the gate. The road leads through private property, and there is only enough room to park two vehicles at the trailhead.

To find the trailhead for BROOKSIDE-McCURDY, do not enter Payne Gulch, but stay on the main gravel road for another 1.2 miles, passing Bailey Picnic Grounds. There is a sign on your left marking Trail #607.

For directions to the southern trailhead for BROOKSIDE-McCURDY, see TARRYALL AREA. For directions to the middle, see JEFFERSON AREA.

The trailhead for BEN TYLER is located on Highway 285, 6.4 miles west of Bailey. Parking for about half a dozen vehicles is on the north side of the highway and the trailhead is on the south side.

CRAIG PARK has no road access and can only be reached via Brookside-McCurdy or Ben Tyler.

CRAIG MEADOW Forest Service #637, 6 miles one-way; elevation gain 1,030 feet, loss 1,200 feet; trailhead #44; located on maps Shawnee D, Windy Peak A; approximate hiking time 3 hours; features scenic meadow with beaver ponds.

Craig Meadow is a grassy park with beaver ponds, a popular spot for the backpacker fishermen who are looking for more scenery than fish. This used to be called Payne Creek Trail, for it begins at Payne Creek on the north, but it does not really follow Payne Creek at all.

Park as best you can near that northern trailhead, and start up the path that used to be a four-wheeler road. It is quite steep and stays high on the hillside, going up through the woods to the ridge above Payne Creek, then down the other side. It picks up a tributary of Craig Creek and follows that down to the meadow.

Your trail makes a bog crossing at Craig Creek and follows the stream where the beavers are at work. Large blue spruce grow widely spaced in the meadow.

Beyond the meadow, the trail crosses Bluestem Creek and then you will find an old road known as Pine Ridge joining the trail from the right. This is now closed to vehicles.

From here you begin climbing a trail uphill through the trees to join Colorado Trail #1776 two miles from the meadow. This is where Craig Meadow trail ends.

One warning: there is no trail between Craig Meadow and Craig Park upstream because this creek plunges through a rock gorge known as Black Canyon where hikers have become lost and injured.

BEN TYLER Forest Service #606, 9.0 miles one-way; elevation gain 3,460 feet, loss 2,040 feet; trailheads #46 and #45; located on maps Shawnee C, Mt. Logan D, Observatory Rock C; approximate hiking time 6 hours; features streamside and high mountain hiking.

The way we heard it, Ben Tyler lived with his family up in the gulch that bears his name, and there he had a lumber operation in the gold rush days. He sawed up timber and hauled it over the high ridge and down the other side to Fairplay. As you hike this spectacular trail, you can thank Ben for showing the way.

You park your vehicle on the north side of Highway 285, then cross the highway to start up the trail. You climb a series of switchbacks, go through a gate that keeps cattle in, and then you head down a path on a grassy hillside that overlooks Ben Tyler Creek. Your trail follows this creek up through the woods, crosses it and continues to follow it past ancient beaver doings toward the place where Tyler's cabins used to be. Only the foundation and some trash remain now. They are located on the west side of the creek.

Your trail continues up the east side, leaves the water and then begins rising very steeply. A short side path returns to the creek higher up, and from there you have a view of the gulch laid out below. The hillsides are practically nothing but aspens, a golden vista in late September.

Now your path becomes a little less distinct (and less popular) because it switchbacks up to a high ridge, where it joins the top of Craig Park Trail. Then it angles down the other side, joins Rock Creek, and follows that down to a road access off East Lost Park Road (See JEFFERSON AREA).

CRAIG PARK Forest Service #608, 7 miles one-way; elevation gain 660 feet, loss 630 feet; trailheads #43 and #45; located on maps Mt. Logan D, Shawnee C, Topaz A, B; approximate hiking time 3 hours; features mountain hiking and timberline scenery.

Few trails in our area are so little traveled as this one. That's because Craig Park has no road access of its own. To reach it, you must hike to it from Ben Tyler or Brookside-McCurdy, which adds many miles to the trail length given above.

But once you get there, you find a long grassy meadow area surrounded by wooded hills and rock outcroppings. The lower part of the trail is very easy going and is interrupted only by several bogs that you must get around. The only steep section is at the west end where the trail climbs up above the headwaters of Craig Creek to a high ridge, where it joins Ben Tyler.

Craig park is normally hiked as part of a long excursion, but if your purpose is to reach Craig Park itself, the most popular route seems to be from the north end of Brookside-McCurdy, a distance of 5.5 miles.

Notice that no trail links Craig Park with Craig Meadow downstream. That is because Craig Creek plunges through a steep gorge known as Black Canyon, where hikers have become lost and injured.

GUANELLA PASS AREA

Road directions for:

THREEMILE TRAIL
BURNING BEAR
SCOTT-GOMER TRAIL TO ABYSS LAKE
SHELF LAKE
SOUTH PARK
ROSALIE (See DEER CREEK AREA)

About 10 1/2 miles west of Bailey on Highway 285 you find the small town of Grant, where a gravel road cuts away to the north marked "Geneva Basin Ski Area" and "Georgetown 24". Six major trailheads are located along this road over Guanella Pass. Note your odometer reading here.

The trailhead for THREEMILE is exactly three miles up this road from Grant. Watch for it on your right.

Drive another 2.1 miles and you find BURNING BEAR on your left. SCOTT-GOMER is located on your right only 0.2 mile farther.

Drive another 1.9 miles and watch for a pair of gravel roads that cut away to the left. Take the second of those two roads and travel 3.2 miles to SHELF LAKE trailhead, which is on your right.

Going higher on the Guanella Pass road, you find a pair of trailheads at the very top. SOUTH PARK strikes out to the west and ROSALIE heads east. For a description of ROSALIE, see DEER CREEK AREA.

THREE MILE CREEK Forest Service #635, 6 miles one-way; elevation gain 2,600 feet, loss 200 feet; trailhead #41; located on maps Mt. Logan A, B, Mt. Evans D; approximate hiking time 4 hours; features streamside hike that leads up to timberline and intersection with Rosalie.

Don't let the name fool you. Threemile Creek Trail is six miles long and even Threemile Creek is longer than three miles. It just happens to be the creek you find three miles up from Highway 285.

This trail is a popular link to the very middle of two other long trails, Rosalie and Scott-Gomer Trail to Abyss Lake, making the whole system more complex.

As the path leaves the parking lot, it climbs steadily up the side of a ridge in order to avoid private property where Threemile Creek crosses the road. The creek is somewhat hidden from view and your trail won't find it for half a mile.

Then you join and cross the creek and begin weaving up it as it passes through small grassy areas and cool forest with rock formations on either side. It's a steady and somewhat rocky climb.

After passing Spearhead Mountain, the main creek and trail swing sharply to the east. Here the trail is a little steeper. The path turns again at a fork of tributaries, following the northern one up to timberline. Four-wheel drive vehicles used to drive around in this area, so here your trail looks like a fading road as it skirts Kataka Mountain to find the saddle ridge between Kataka and Tahana Mountains.

There on the saddle, Threemile Trail ends at a junction with Rosalie. The altitude is 11,660 and you may have to look for a wooden post to make sure you've found Rosalie. A shelter lies about a mile and a half beyond this point. It is located on Rosalie Trail past its intersection with Scott-Gomer. See ROSALIE for instructions.

BURNING BEAR Forest Service #601, 5 miles one-way; elevation gain 1,160 feet, loss 1,120 feet; trailheads #40 and #39; located on maps Jefferson B, Montezuma D, Mt. Evans C; approximate hiking time 2.5 hours; features popular stroll beside valley and through forest, excellent for cross-country skiing.

This is a good trail for easy strolling or cross-country skiing because it is very gentle for a long way. The trailhead is located beside Geneva Creek on the road to Geneva Ski Basin, so skiers should always find the road open, though parking may be limited by snowbanks. Here, Geneva Creek winds through a long valley where cattle graze. Enter the fence near the stream and follow Geneva upstream to a wooden bridge.

After crossing, you continue upstream on a trail that stays just inside the trees. This area is used for judging snowpack depth, so please stay on the trail when snow is on the ground. As you travel this section, you pass gaps in the trees where you can look out across the wide valley toward the mountains beyond.

Eventually your trail turns up the tributary that flows from Burning Bear Gulch, a stream too small for fishing. Even here the trail is fairly gentle as it climbs slowly through the forest. You pass the remains of a log cabin, and finally cross to the south (or left) side of the stream, where you find a mild set of switchbacks that lead up and over the wooded ridge into another watershed.

From here it is downhill all the way. You follow a tributary to Lamping Creek, then down Lamping Creek itself to a rough gravel road. This is Park County 60, which joins Highway 285 at Webster, about 14 miles west of Bailey.

SCOTT-GOMER TRAIL TO ABYSS LAKE Forest Service #602, 8 miles one-way; elevation gain 3,050 feet; trailhead #38; located on maps Mt. Evans C, D, B; approximate hiking time 5.4 hours; features high mountain fishing lakes and link to other long trails.

First of all, we have to warn you about the apparent shortcut shown on many maps. You can actually see Abyss Lake from one of the switchbacks on the side of Mount Evans, but in order to reach the lake from there, you would have to scramble down a rockslide area for a long way. This is very dangerous because the rocks are loose and you may easily start a slide toward one of your companions below, or you may be struck by rocks dislodged (or thrown) by visitors on the overlook above. This route appears on official maps, but is CLOSED.

So our description will begin at the main trailhead on the Guanella Pass road. You climb up through the forest on a trail that resembles an old road. The forest is very young and you don't find the creek for quite a ways. When you do, you may be surprised at how little you see of Scott-Gomer Creek. This is a wide stream often used by fly fishermen who can wade up its middle, but the trail gives only a glimpse of it through the brush and only crosses in two places.

After the first stream crossing, the real scenery begins with high mountains crowning the trees ahead. After the second crossing, you begin climbing an old road again through very round aspen. You arrive at a place where tributaries join the creek from the left. An unmarked trail leads up the first tributary and Rosalie Trail leads up the second toward a Forest Service shelter that is open on a first-come basis.

Your trail stays to the left of the main creek, climbing in the trees to avoid bogs in the grassy areas above. There were fresh bear tracks in this area at the time of our visit.

The higher you go, the more faint the trail becomes. Yet the ground is very open at this altitude and is surrounded by high landmarks such as Mount Evans ahead. Blue mountain gentian can be found blooming in many areas above timerline, but in this area a white variety can be found.

There is no trail at all once you are near either Frozen Lake or Abyss Lake. Simply follow their drainage.

SHELF LAKE Forest Service #634, 3.5 miles one-way; elevation gain 1,880 feet; trailhead #42; located on map Montezuma B; approximate hiking time 2.3 hours; features high fishing lake.

The State of Colorado uses airplanes to stock this lake with native cutthroat trout, but the only way you can get there is by climbing a very steep and rocky trail to the 12,000-foot level. The trail begins next to a large heap of smelter's slag that looks like coal, and it climbs through aspens, heading up Smelter Gulch. Some of the toughest going is in the first half-mile.

Your trail becomes a little less rugged as you hike a meadow area there, but most of your trail stays just inside the trees.

Finally you cross the creek near some beaver workings. The large pond shown on topo maps had been replaced by a marsh when we explored here.

Follow the water as it curves to the left above timberline and find the big green basin known as Smelter Basin. Here the trail becomes faint, but to your left you see where the main stream tumbles down a steep ridge. Shelf Lake is up above that ridge, so get ready for some steep climbing.

If you sit quietly near the shore, pika may come out and feed on the grass. These high altitude members of the rabbit family look something like guinea pigs with round ears. They store grass by making little haystacks under the protection of rocks. There are quite a few at Shelf Lake.

SOUTH PARK TRAIL TO SQUARE TOP LAKES Forest Service #600, 2 miles one-way; elevation gain 375 feet; trailhead #37; located on map Mt. Evans A; approximate hiking time 1.3 hours; features tundra hike to high fishing lakes.

South Park Trail is very old and used to be about 26 miles long, but after 20 years of neglect it has become overgrown and difficult to follow. The top two miles exist in slow-growing tundra, but actually you will be following the ruts made by trucks that were once used to stock the lakes with fish. The State of Colorado now uses airplanes to stock the lakes with native cutthroat trout.

The trailhead is located at the very top of Guanella Pass, well above timberline. Park on the west side of the road and proceed west downhill to the boggy region that feeds Duck Lake below. Duck Lake is private property and can be seen from the road.

After crossing the boggy stream, you climb again and incline to the left. It's a strange hike, in that you can go for a long ways and still look back to see your car. At last you climb up to the pocket where the lower lake hides. A small glacier on the far side feeds the lake, and the water is deepest over there. The other lake is located just above.

The altitude of the LOWER lake is 12,046 feet, so take it easy. Please stay on the trail to avoid damaging delicate tundra.

JEFFERSON AREA

Road directions for:

GIBSON LAKE
BURNING BEAR (See GUANELLA PASS AREA)
JEFFERSON LAKE
BEN TYLER (See BAILEY AREA)
BROOKSIDE-McCURDY (MIDPOINT, See TARRYALL AREA)
WIGWAM (See WELLINGTON LAKE AREA)
CRAIG PARK (See BAILEY AREA)

The turnoff toward GIBSON LAKE and the lower trailhead for BURNING BEAR is located 13.7 miles west of Bailey on Highway 285 and is called Park County 62. Signs warn that the road is not suitable for passenger cars, but passenger cars can reach BURNING BEAR trailhead, which is almost three miles from the highway, where Lamping Creek crosses the road. The creek is small and hidden by trees, so watch the lay of the land to predict where it will cross. Park to the right just after passing a house. There is only enough room for one or two vehicles, and the only sign marking the trail is located on a fence gate well back from the road.

The road grows worse as you travel toward GIBSON LAKE trailhead, which is located 6.4 miles from the Highway, just past Hall Valley Campground. This is an elaborate trailhead.

The turnoff for JEFFERSON LAKE is located at Jefferson on Highway 285 and is well marked all the way. The road is good. Distance: 8 miles.

Slightly more than a mile north of Jefferson is a turnoff for Lost Park Road. Travel eastward for 7.3 miles and you will see a turnoff to BEN TYLER'S southern trailhead, which is also an approach to CRAIG PARK TRAIL #608, and the mid-point of COLORADO TRAIL #1776. The Lost Park Campground, with its western trailhead for WIGWAM and

and access to the center of BROOKSIDE-McCURDY, is located 19.1 miles from Highway 285. Horse trailers often park along the road near the campground.

GIBSON LAKE Forest Service #633, 2.5 miles one-way; elevation gain 1,760 feet; trailhead #48; located on map Jefferson A; approximate hiking time 1.7 hours; features alpine fishing lake.

This may seem like one of the longest 2.5-mile hikes in our area because Gibson Lake Trail is a steady climb over rocky ground at high altitude. The actual length of this trail depends on the kind of vehicle you bring. If you have a passenger car, you won't be able to get near the actual trailhead, so you'll have to walk extra miles. If you drive a vehicle with high ground clearance, you may be able to negotiate the rocky track that leads to the trailhead.

Oddly enough, this primitive track leads to a rather elaborate trailhead with good parking, notice board, outhouses, picnic tables and a loading chute for horses. You cross the North Fork of the South Platte on a fine wooden bridge, and there the improvements end. You're in backcountry once more.

The trail itself is wide and rocky, a ghost of an old mining road. It follows the Lake Fork closely so you have frequent glimpses of the noisy waterfalls and fishing pools along the way.

You follow this water up above timberline toward a pocket at the base of granite walls. The trail grows more faint above timberline, but stacked rocks mark the way. The creek splits up at this high level, but you curve to the left. You cannot see the lake until you are very close.

On the day of our exploration, a mountain lion scampered away from a ledge overlooking the lake, and this is one of the few places where we have seen beaver activity above timberline. This is unusual because beaver literally eat trees, but at Gibson Lake they eat shrubs and use marsh willow and mud to dam the water coming from a tiny lake located above Gibson Lake.

Gibson Lake has a self-sustaining brook trout population.

JEFFERSON LAKE Forest Service #642, 1.5 miles in loop-trail; elevation gain 40 feet; trailhead #49; located on map Jefferson A; approximate hiking time 0.6 hour; features access to shores of stocked fishing lake.

The State of Colorado stocks Jefferson Lake with rainbow trout and the road extends all the way to the lake, so this is a very popular spot with picnic tables and restrooms and quite a bit of parking. Because of this heavy use, no camping is allowed near the lake itself, but you will pass several auto campgrounds on the way to the lake.

The lake is surrounded by scenic mountains, of course, and the only way to see this scenery from every angle is to hike the 1.5 mile trail that circles the lake. A stream and a smaller brook enter the lake on the far side.

The trail is best on the eastern shore and makes a nice stroll for persons who do not ordinarily hike. The trail on the western shore was rocky and indistinct at the time of this writing.

We cannot exclude this area because of mere popularity, but this area is already considered over-used by the Forest Service and cannot be recommended as a place to "get away from it all".

Perhaps the best view of the lake is from Colorado Trail #1776, a better trail for hikers.

RICH-TUMBLE CREEK CIRCUIT

Road directions for:

RICH CREEK TRAIL
ROUGH AND TUMBLING CREEK TRAIL
(often called simply Tumbling Creek)

Both these trails share a common trailhead, so they can be hiked as a circuit, if you're willing to do a little bushwhacking at a saddle ridge. To find the trailhead, take

Highway 285 between Antero Junction and Fairplay. Two country roads lead away from this highway toward Weston Pass; you may take either, depending on which direction you are coming from. Both Park County 22 and Park County 5 head into the woods for about 7 miles, then join. Three miles west of this union, look for a tiny parking area beside the South Platte, which is more of a stream than a river at this point. The USGS topo maps mark this spot as Rich Creek Campground, but there is no campground and hardly enough room for half a dozen cars. Cross the river on a footbridge constructed by South Park High School students, follow the path upriver for a few yards and you come to a fork marked "TUMBLE CREEK" to the left and "RICH CREEK" to the right. The sign says "TUMBLE CREEK, 2 miles", but that means it is two miles to the creek itself.

If you wish to hike these trails as a circuit, we recommend that you start up Rich Creek because there is less chance of getting lost that way.

RICH CREEK Forest Service #616, 6 miles one-way, but can be hiked as an 11 1/2 mile circuit with Rough and Tumbling Creek; elevation gain 1,890 feet, loss 520 feet; trailhead #50; located on maps Jones Hill A, South Peak B, D; approximate hiking time 3 hours; features mountain meadow hiking with grand vista of South Park region.

For some reason, Rich Creek becomes known as the South Fork of the South Platte River even before any major streams join it. So when you cross the footbridge at the Rich Creek trailhead, you are actually crossing the South Platte, though as you hike upstream, it magically changes to Rich Creek. Same water.

Soon the trail crosses and recrosses Rich Creek, then steepens before breaking out of the timber into the high valley. From the edge of the valley you can look back toward the mountains and flats of the South Park region. A weathered snag has toppled beside the trail to add itself to the vista.

Ahead lies a long, curving valley, wide open and green, with Rich Creek often hidden in the boggy brush at the valley center. Here your trail turns into a cattle path, for cattle often graze this valley under permit from the Forest Service.

As you start up the headwaters basin, your cattle path fades into brush where cattle graze and retreat again. So eventually you have to cross the stream. This path will fade in the brushy marsh also. You could spend hours trying to fight your way through that stuff, so instead climb the hillside to your left and walk just inside the trees. There is no trail there, either, but oddly enough, the ground in the forest is quite clear, while the ground in the clearing is all a tangle.

You are headed for the low wooded saddle that separates the Rich Creek headwaters from the watershed beyond. Now you see why we recommend hiking the circuit in this direction. If you were coming from the other direction, it might be hard to pick the right tributary that would lead you to this same ridge saddle, but as you hike up Rich Creek, there is no question that's where Rich Creek leads.

To complete the circuit, hike over this wooded saddle and bear to your left as you stay in the trees. More brushy bog awaits you in the clearing. The tributary in the center of that brush leads down to Rough and Tumbling Creek, known locally as Tumble Creek.

TUMBLE CREEK Forest Service #617, about 6 miles one-way to Buffalo Meadows and the junction that links this trail with Rich Creek; elevation gain 1,670 feet; trailhead #50; located on maps Jones Hill A, C, South Peak D; approximate hiking time 3 hours; features many beaver ponds and stream fishing.

The National Forest Visitor Map shows this trail to be very long, but the upper end is so indistinct that there is no use trying to describe it as a trail. We have told you how to use Rich Creek to join this trail high up to make a long circuit, but we will describe Tumble Creek from the bottom trailhead for the benefit of those not hiking the circuit.

Cross the footbridge at the Rich-Tumble Trailhead and take the left fork that is marked "Tumble Creek, 2 miles".

Hike up and over a high ridge, dropping down into the Tumble Creek watershed. As soon as you arrive, you will see beaver ponds extending up and down the valley. Some will be abandoned, others active.

Stop and take a good look at the place where you join this stream for you don't want to miss this turnoff on the way back. If you do, you could hike down the fishermen's trail that follows Rough and Tumble for miles, leading you far away from your car.

Follow the creek upstream. There is no definite place to cross, but do cross and look for another trail on the other side. Fishermen and campers have obscured "the trail" by making others.

About 3/4 mile upstream you find a tiny stream (Lynch Creek) coming down from a side drainage to join Rough and Tumble. Less than 100 yards farther another tributary enters Tumble Creek from the southwest. At this point the trail veers away from Tumble and follows the tributary a short distance before continuing up the ridge that separates the two streams. For a while you are away from both creeks, then the path takes you to a log crossing Rough and Tumble.

Here the creek earns its name, tumbling down rocks in a narrow gorge. And here you start up switchbacks beside that stream. This is the most difficult part of the trail, but perhaps the most beautiful.

Above lies a wide-open valley where Rough and Tumble snakes along, growing slower as you follow it up. Soon the trail is only a cattle path that may wander anywhere, so you simply follow the valley as far as you please.

The third tributary on your right is the one that leads to the saddle ridge connecting to Rich Creek, but the number of active tributaries may change in wet or dry times.

The Tumble Creek Trail may also be approached from the Buffalo Peaks Road (#431) which leaves Highway 285 about 13 miles south of Fairplay. A National Forest access sign marks the junction.

Just over 8.5 miles off the highway, the road enters a clearing where a sawmill once stood. The road then becomes primitive. Passenger cars may proceed about 1/2 mile farther, stopping at the top of a steep hill overlooking Lynch Creek.

After crossing Lynch Creek, the road leads about 3/4 mile down to a point where the southwestern tributary mentioned earlier joins Tumble Creek and the main trail. Turn left to climb the main trail toward Buffalo Meadows. This approach saves a couple of miles.

TRAIL INDEX

TRAIL NAME	LENGTH IN MILES	ELEVATION GAIN	ELEVATION LOSS	HIKING TIME APPROX. IN HRS.	TRAIL HEAD 1	TRAIL HEAD 2	TOPOGRAPHIC MAPS
CHEYENNE CANYON–HIGH DRIVE AREA							
Columbine	2.0	620	200	1.2	5		Manitou Springs D
Mount Cutler	1.0	600		.5	6		Manitou Springs D
							Colorado Springs C
North Cheyenne Canyon	2.5	1,800		1.3	7		Manitou Springs D, C
North Cheyenne Cutoff	.5	200		.2	7	10	Manitou Springs D, C
Saint Mary's Falls	4.5	2,700		2.5	8		Manitou Springs D
							Mount Big Chief B, A
Saint Peter's Dome	.7	400		.5	9		Mount Big Chief B
Bear Creek	3.0	1,980		1.5	10		Manitou Springs D, C
Palmer–Redrock Loop	4.7	620	1,140	2.7	11		Manitou Springs B
PIKES PEAK VICINITY							
Barr Trail	12.0	7,258		8.0	12		Manitou Springs B, A
							Pikes Peak B
Bottomless Pit	2.0	760		1.0	12		Pikes Peak B
Mountain View	1.5	220		.6	12		Manitou Springs A
							Pikes Peak B
Manitou Reservoir	2.5	275	900	1.3	12		Manitou Springs A
							Cascade C
Fremont Experimental Forest	.5	380		.3	12		Manitou Springs A
Incline	.5	120		.2	12		Manitou Springs A
Eagles Nest – Mt. Crest Crag	.6	650		.3	12		Manitou Springs A
Elk Park	6.0	200	1,680	3.4	14		Woodland Park C
							Pikes Peak B
Ute Indian	3.7	1,040	340	2.0	15	16	Manitou Springs B, A
							Cascade C
Waldo Canyon	7.0	1,280		3.5	17		Cascade C, D

TRAIL NAME	LENGTH IN MILES	ELEVATION GAIN	ELEVATION LOSS	HIKING TIME APPROX. IN HRS.	TRAIL HEAD 1	TRAIL HEAD 2	TOPOGRAPHIC MAPS
AIR FORCE ACADEMY AREA							
Falcon	12.0	880		4.8	18		Pikeview A
							Cascade B
							Palmer Lake D
							Monument C
Stanley Canyon	3.0	1,500		2.0	19		Cascade B
							Palmer Lake D
RAMPART RESERVOIR AREA							
Rainbow Gulch	1.2	140	120	.5	20	21	Woodland Park B
							Cascade A
BPW Nature	.3	40		.1	22		Cascade A
Nichols	2.0	40		.8	20	21	Cascade A
West Monument Creek	6.0	2,000	60	3.4	21	20	Cascade B, A
Lake Shore	12.0	40	40	4.8	20	21	Cascade A
MONUMENT AREA							
Mt. Herman	8.1	200	1,200	4.6	23		Palmer Lake B, A
CRIPPLE CREEK AREA							
Crags	4.5	700		2.3	24		Pikes Peak A
							Woodland Park C
Horsethief Park	4.5	1,400	900	2.5	25		Cripple Creek North B
							Pikes Peak A, C
FLORISSANT AREA							
Sawmill	2.7	200	200	1.5	26		Lake George D
TARRYALL AREA							
Brookside – McCurdy	37.0	5,750	4,180	24.0	27	43	McCurdy Mountain C, A
							Farnum Peak B
							Topaz Mountain D, B
							Shawnee D
Ute Creek	3.5	400		2.0	28		Farnum Peak B

TRAIL NAME	LENGTH IN MILES	ELEVATION GAIN	ELEVATION LOSS	HIKING TIME APPROX. IN HRS.	TRAIL HEAD 1	TRAIL HEAD 2	TOPOGRAPHIC MAPS
LOST CREEK SCENIC AREA							
Hankins Pass	5.9	1,820	1,040	2.9	30		McCurdy Mountain D, C
Lake Park	3.0	1,480	720	2.0	30		McCurdy Mountain D, B, A
McCurdy Park	5.3	400	1,080	3.0	27		McCurdy Mountain A, B
Goose Creek	11.8	2,000	780	6.7	30		McCurdy Mountain D, B
							Windy Peak D
WELLINGTON LAKE AREA							
Rolling Creek	9.0	2,560	1,200	4.5	31		Windy Peak B, D
Wigwam	13.3	2,220	500	7.0	32	29	Cheesman Lake A
							Green Mountain C
							Windy Peak D, C
							Topaz D
Colorado Trail	47.0	6,110	4,250	30.0	33	47	Windy Peak B, A, C
							Topaz Mountain D, B, A
							Observatory Rock B, A
							Mount Logan D, C
							Jefferson D, C
							Boreas Pass D, B
DEER CREEK AREA							
Meridian	3.0	1,600		2.5	34		Harris Park D
Rosalie	12.0	3,560	1,120	8.3	35	36	Harris Park C
							Mount Evans D, B, A
Tanglewood	5.0	2,680	160	3.3	35		Harris Park C
BAILEY AREA							
Craig Meadow	6.0	1,030	1,200	3.0	44		Shawnee D
							Windy Peak A
Ben Tyler	9.0	3,460	2,040	5.5	46	45	Shawnee C
							Mount Logan D
							Observatory Rock B

TRAIL NAME	LENGTH IN MILES	ELEVATION		HIKING TIME APPROX. IN HRS.	TRAIL HEAD		TOPOGRAPHIC MAPS
		GAIN	LOSS		1	2	
Craig Park	5.5	660	630	3.0	43	45	Mount Logan D Shawnee C Topaz Mountain A, B
GUANELLA PASS AREA							
Three Mile Creek	6.0	2,600	200	4.0	41		Mount Logan A, B Mount Evans D
Burning Bear	5.0	1,160	1,120	2.5	40	39	Jefferson B Montezuma D Mount Evans C
Scott Gomer to Abyss Lake	8.0	3,050		5.4	38		Mount Evans C, D, B
Shelf Lake	3.5	1,880		2.3	42		Montezuma B
South Park	2.0	375		1.3	37		Mount Evans A
JEFFERSON AREA							
Gibson Lake	2.5	1,760		1.7	48		Jefferson A
Jefferson Lake	1.5	40		.6	49		Jefferson A
RICH–TUMBLE CREEK CIRCUIT							
Rich Creek	6.0	1,890	520	3.0	50		Jones Hill A South Peak B, D
Tumble Creek	6.0	1,670		3.0	50		Jones Hill A, C South Peak D

MAPS

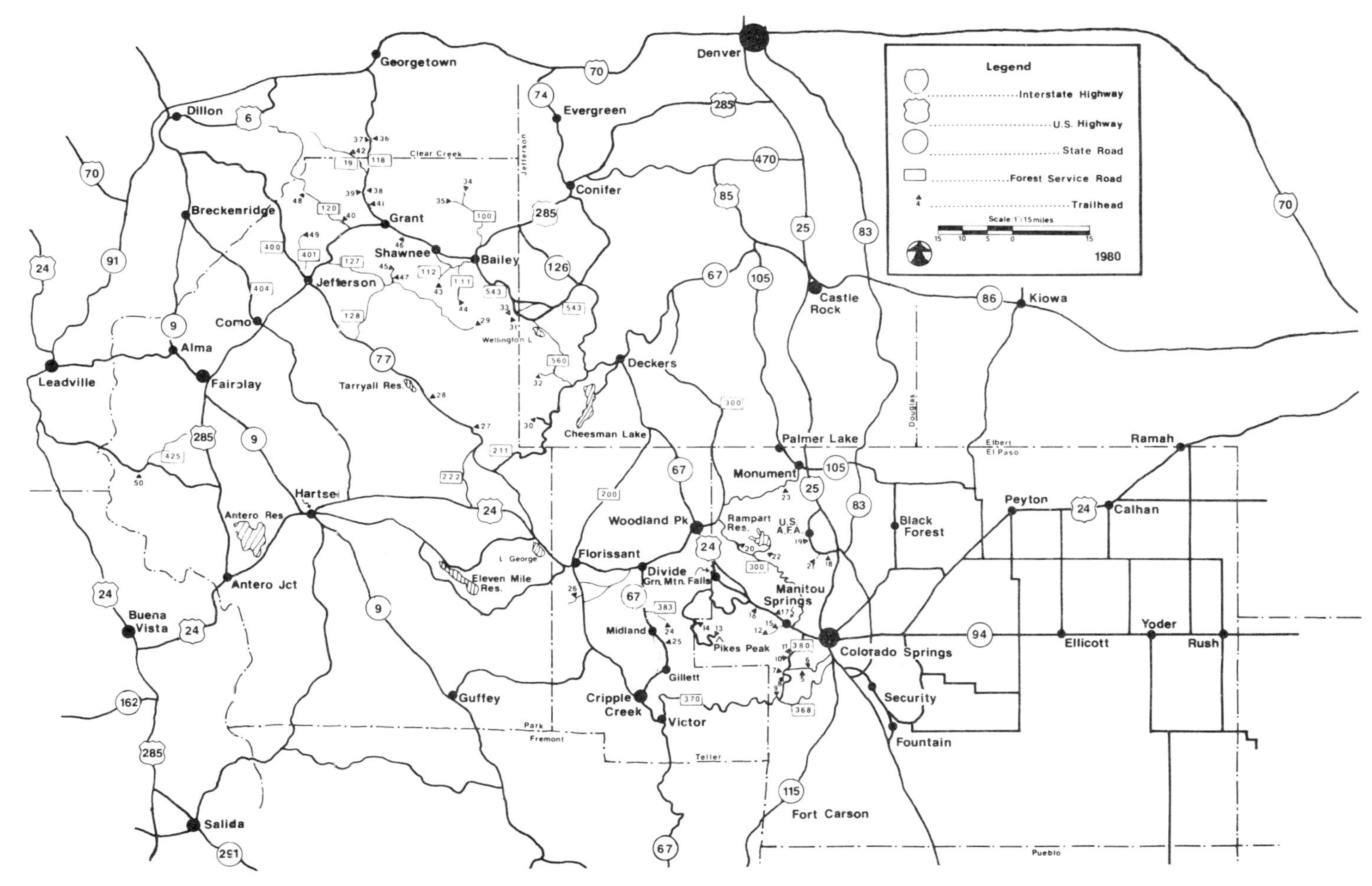

Legend
Interstate Highway
U.S. Highway
State Road
Forest Service Road
Trailhead
Scale 1:15 miles
1980
Denver
Evergreen
Conifer
Georgetown
Dillon
Breckenridge
Grant
Shawnee
Bailey
Jefferson
Como
Alma
Fairplay
Leadville
Hartsel
Antero Jct
Antero Res
Buena Vista
Salida
Guffey
Cripple Creek
Victor
Gillett
Midland
Divide
Grn. Mtn. Falls
Florissant
Woodland Pk
Deckers
Cheesman Lake
Tarryall Res.
Eleven Mile Res.
L George
Wellington L
Clear Creek
Castle Rock
Kiowa
Palmer Lake
Monument
Rampart Res.
U.S. A.F.A.
Manitou Springs
Pikes Peak
Black Forest
Colorado Springs
Security
Fountain
Fort Carson
Peyton
Calhan
Ramah
Ellicott
Yoder
Rush
Elbert
El Paso
Douglas
Teller
Park
Fremont
Pueblo

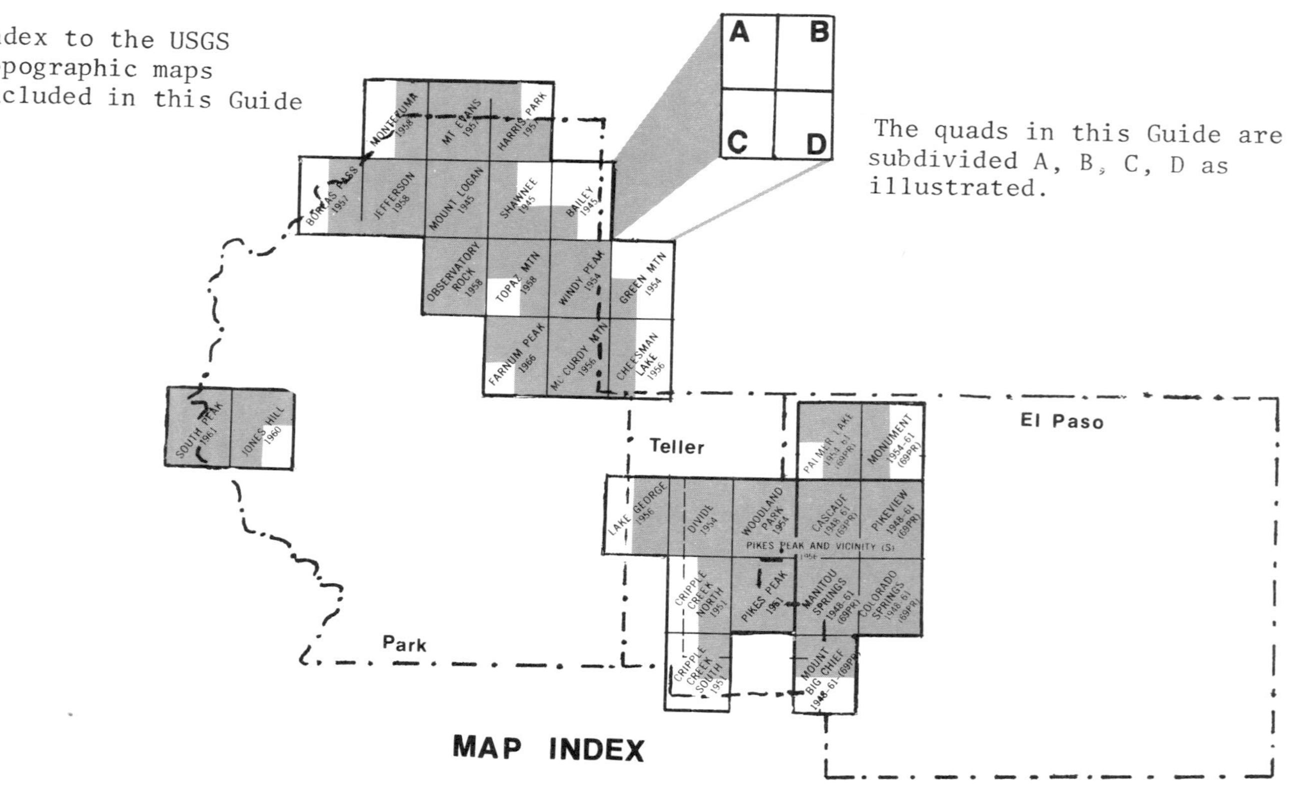
Index to the USGS
topographic maps
included in this Guide
A
B
C
D
The quads in this Guide are
subdivided A, B, C, D as
illustrated.
MONTEZUMA 1958
MT EVANS 1957
HARRIS PARK 1957
BOREAS PASS 1957
JEFFERSON 1958
MOUNT LOGAN 1945
SHAWNEE 1945
BAILEY 1945
OBSERVATORY ROCK 1958
TOPAZ MTN 1958
WINDY PEAK 1954
GREEN MTN 1954
FARNUM PEAK 1966
McCURDY MTN 1956
CHEESMAN LAKE 1956
SOUTH PEAK 1961
JONES HILL 1960
Teller
El Paso
PALMER LAKE 1954-61 (69PR)
MONUMENT 1954-61 (69PR)
LAKE GEORGE 1956
DIVIDE 1954
WOODLAND PARK 1954
CASCADE 1948-61 (69PR)
PIKEVIEW 1948-61 (69PR)
PIKES PEAK AND VICINITY (S) 1956
CRIPPLE CREEK NORTH 1951
PIKES PEAK 1951
MANITOU SPRINGS 1948-61 (69PR)
COLORADO SPRINGS 1948-61 (69PR)
CRIPPLE CREEK SOUTH 1951
MOUNT BIG CHIEF 1948-61 (69PR)
Park
MAP INDEX

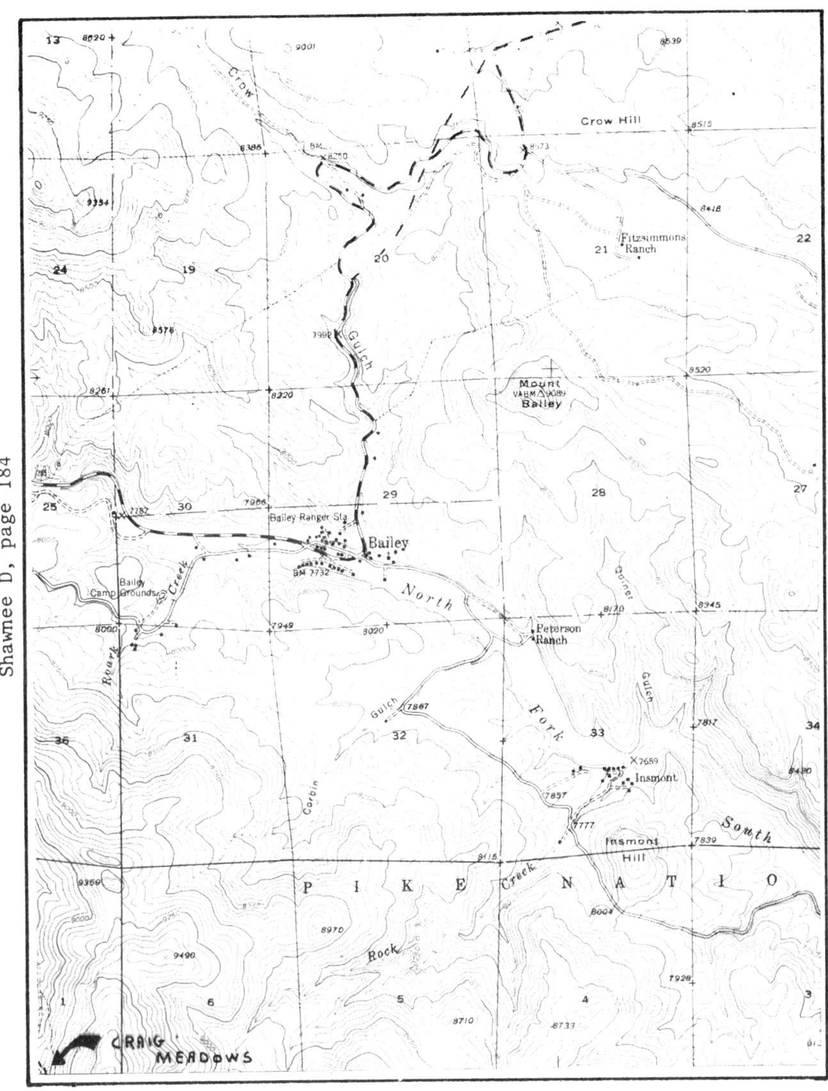

Shawnee D, page 184

Windy Peak A, page 190

GN
MN
0°17'
5 MILS
14½°
258 MILS

Bailey C

1 ½ 0 1 MILE
1000 0 1000 2000 3000 4000 5000 6000 7000 FEET
1 .5 0 1 KILOMETER

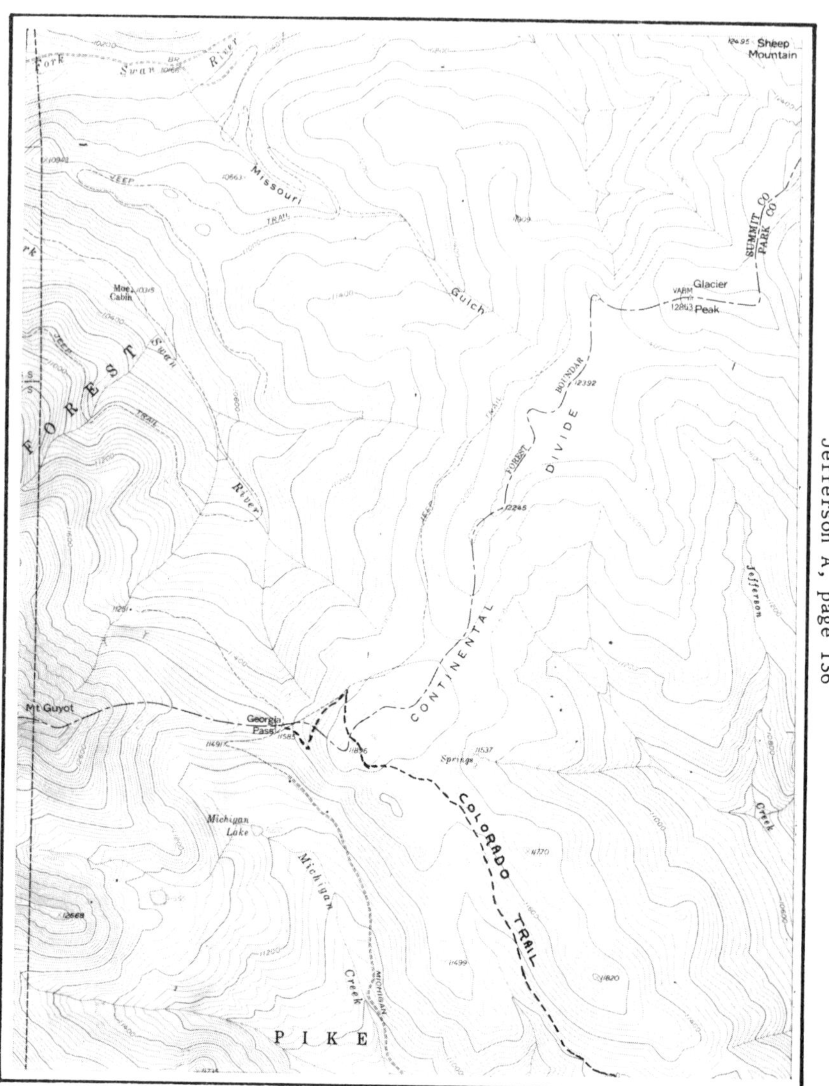

Jefferson A, page 136

Boreas Pass D, page 111

GN

MN

0°36'
11 MILS

14°
249 MILS

Boreas Pass B

1 ½ 0 1 MILE

1000 0 1000 2000 3000 4000 5000 6000 7000 FEET

1 .5 0 1 KILOMETER

Boreas Pass B, page 110

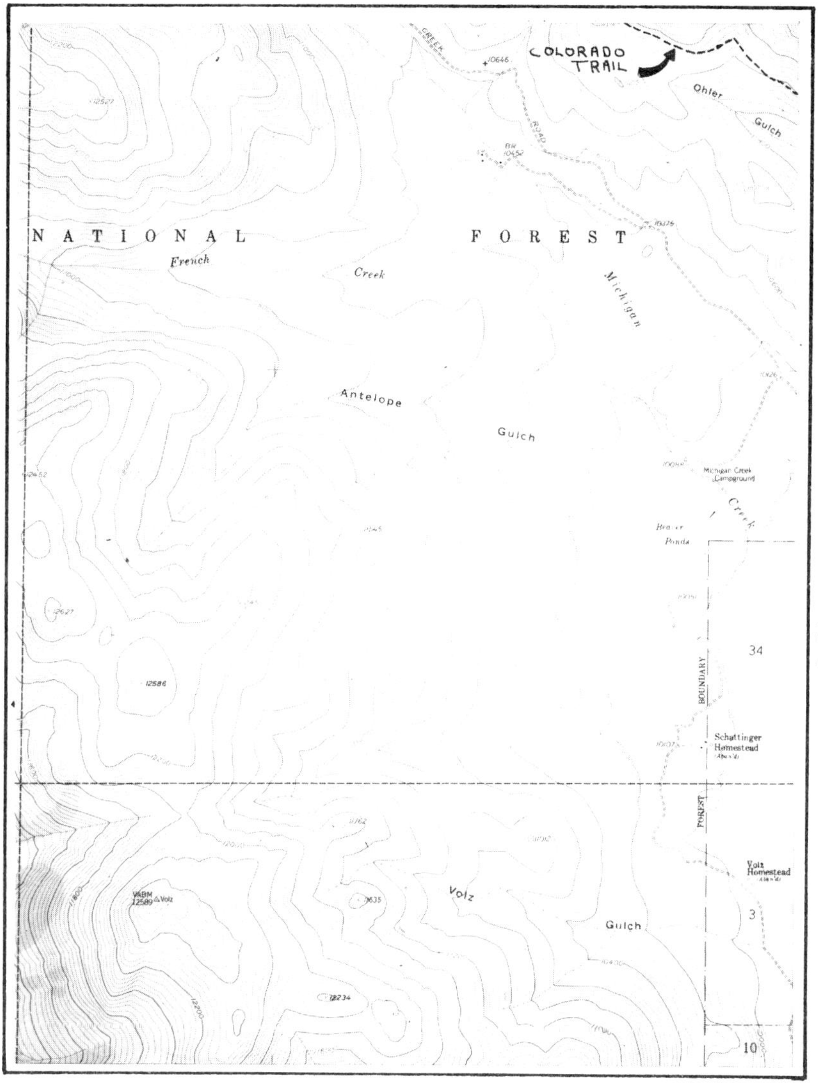

COLORADO TRAIL

Ohler Gulch

NATIONAL FOREST

French Creek

Michigan

Antelope Gulch

Michigan Creek Campground

Creek

Beaver Ponds

34

BOUNDARY

Schattinger Homestead

FOREST

Volz Homestead

3

VABM 12589 △Volz

Volz Gulch

10

Jefferson C, page 138

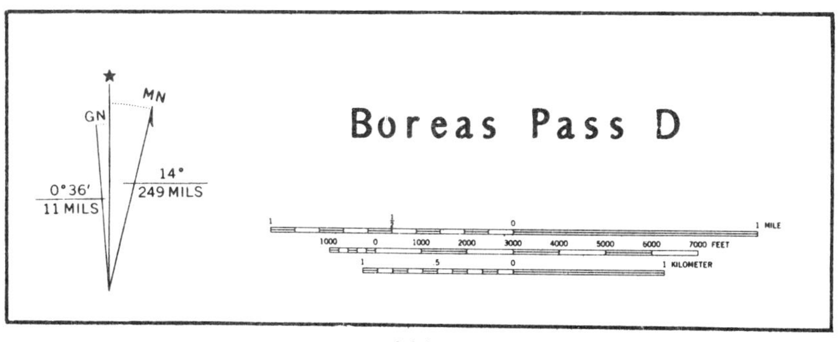

Woodland Park B, page 195

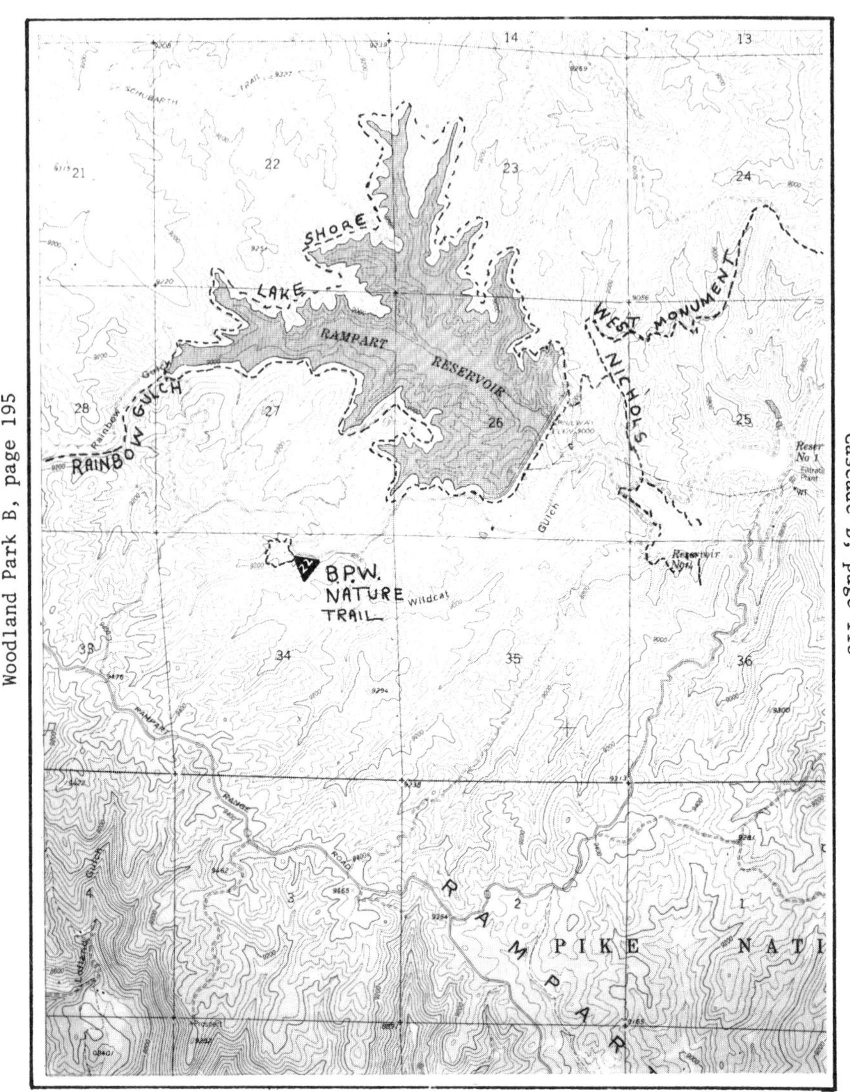

Cascade B, page 113

Cascade C, page 114

Cascade A

GN MN
0°02′ 1 MILS
12½° 222 MILS

1 ½ 0 1 MILE
1000 0 1000 2000 3000 4000 5000 6000 7000 FEET
1 .5 0 1 KILOMETER

Palmer Lake D, page 173

STANLEY CANYON
19
FALCON TRAIL
WEST MONUMENT CREEK
20
UNITED STATES AIR FORCE ACADEMY
Reservoir No 2
Blodgett Peak 9423
Devils Kitchen
Dry Creek
Mount St Francis BM 6901
NATIONAL FOREST

Cascade A, page 112

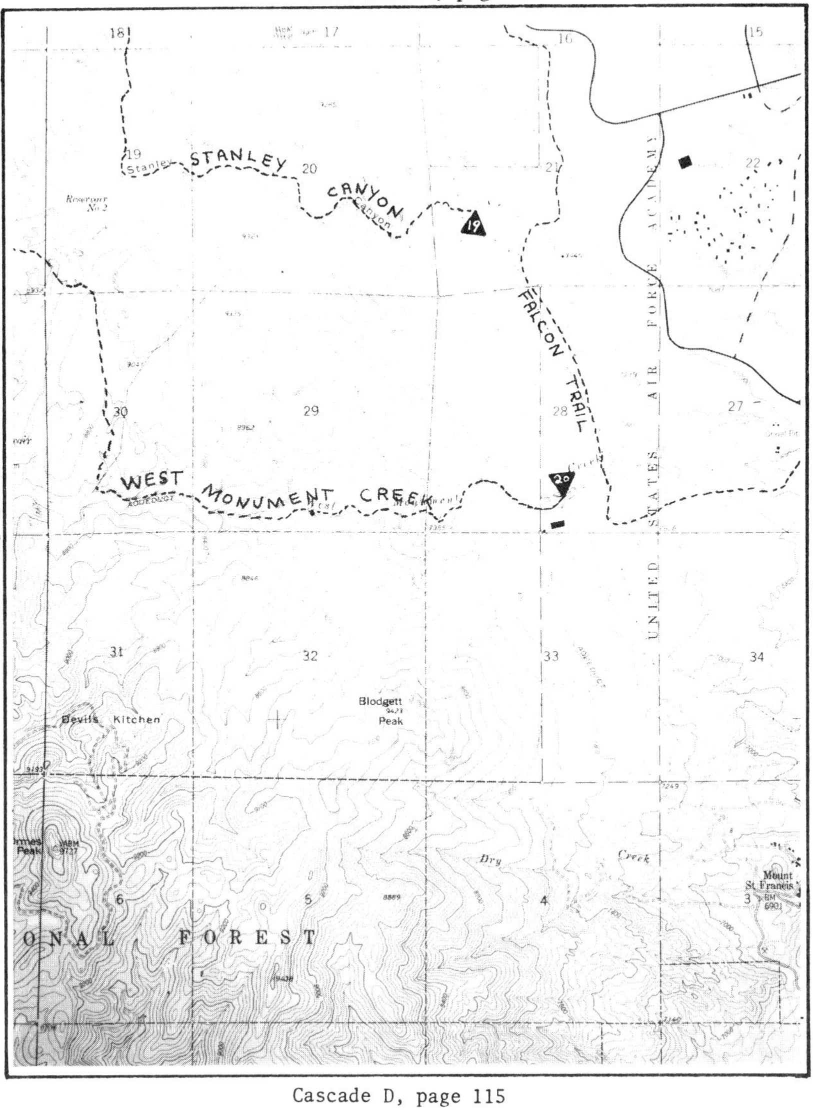

Pikeview A, page 178

Cascade D, page 115

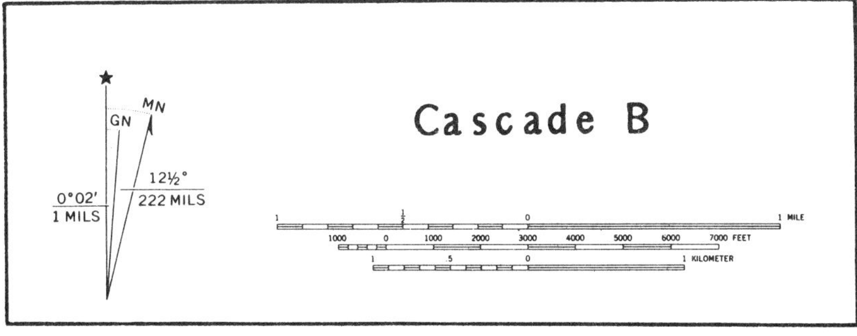

Cascade A, page 112

Woodland Park D, page 197

Cascade D, page 115

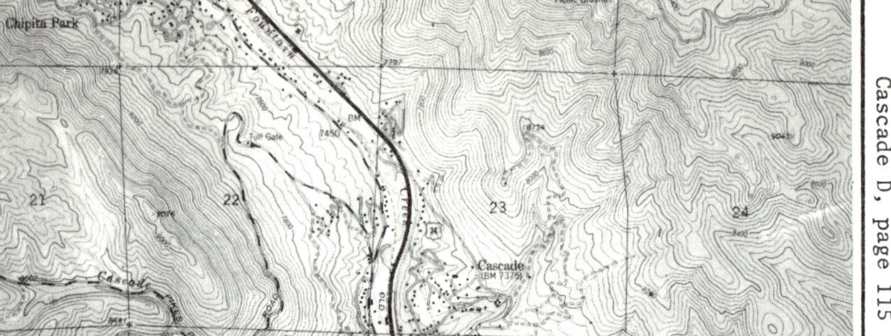

Manitou Springs A, page 145

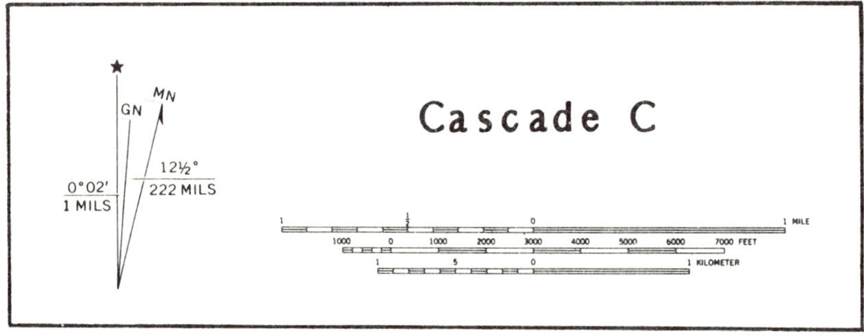

Cascade C

Cascade B, page 113

Cascade C, page 114

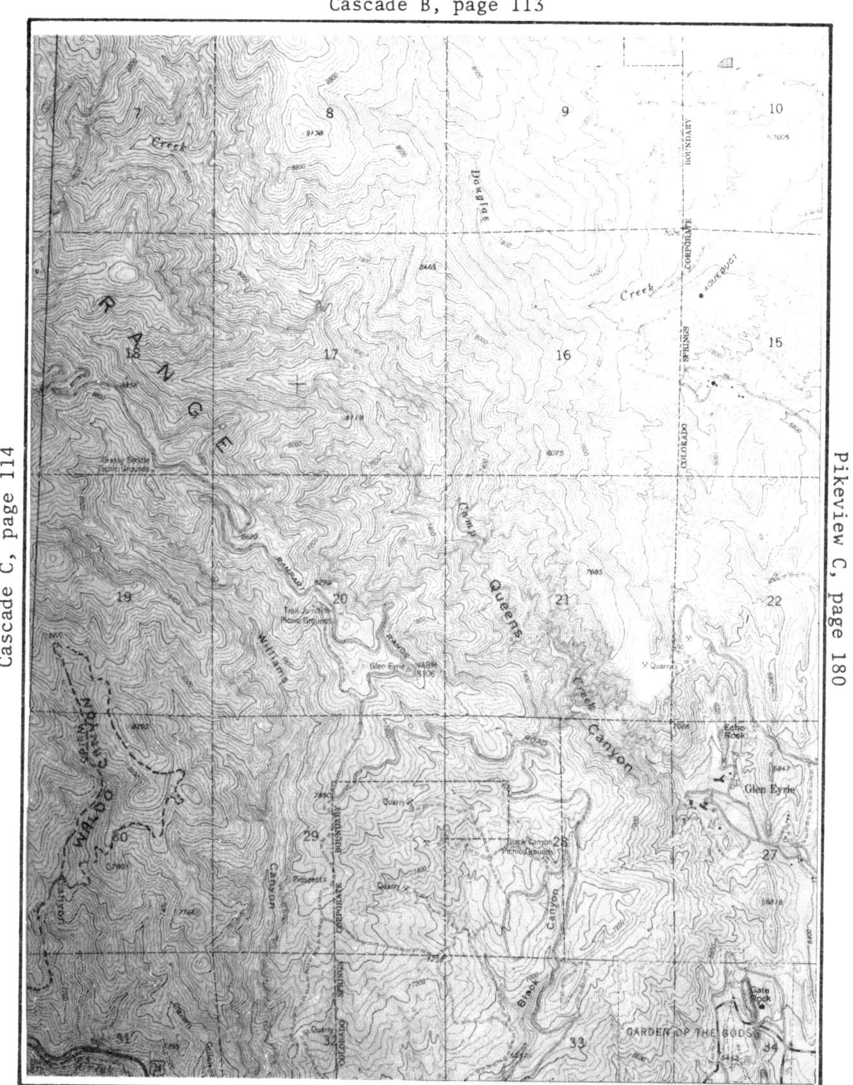

Pikeview C, page 180

Manitou Springs B, page 146

Cascade D

GN
MN
0°02′
1 MILS
12½°
222 MILS

1 MILE
1000 0 1000 2000 3000 4000 5000 6000 7000 FEET
1 KILOMETER

Green Mountain C, page 132

McCurdy Mountain B, page 150

Cheesman Lake C, page 117

Cheesman Lake A

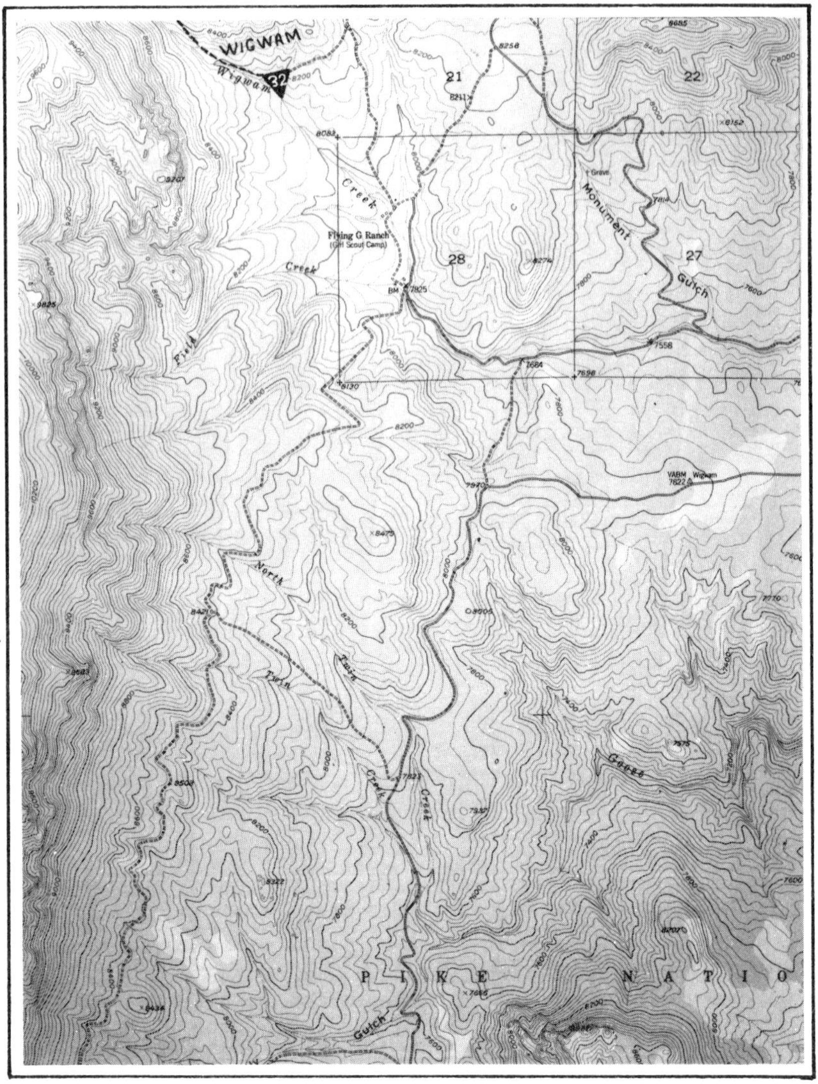

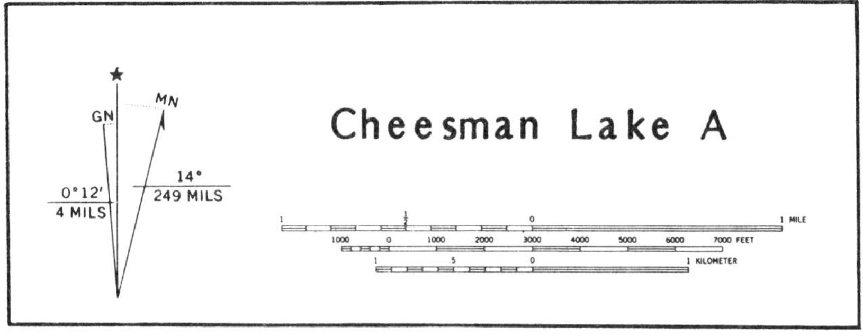

Cheesman Lake A, page 116

McCurdy Mountain D, page 152

Cheesman Lake C

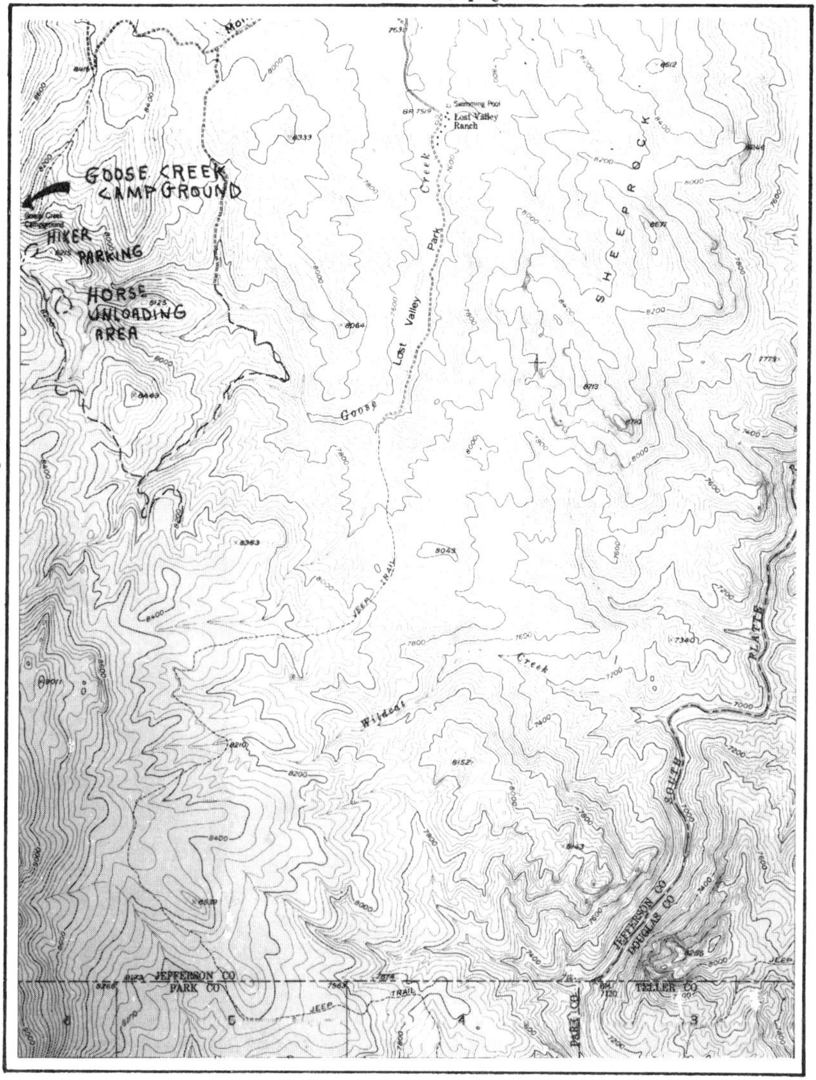

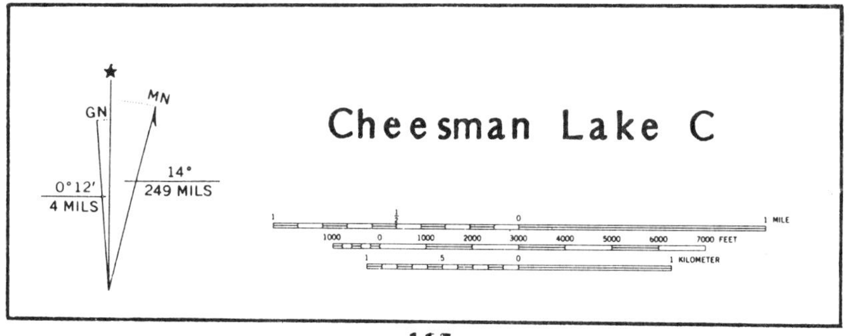

Pikeview C, page 180

Manitou Springs B, page 146

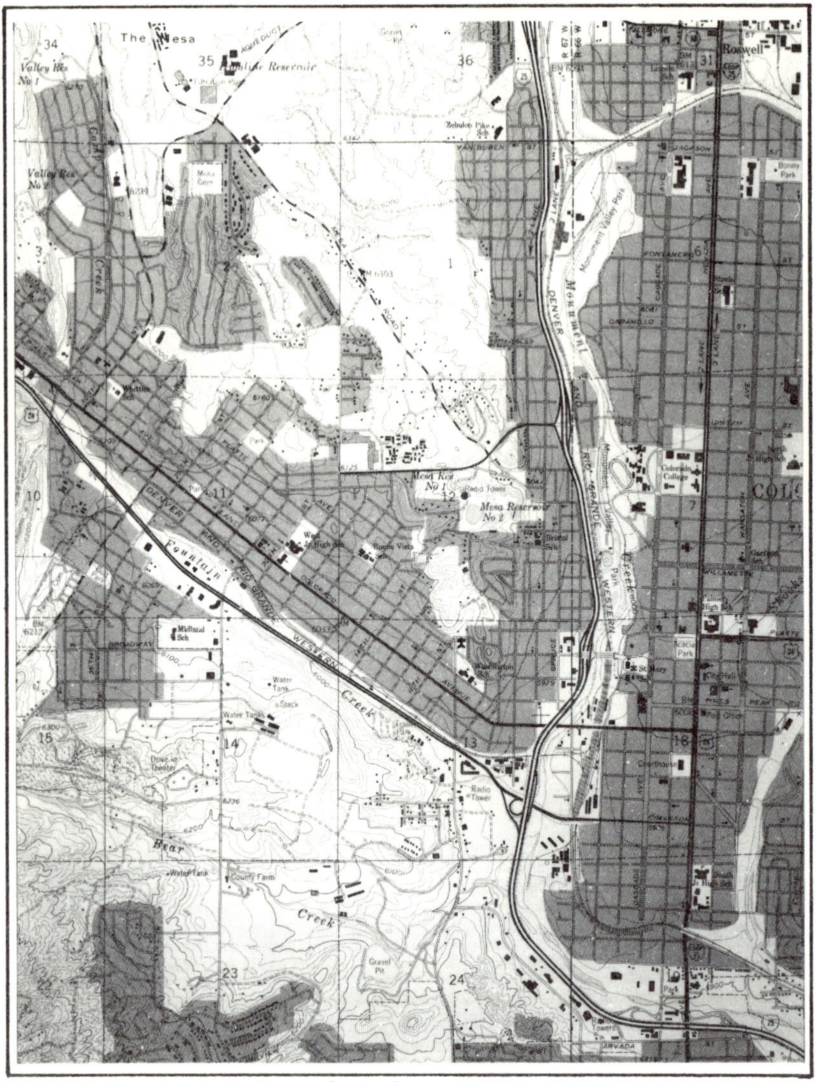

Colorado Springs B, page 119

Colorado Springs C, page 120

Colorado Springs A

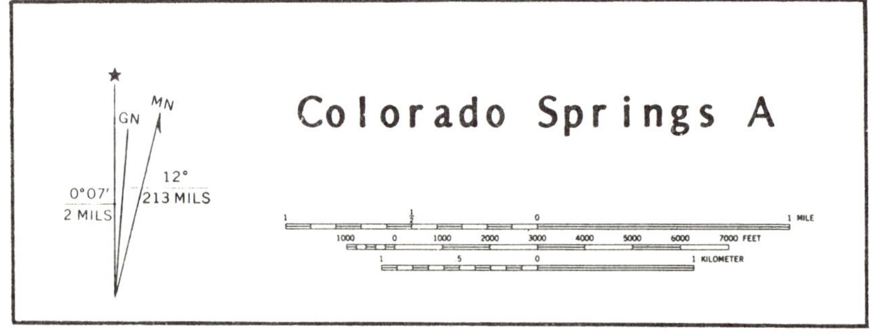

Pikeview D, page 181

Colorado Springs A, page 118

Colorado Springs D, page 121

Colorado Springs B

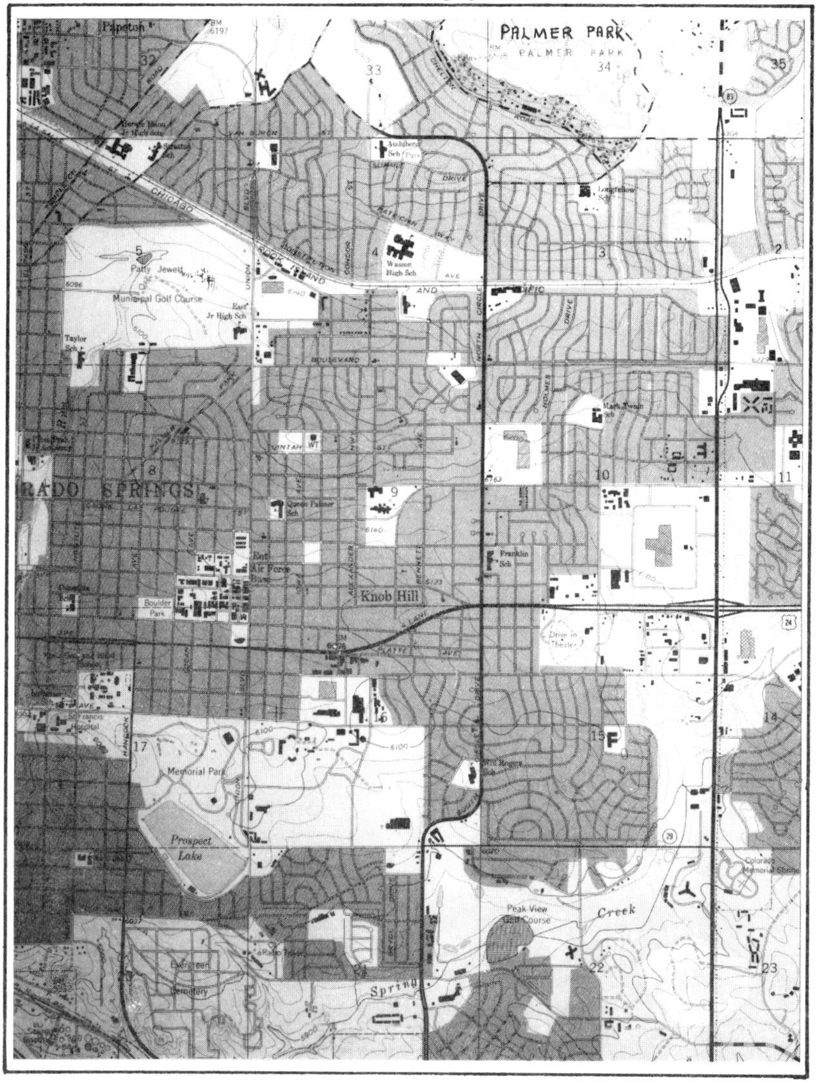

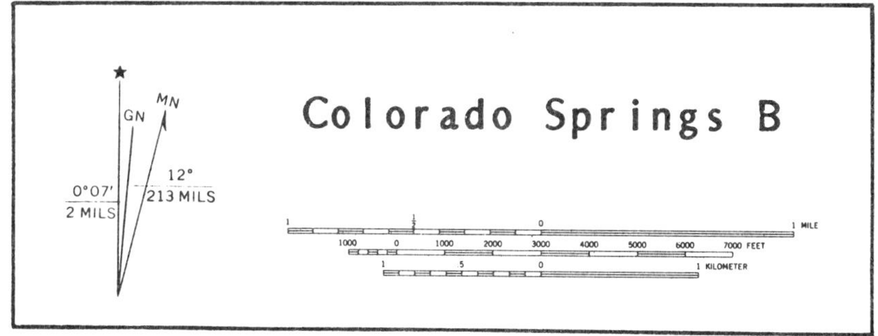

Colorado Springs A, page 118

Manitou Springs D, page 148

Colorado Springs D, page 121

Colorado Springs C

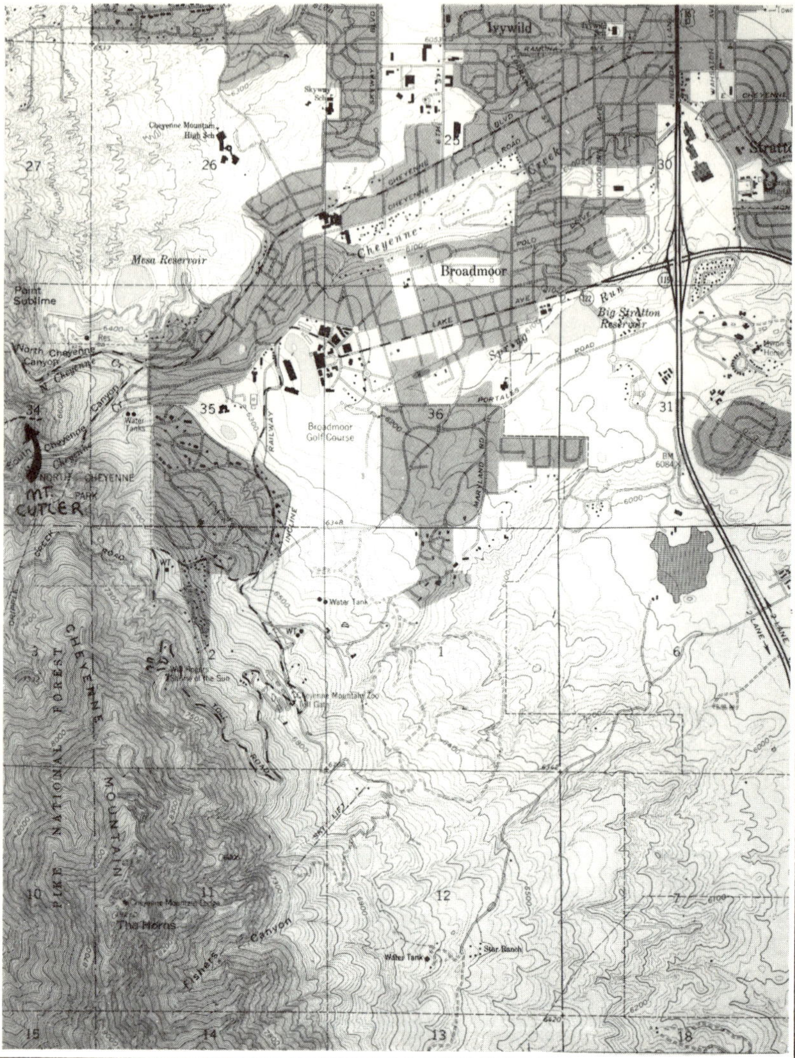

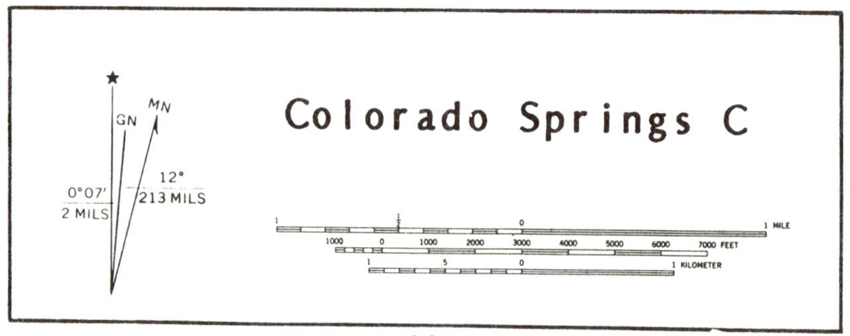

Colorado Springs B, page 119

Colorado Springs C, page 120

Colorado Springs D

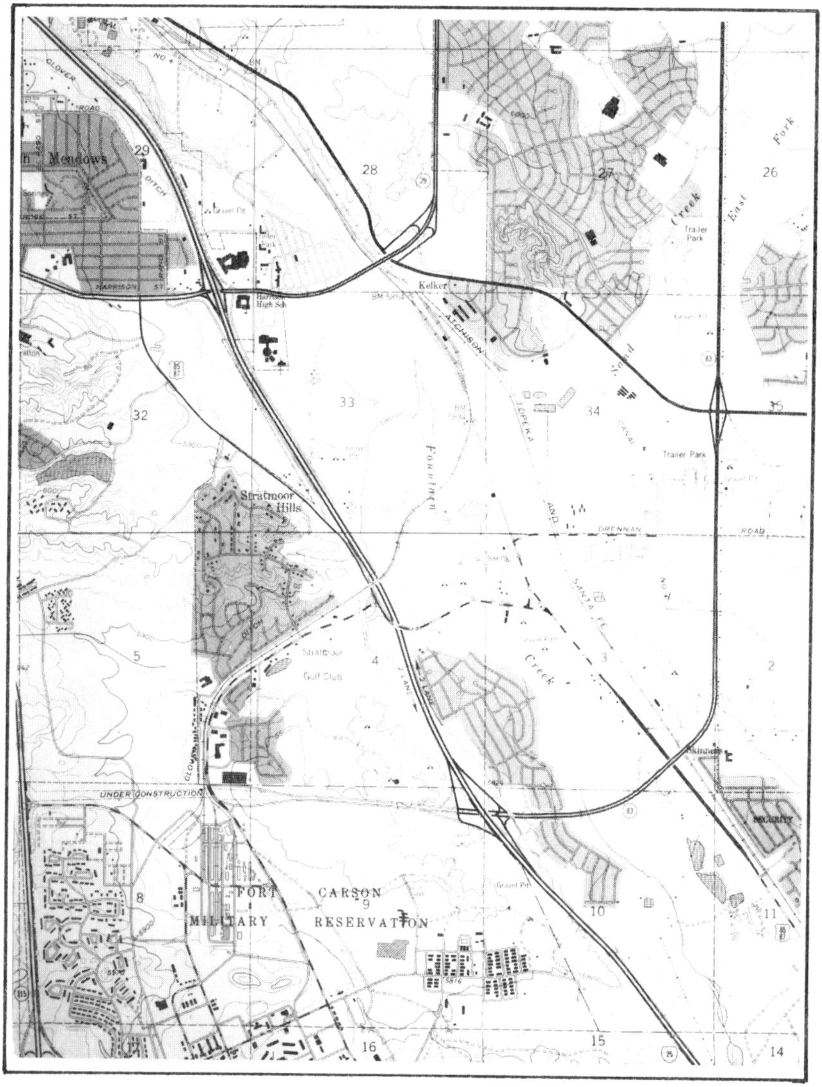

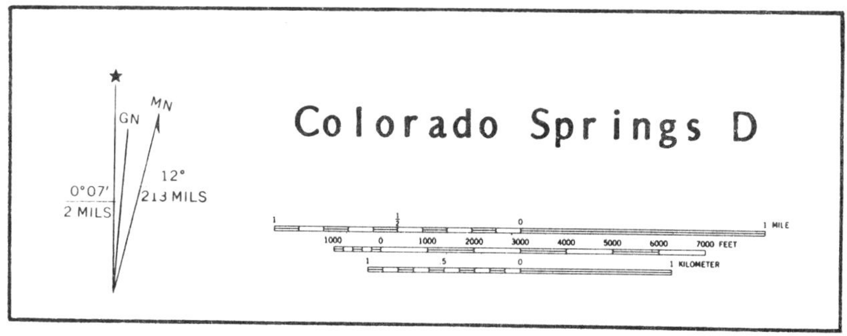

Divide D, page 128

Pikes Peak A, page 174

Cripple Creek North D, 123

Cripple Creek North B

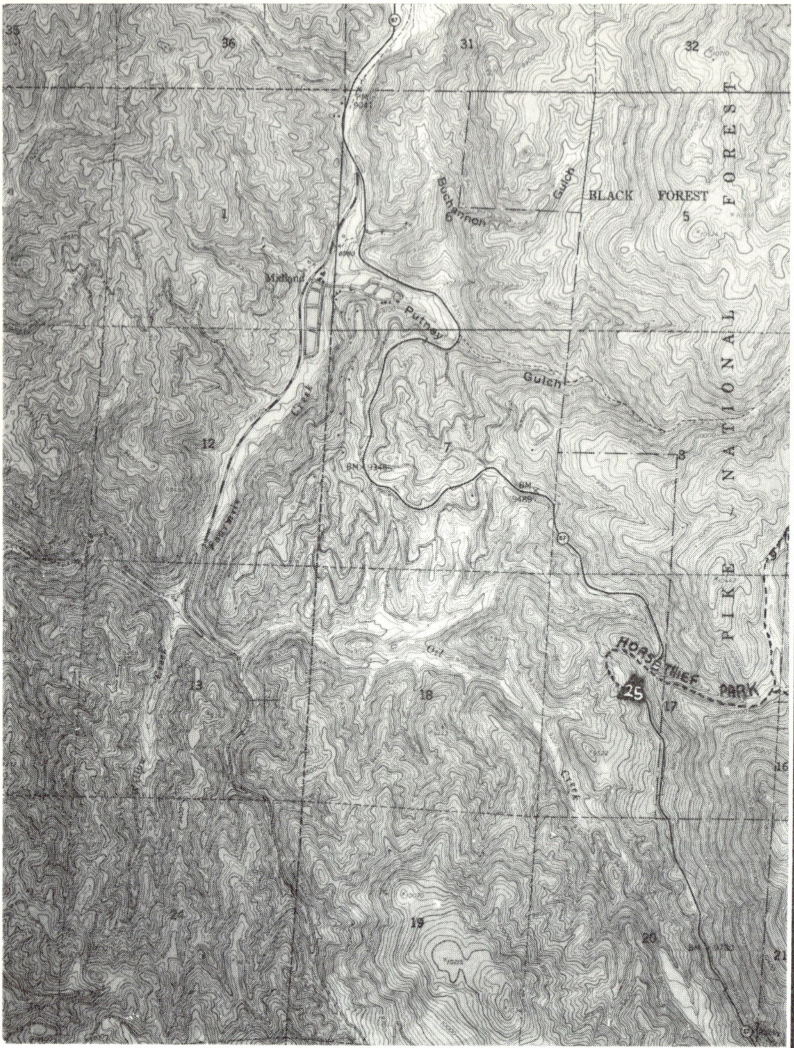

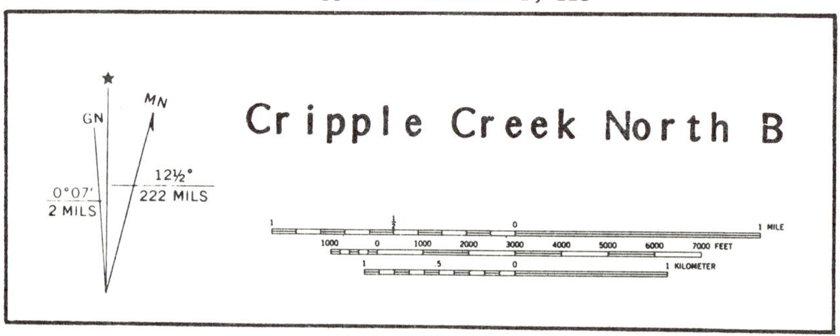

Cripple Creek North B, page 122

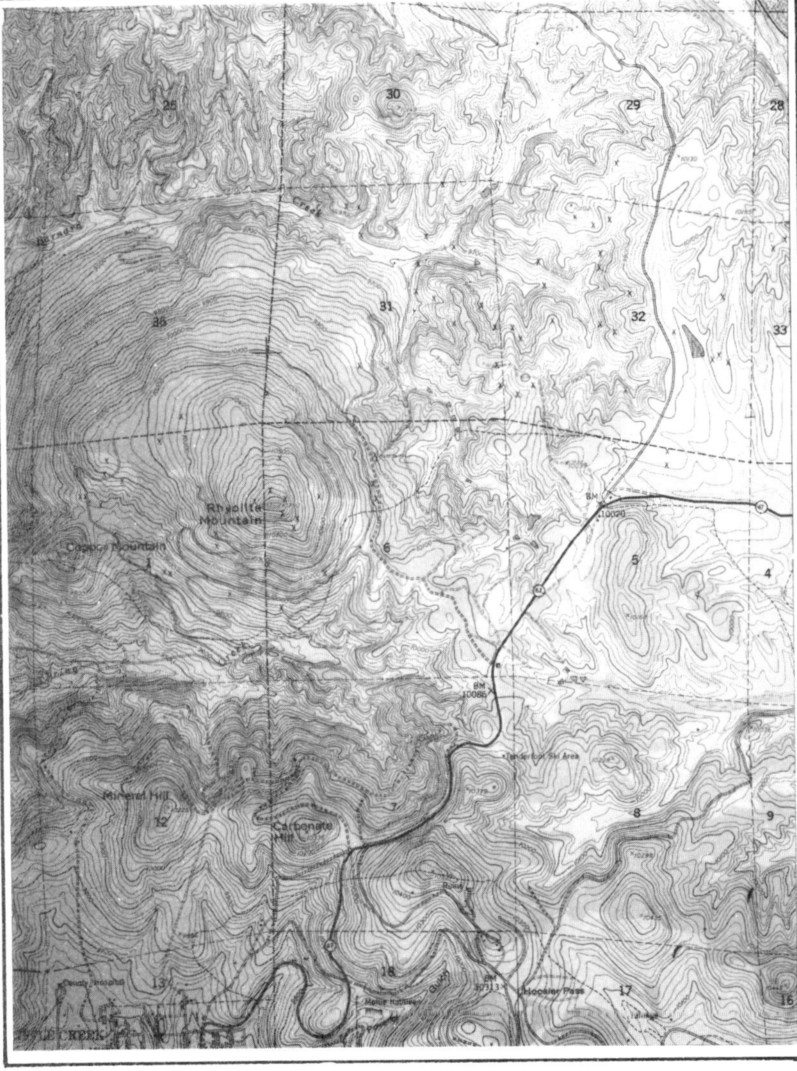

Pikes Peak C, page 176

Cripple Creek South B, page 124

Cripple Creek North D

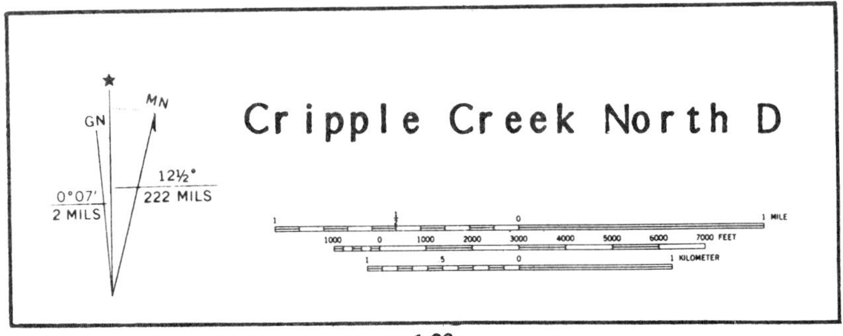

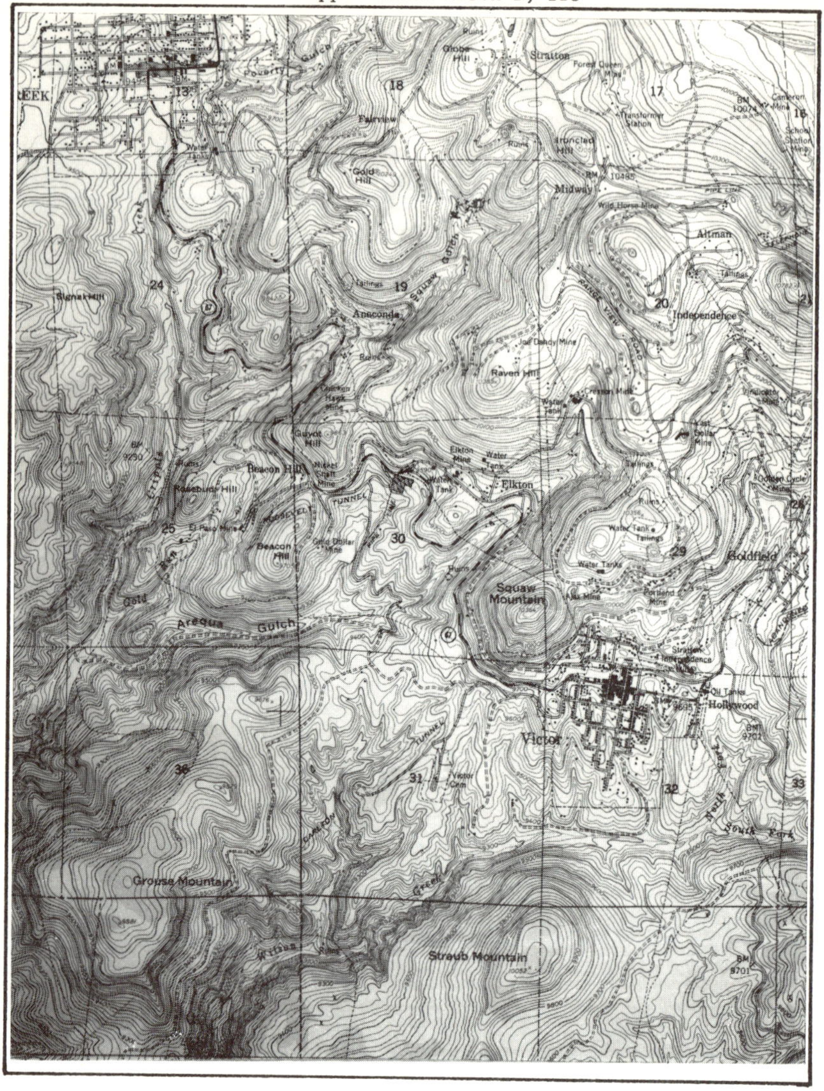

Cripple Creek North D, 123

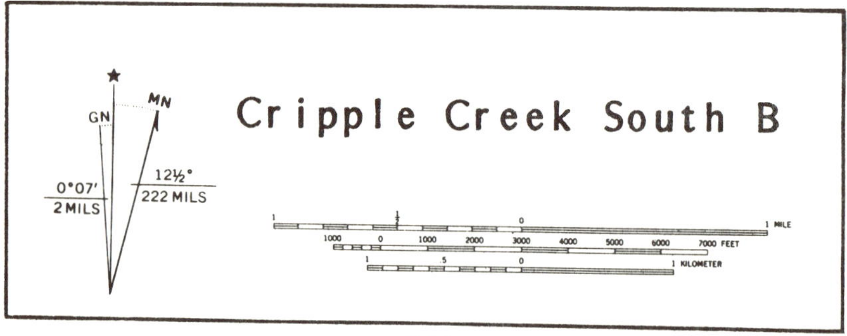

Lake George B, page 143

Divide B, page 126

Divide C, page 127

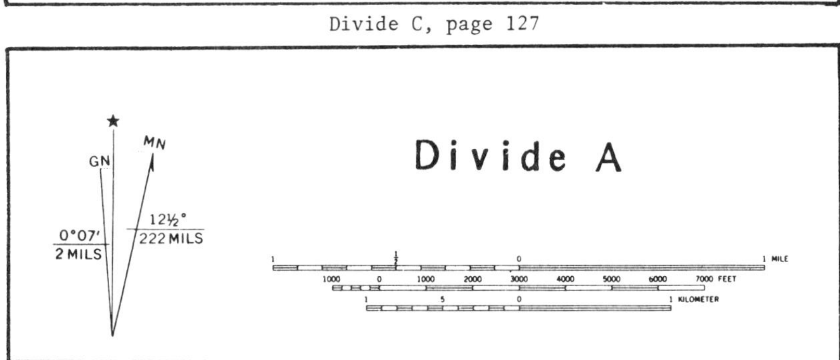

Divide A, page 125

Woodland Park A, page 194

Divide D, page 128

GN
MN
0°07'
2 MILS
12½°
222 MILS

Divide B

1 ½ 0 1 MILE
1000 0 1000 2000 3000 4000 5000 6000 7000 FEET
1 .5 0 1 KILOMETER

Divide A, page 125

Lake George D, page 144

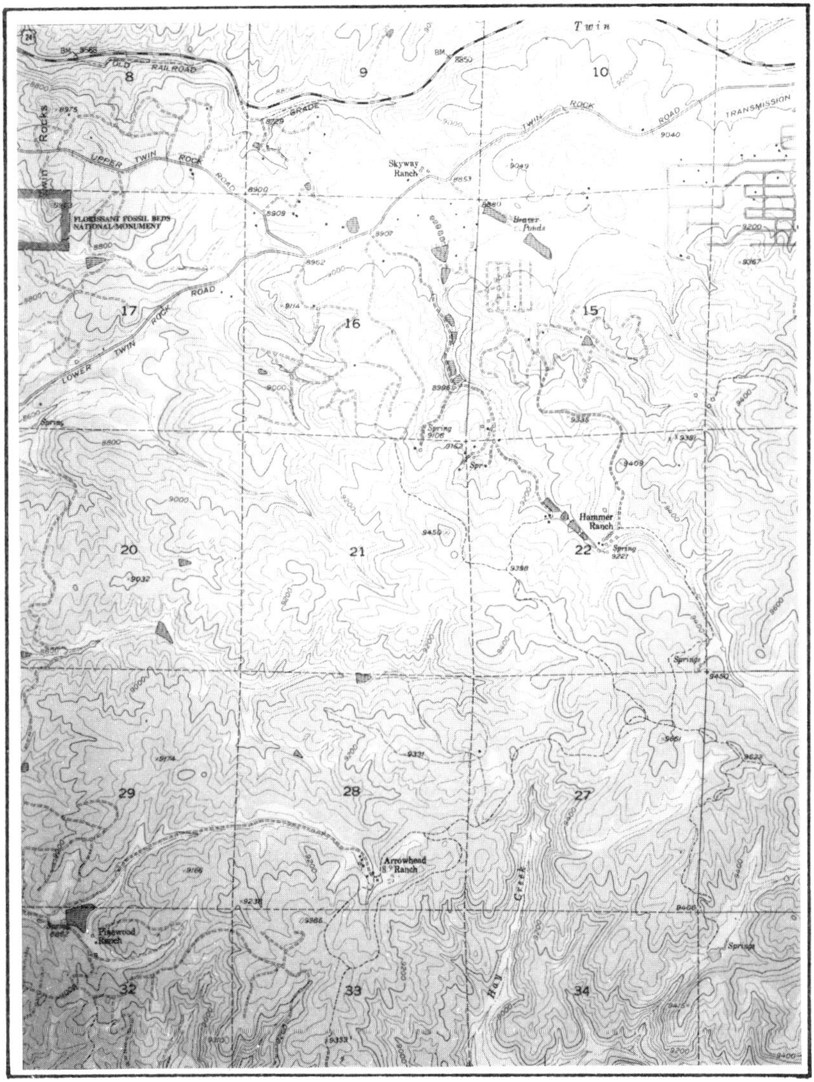

Divide D, page 128

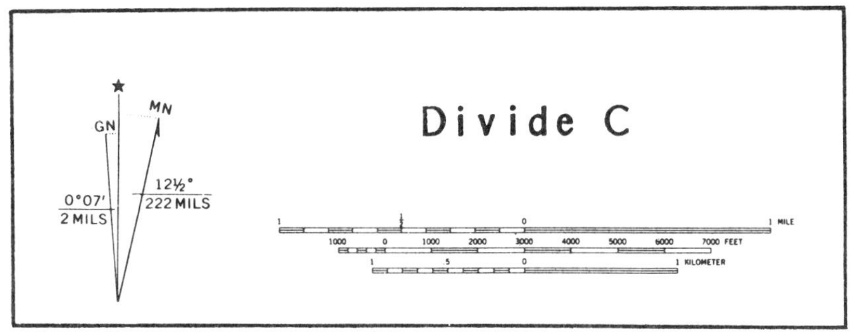

Divide C

Divide B, page 126

Divide C, page 127

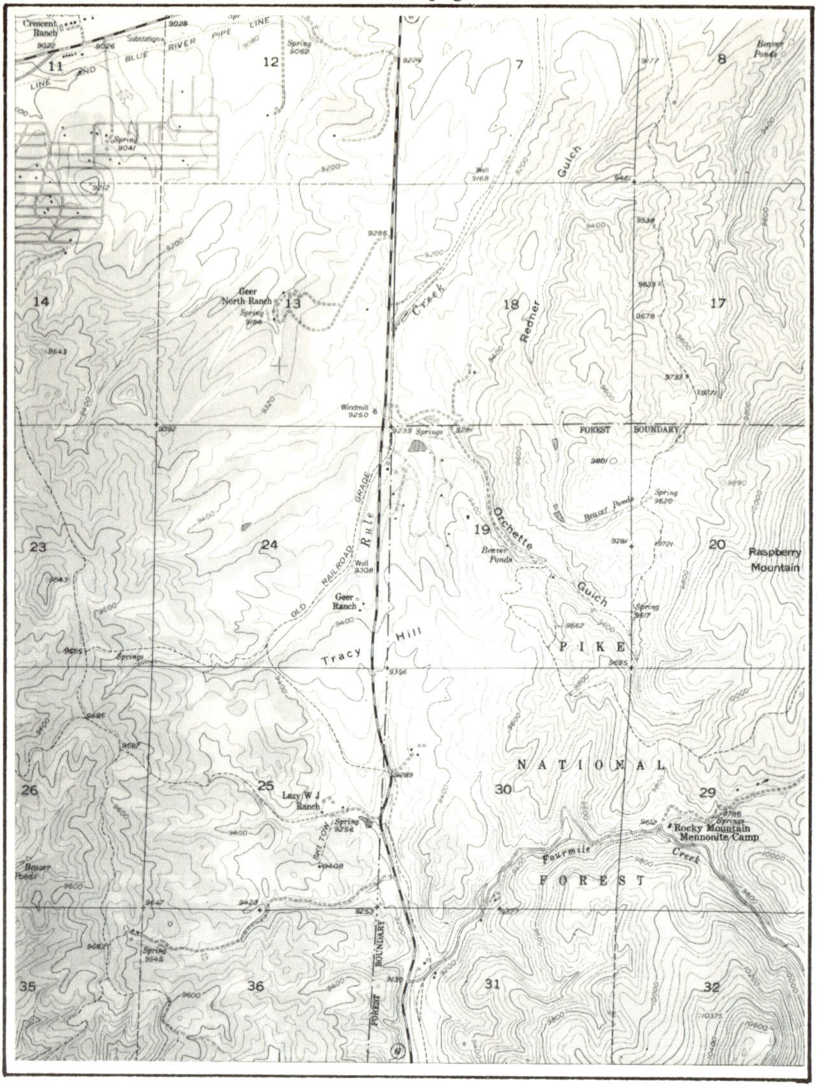

Woodland Park C, page 196

Cripple Creek North B, page 122

Divide D

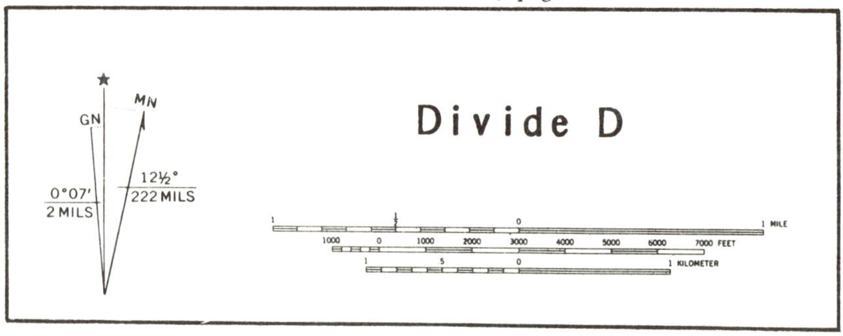

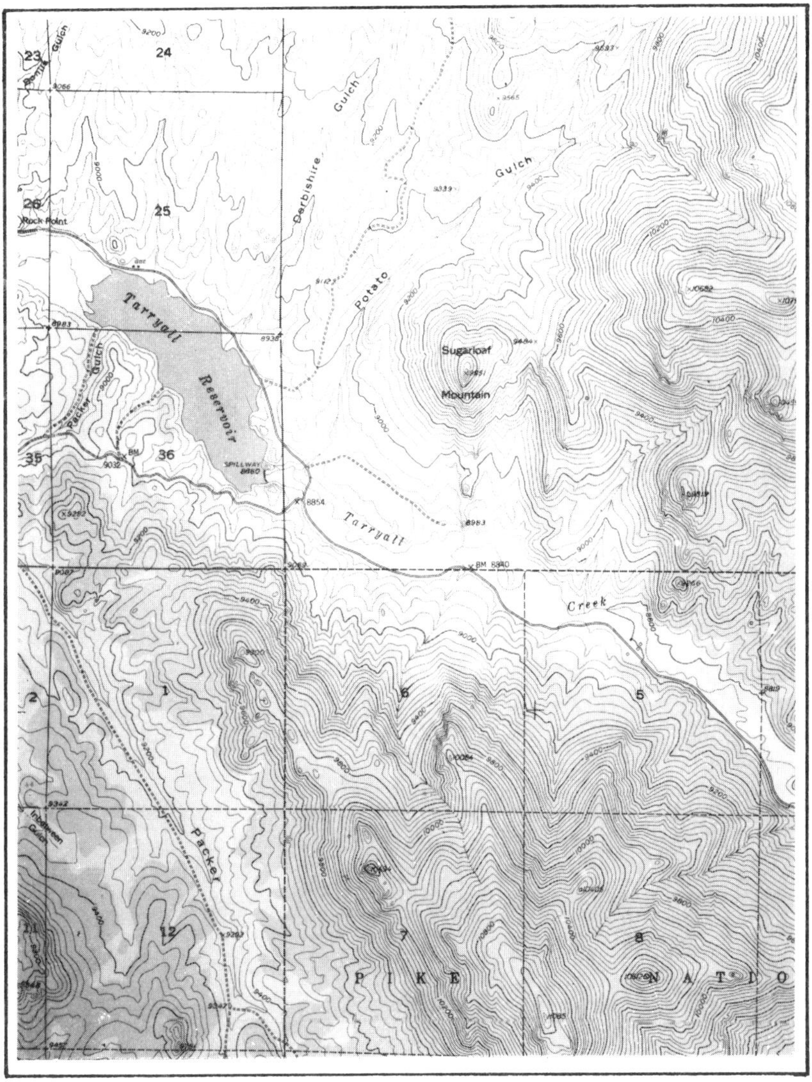

Farnum Peak B, page 130

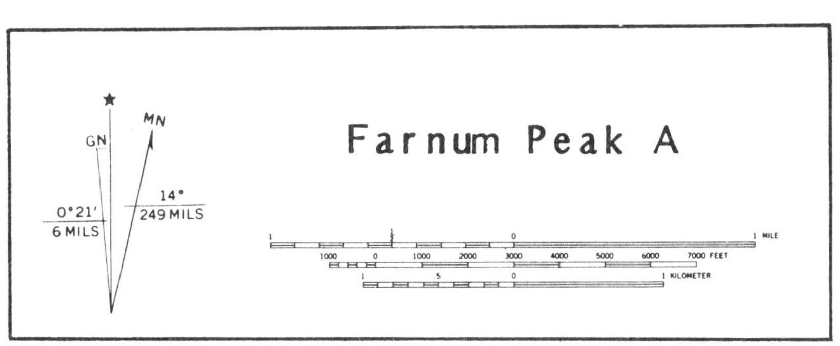

Topaz D, page 189

Farnum Peak A, page 129

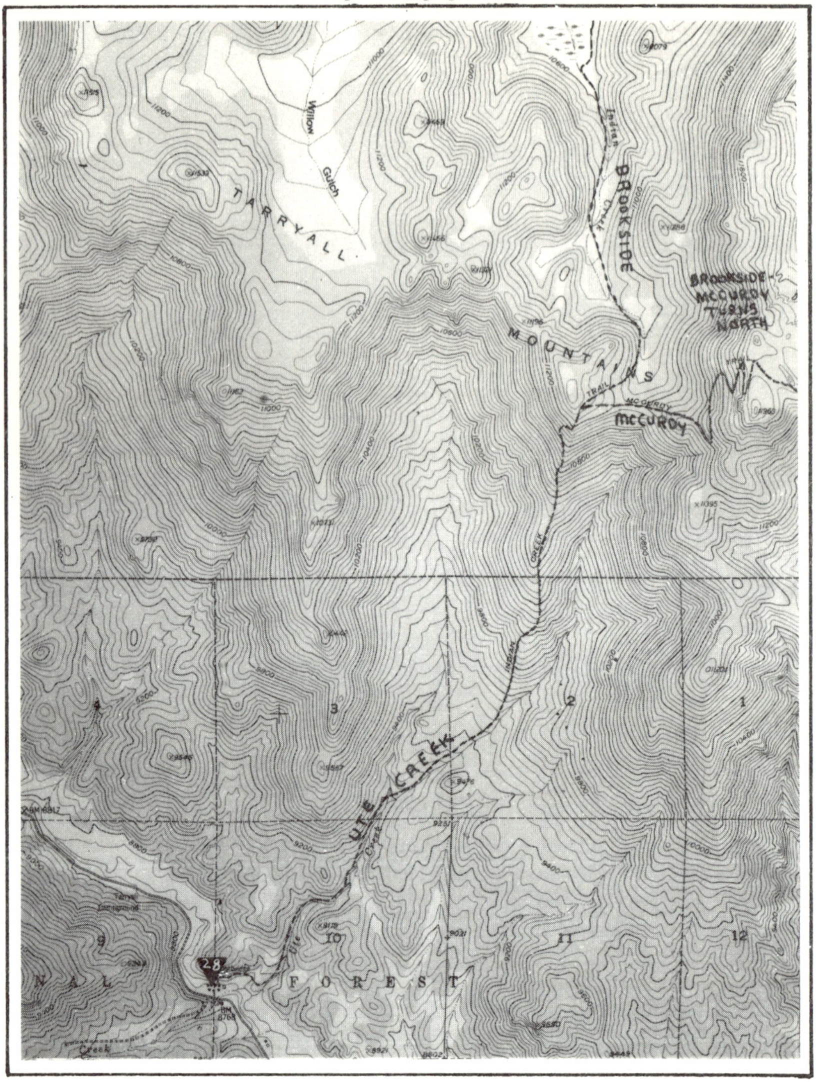

McCurdy Mountain A, page 149

Farnum Peak D, page 131

Farnum Peak B

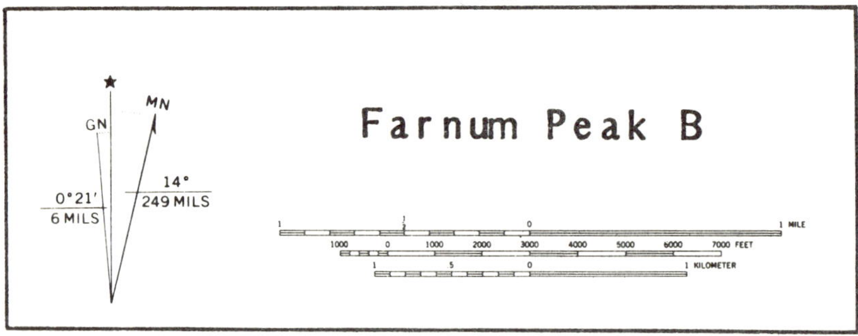

Farnum Peak B, page 130

McCurdy Mountain C, page 151

Farnum Peak D

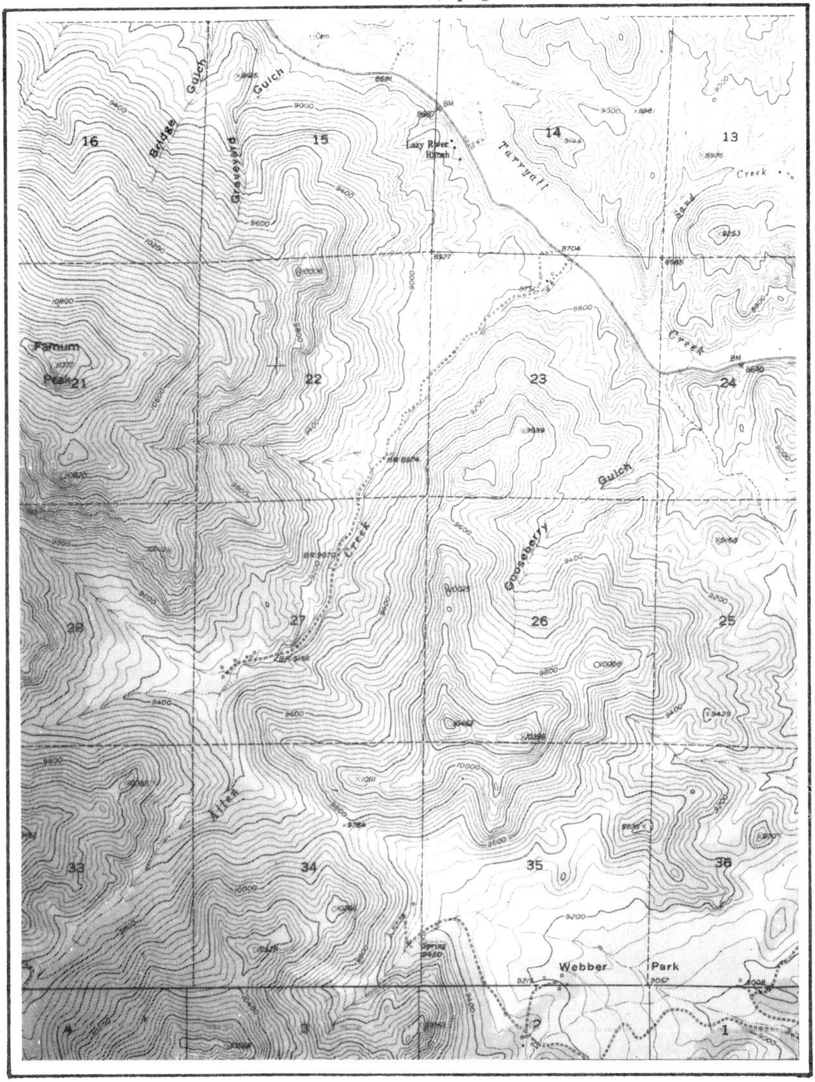

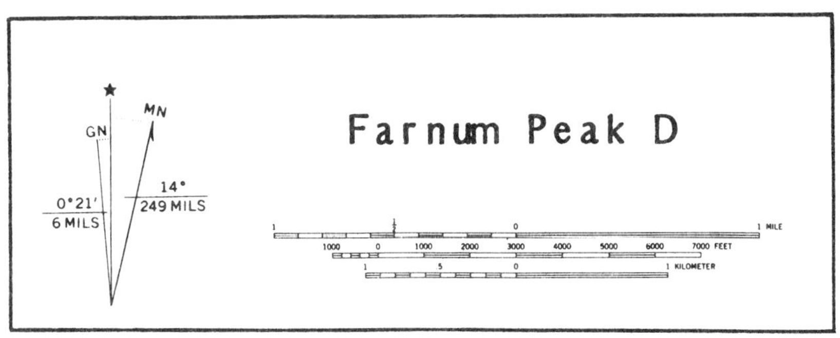

Windy Peak D, page 193

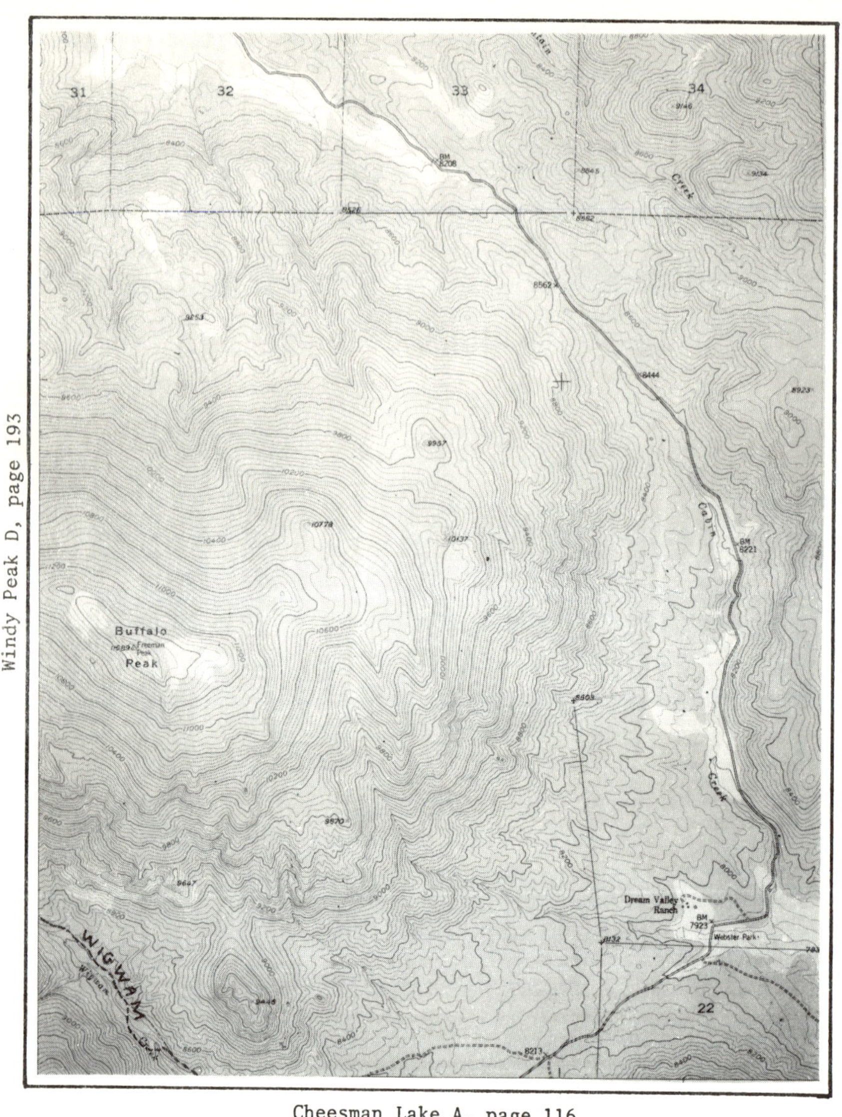

Cheesman Lake A, page 116

Green Mountain C

GN MN

0°12'
4 MILS

14°
249 MILS

1 ½ 0 1 MILE

1000 0 1000 2000 3000 4000 5000 6000 7000 FEET

1 .5 0 1 KILOMETER

Mt. Evans B, page 160

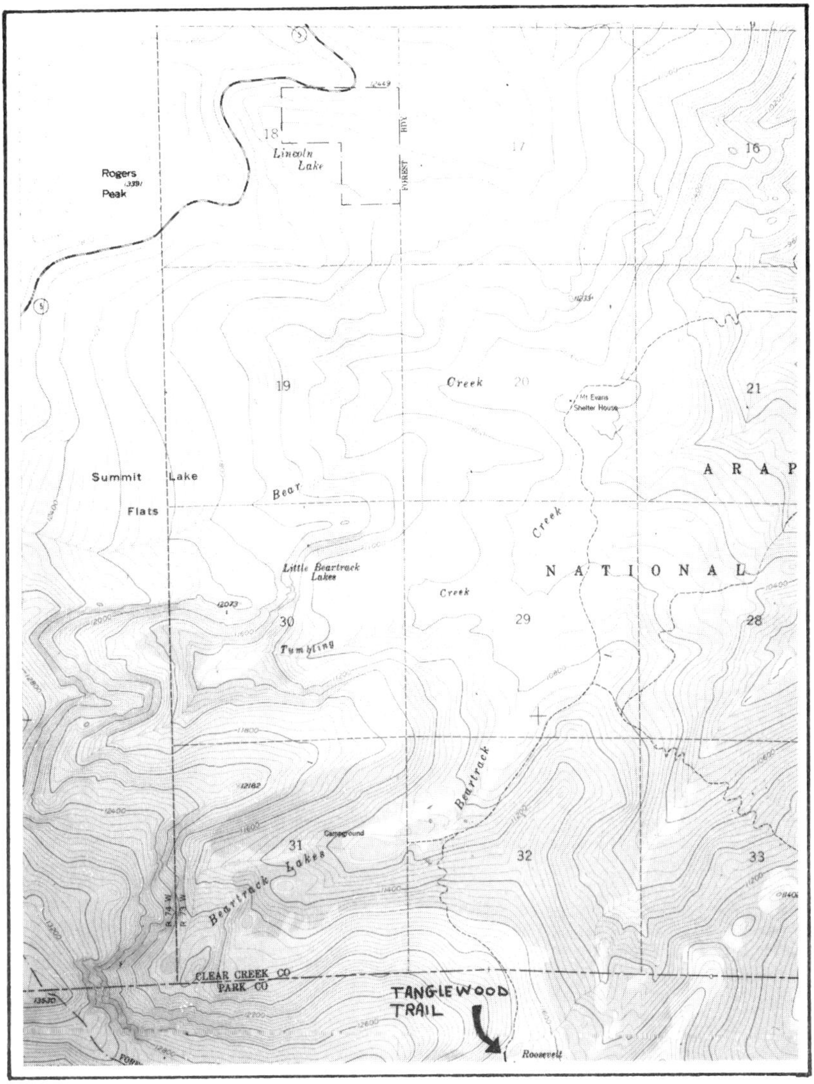

Rogers Peak

Lincoln Lake

Summit Lake Flats

Little Beartrack Lakes

Bear Creek

Tumbling Creek

Beartrack Lakes

Mt Evans Shelter House

Campground

NATIONAL

CLEAR CREEK CO
PARK CO

TANGLEWOOD TRAIL

Roosevelt

Harris Park C, page 134

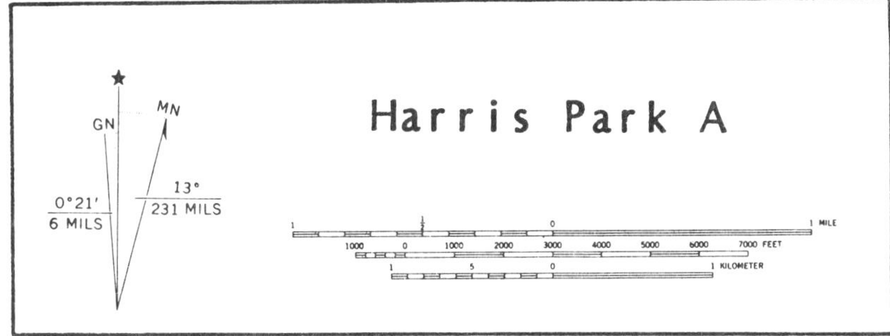

Harris Park A, page 133

Mt. Evans D, page 162

Harris Park D, page 135

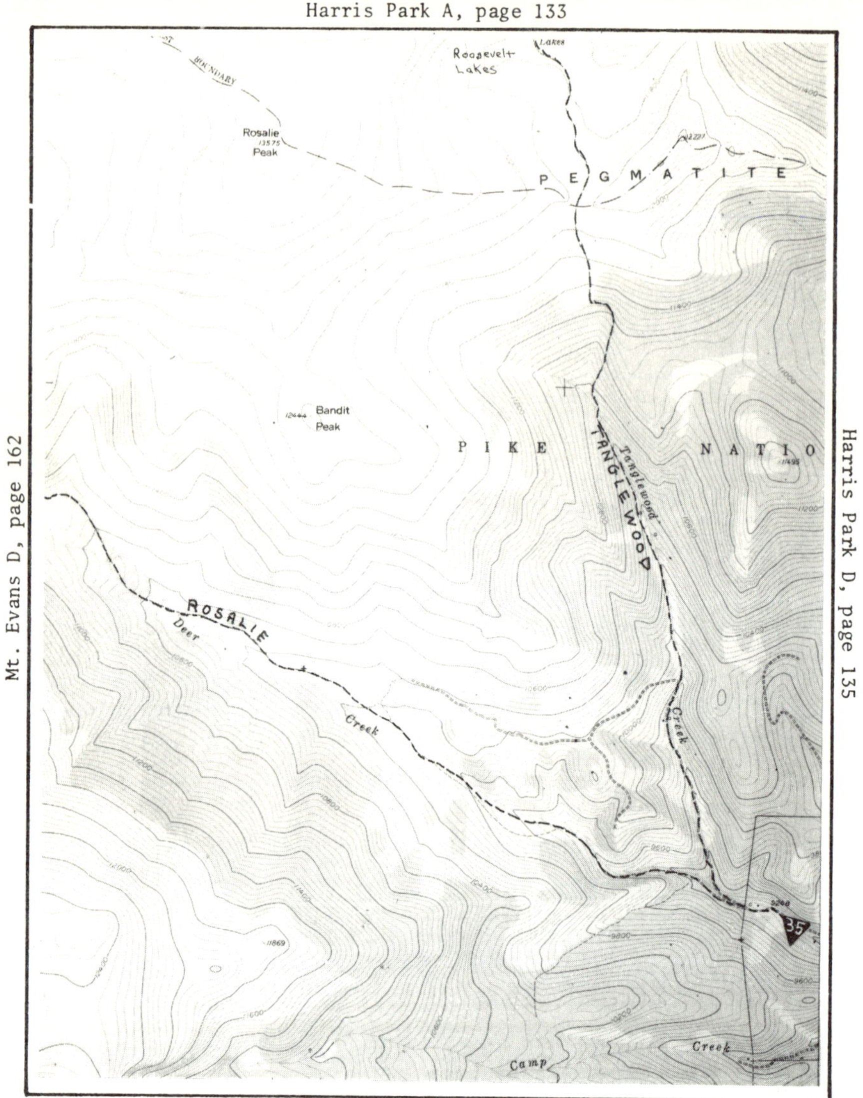

Shawnee A, page 182

GN

MN

0°21′
6 MILS

13°
231 MILS

Harris Park C

1 ½ 0 1 MILE

1000 0 1000 2000 3000 4000 5000 6000 7000 FEET

1 .5 0 1 KILOMETER

Harris Park C, page 134

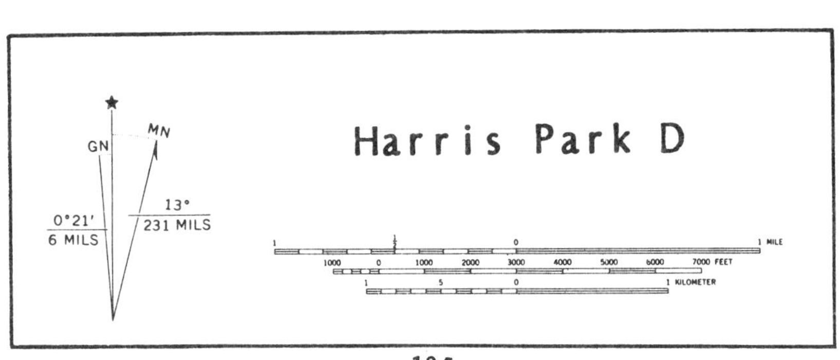

Boreas Pass B, page 110

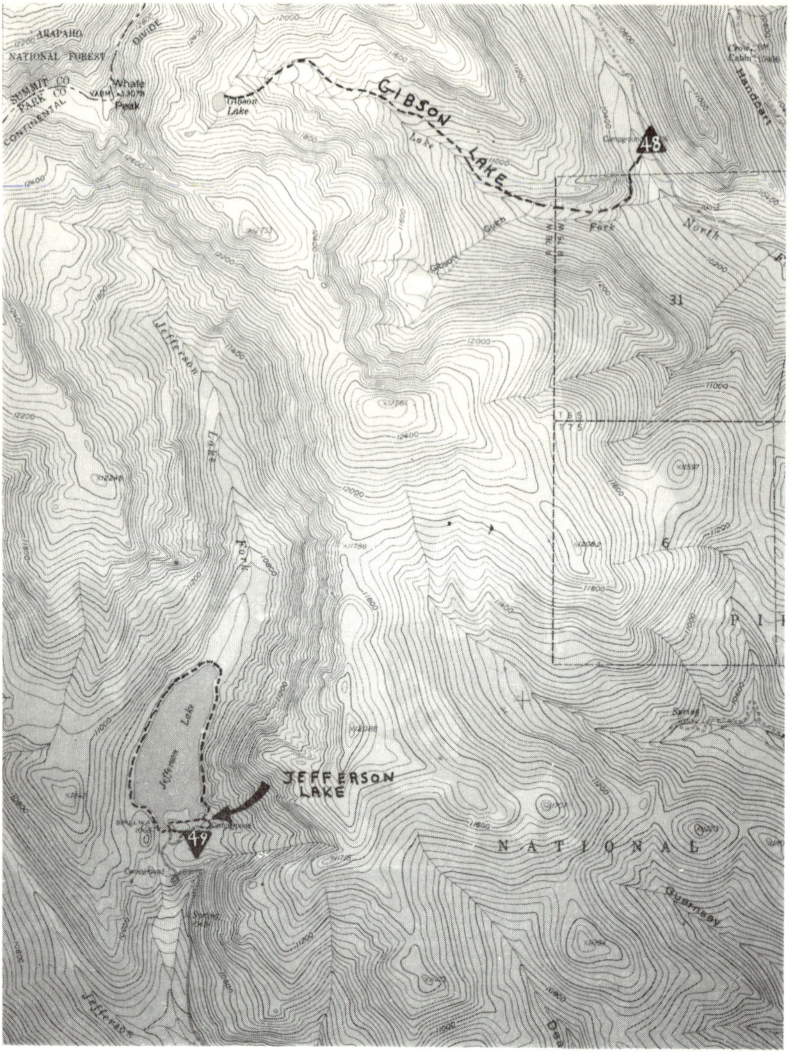

Jefferson B, page 137

ARAPAHO NATIONAL FOREST

SUMMIT CO

PARK CO

CONTINENTAL DIVIDE

Whale Peak

Gibson Lake

GIBSON LAKE

48

Handcart

North Fork

Gibson Gulch

Jefferson Lake Fork

Jefferson Lake

JEFFERSON LAKE

49

NATIONAL

Guernsey

Jefferson

Jefferson C, page 138

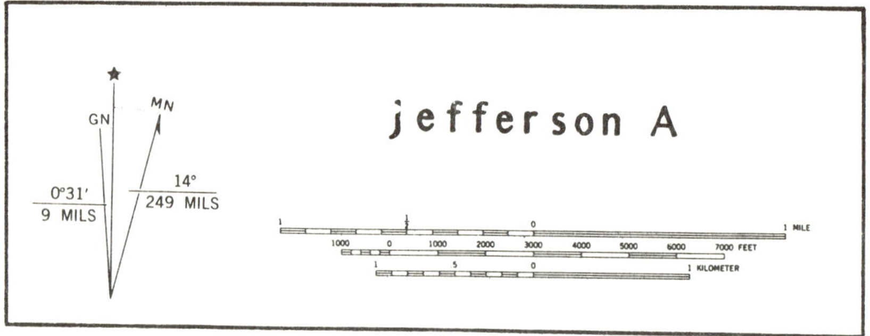

Montezuma D, page 156

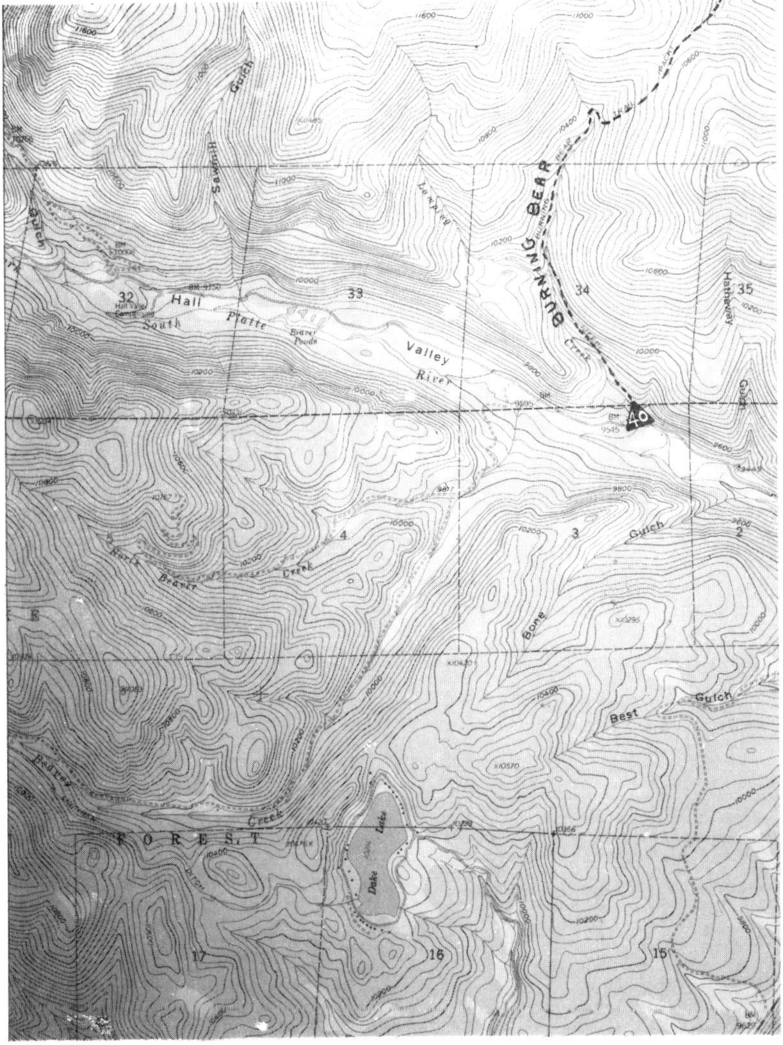

Jefferson A, page 136

Mt. Logan A, page 163

Jefferson D, page 139

Jefferson B

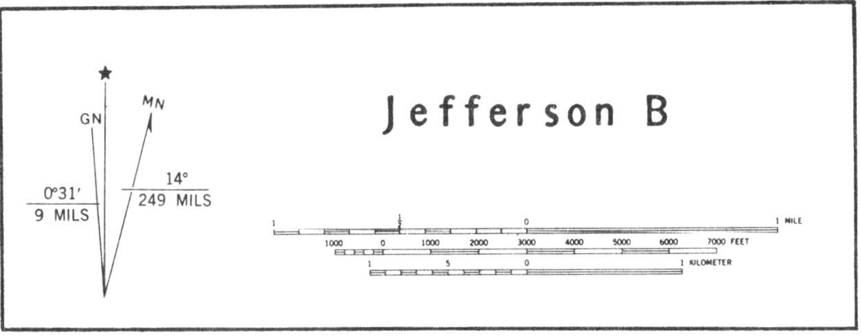

Jefferson A, page 136

Boreas Pass D, page 111

Jefferson D, page 139

Jefferson C

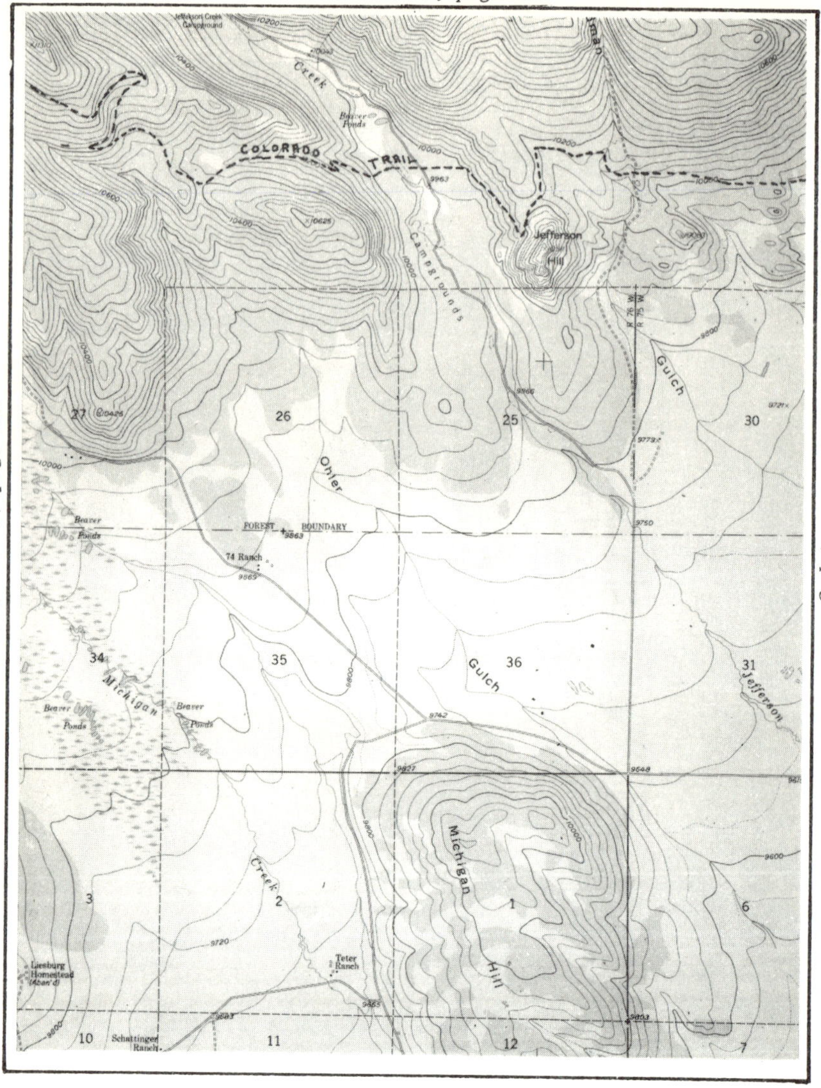

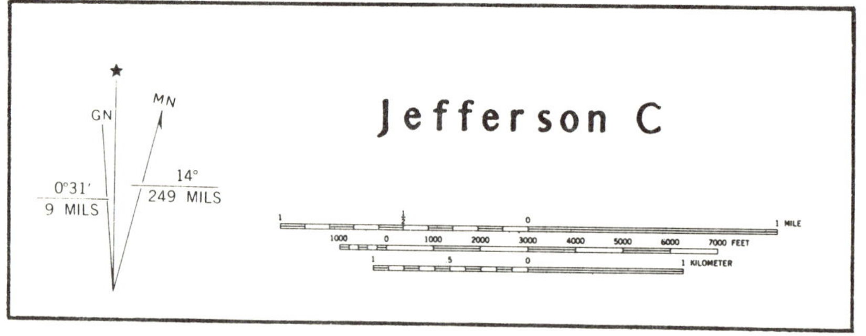

Jefferson B, page 137

Jefferson C, page 138

Mt. Logan C, page 165

Jefferson D

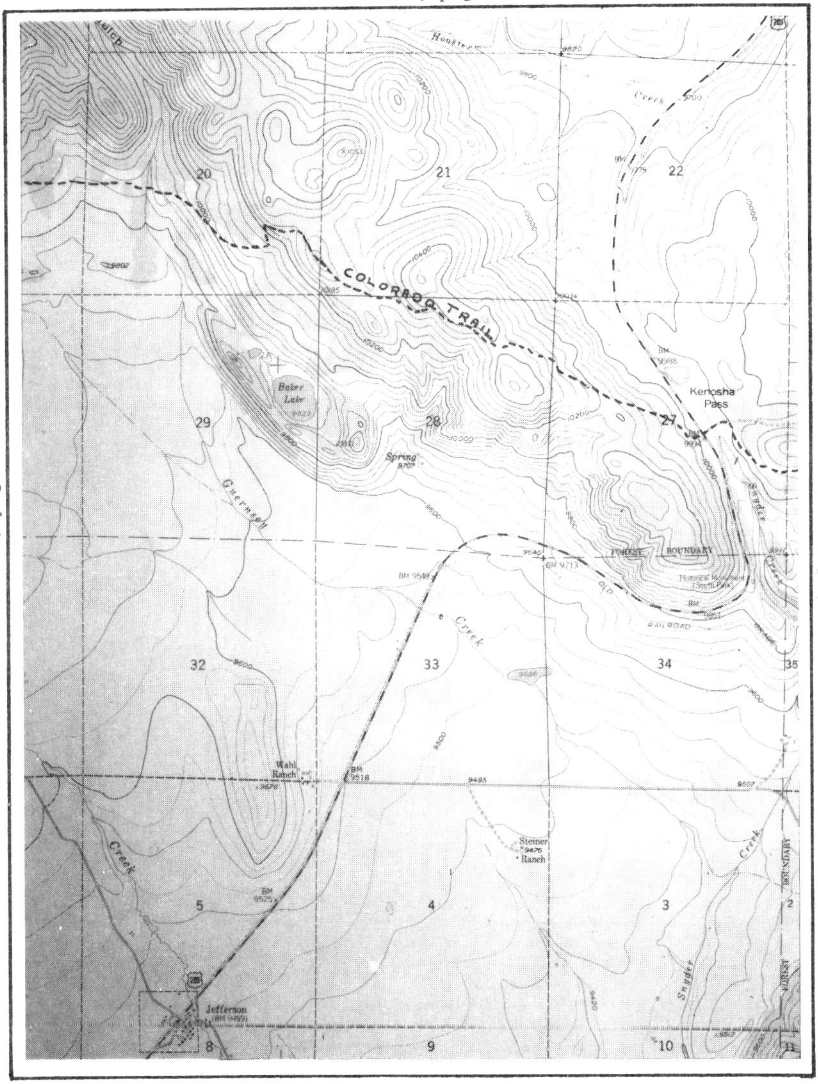

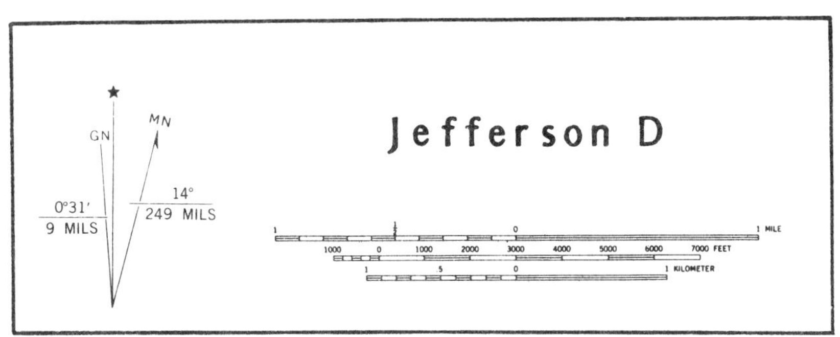

South Peak B, page 185

Jones Hill B, page 141

Jones Hill C, page 142

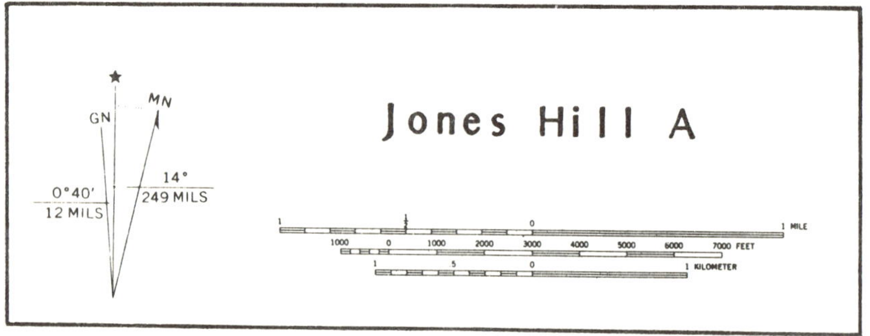

Jones Hill A, page 140

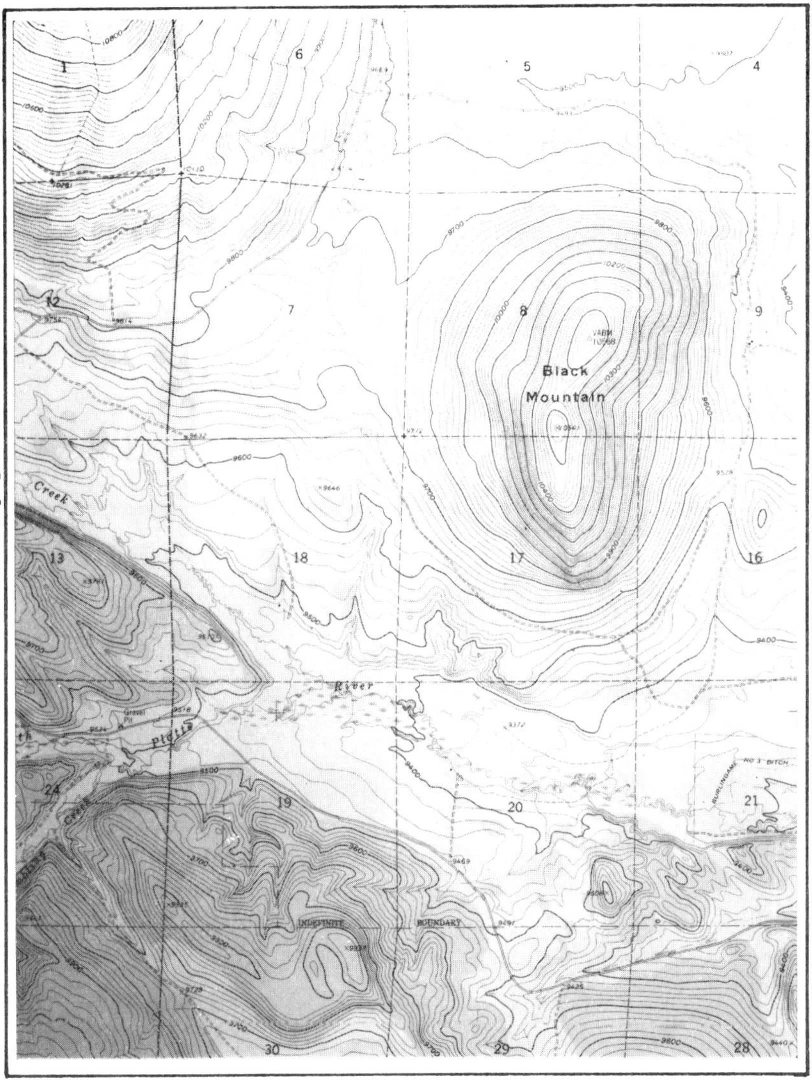

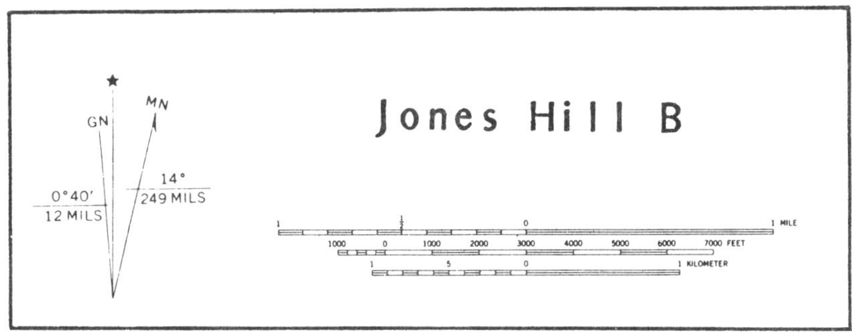

Jones Hill B

Jones Hill A, page 140

South Peak D, page 186

Jones Hill C

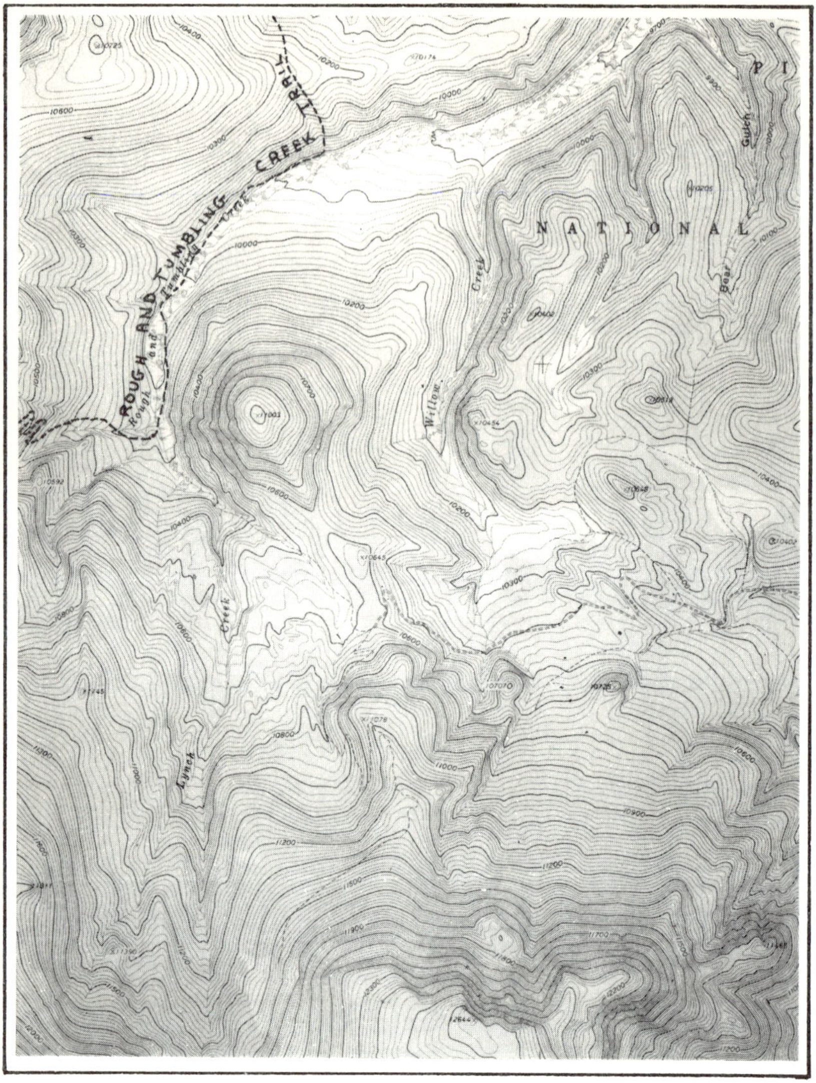

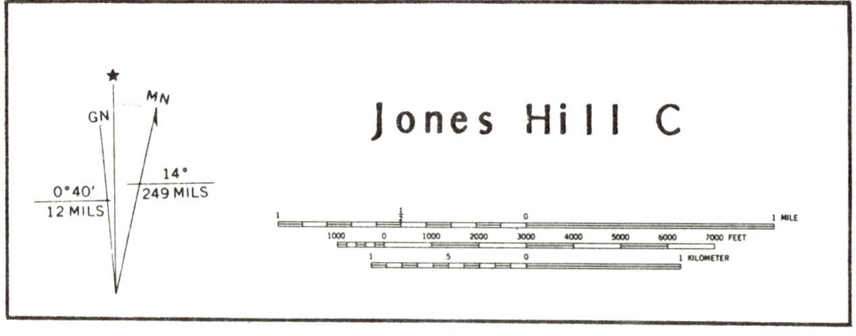

Divide A, page 125

Lake George D, page 144

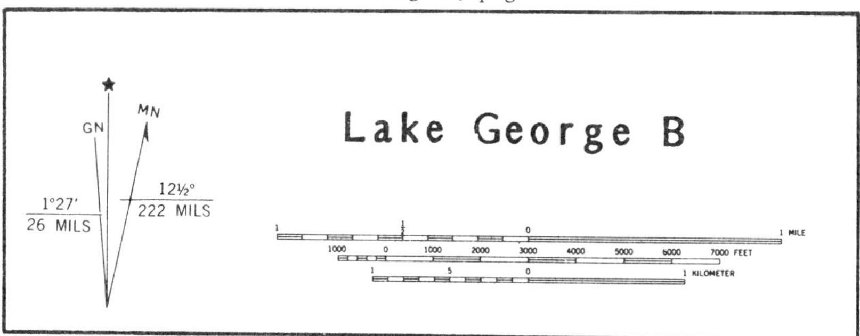

Lake George B, page 143

Divide C, page 127

Lake George D

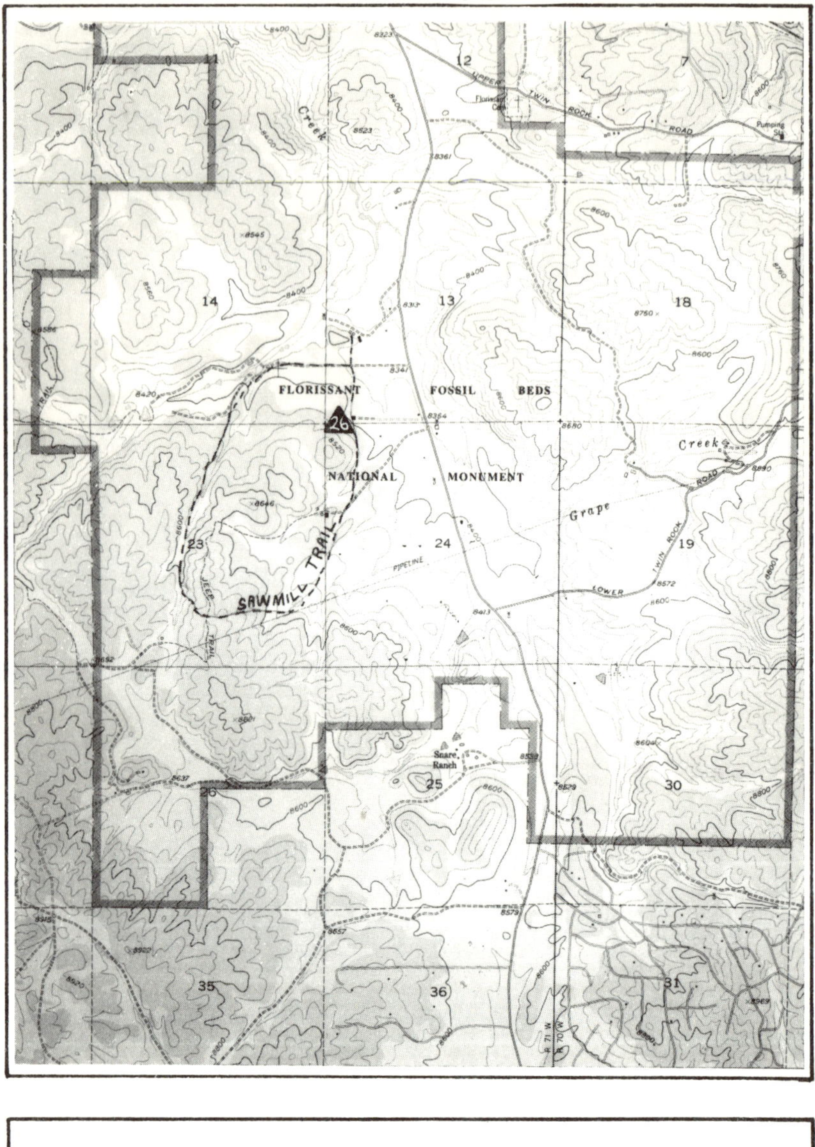

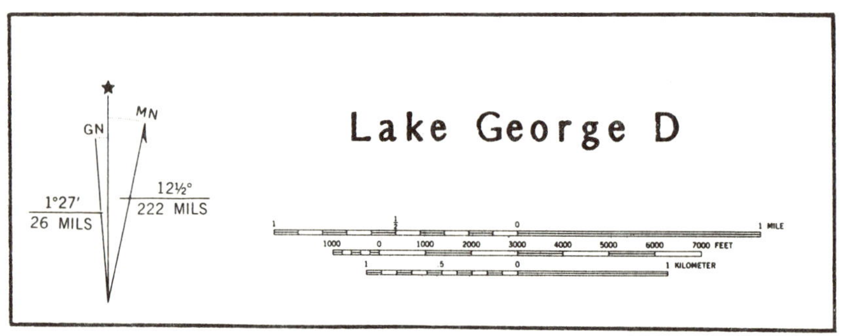

Cascade C, page 114

Pikes Peak B, page 175

Manitou Springs B, page 146

Manitou Springs C, page 147

Manitou Springs A

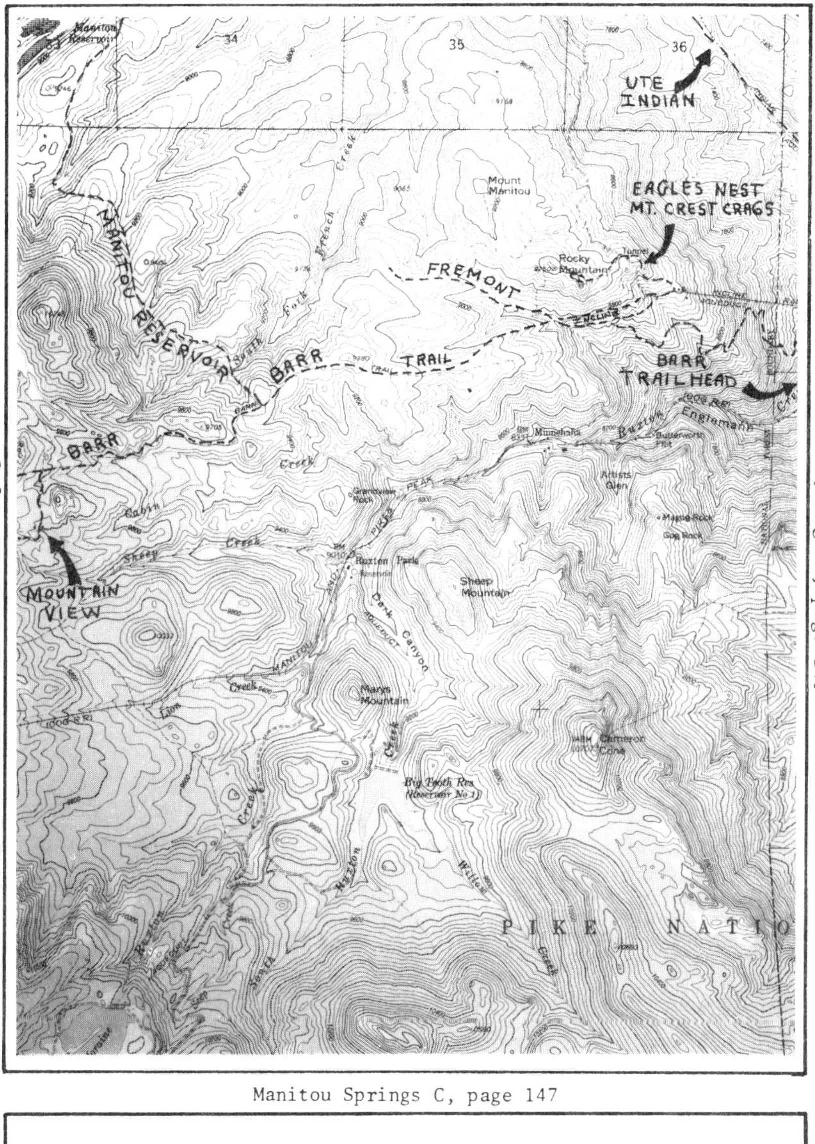

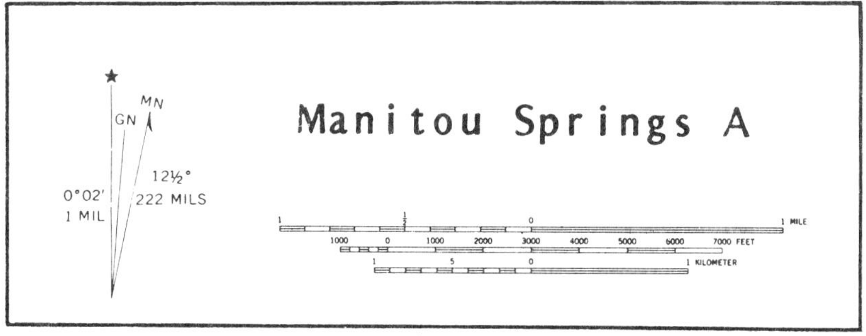

Cascade D, page 115

Manitou Springs A, page 145

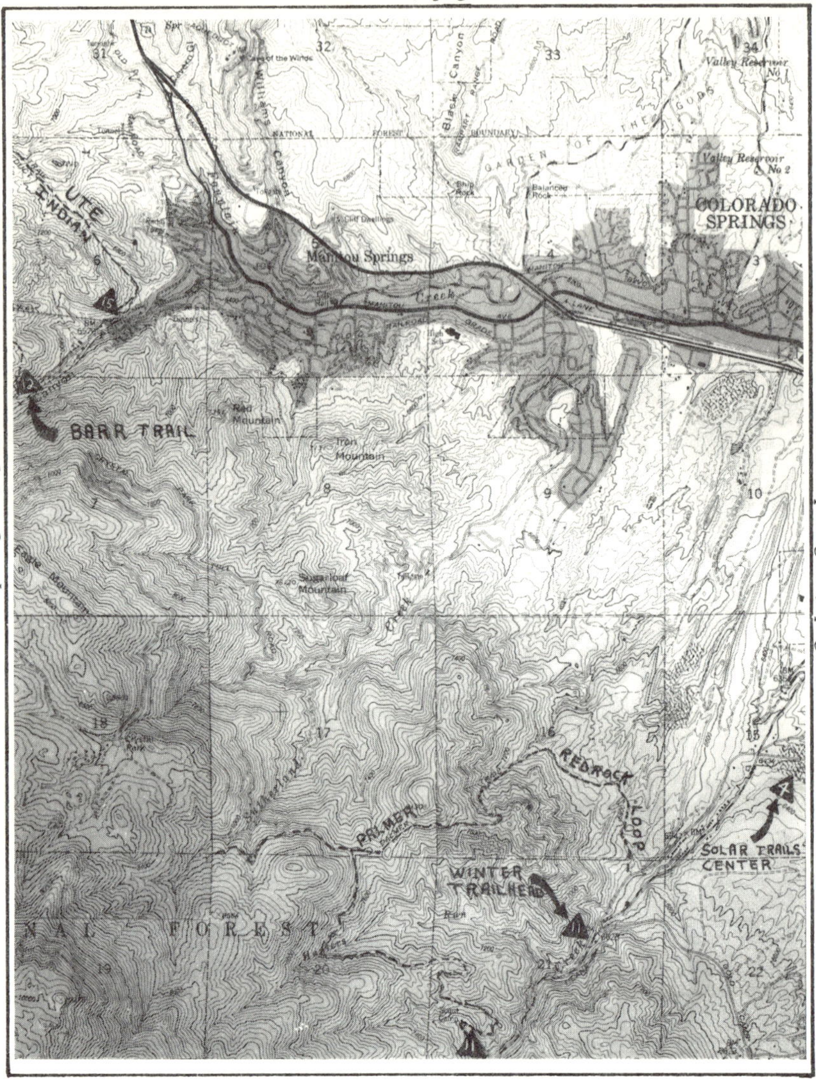

Colorado Springs A, page 118

Manitou Springs D, page 148

Manitou Springs B

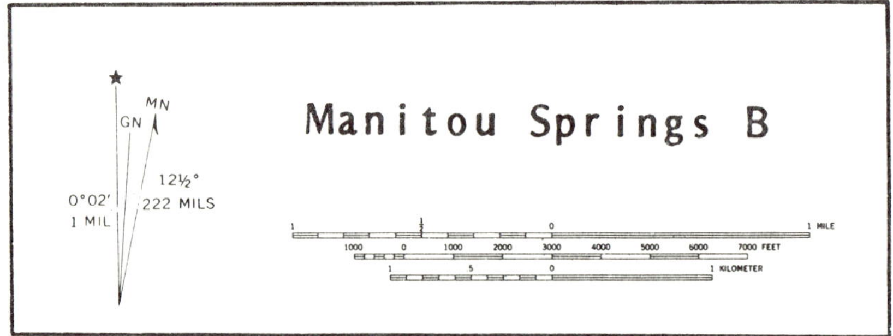

Manitou Springs A, page 145

Pikes Peak D, page 177

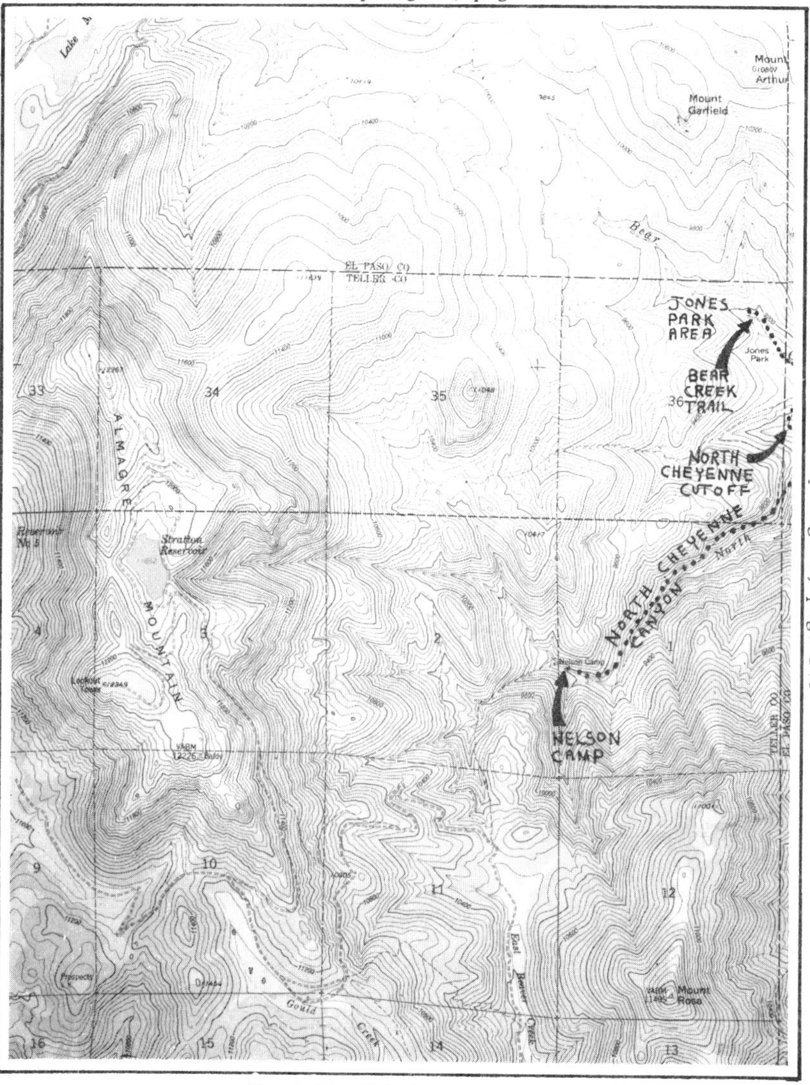

Manitou Springs D, page 148

Mount Big Chief A, page 157

Manitou Springs C

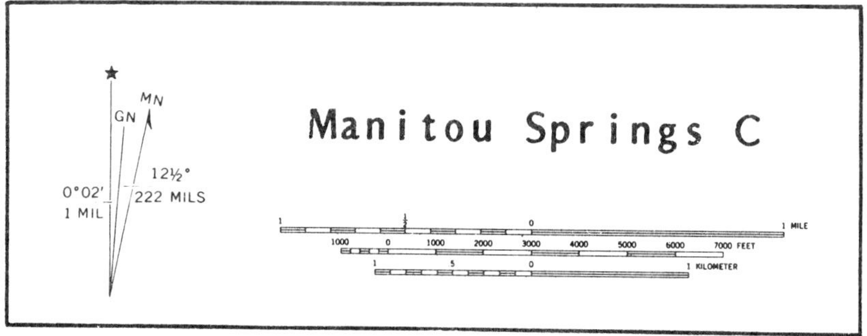

Manitou Springs B, page 146

Manitou Springs C, page 147

Colorado Springs C, page 120

Mount Big Chief B, page 158

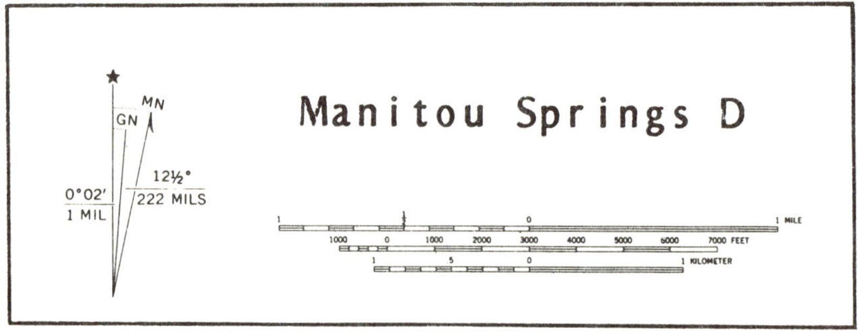

Manitou Springs D

Windy Peak C, page 192

Farnum Peak B, page 130

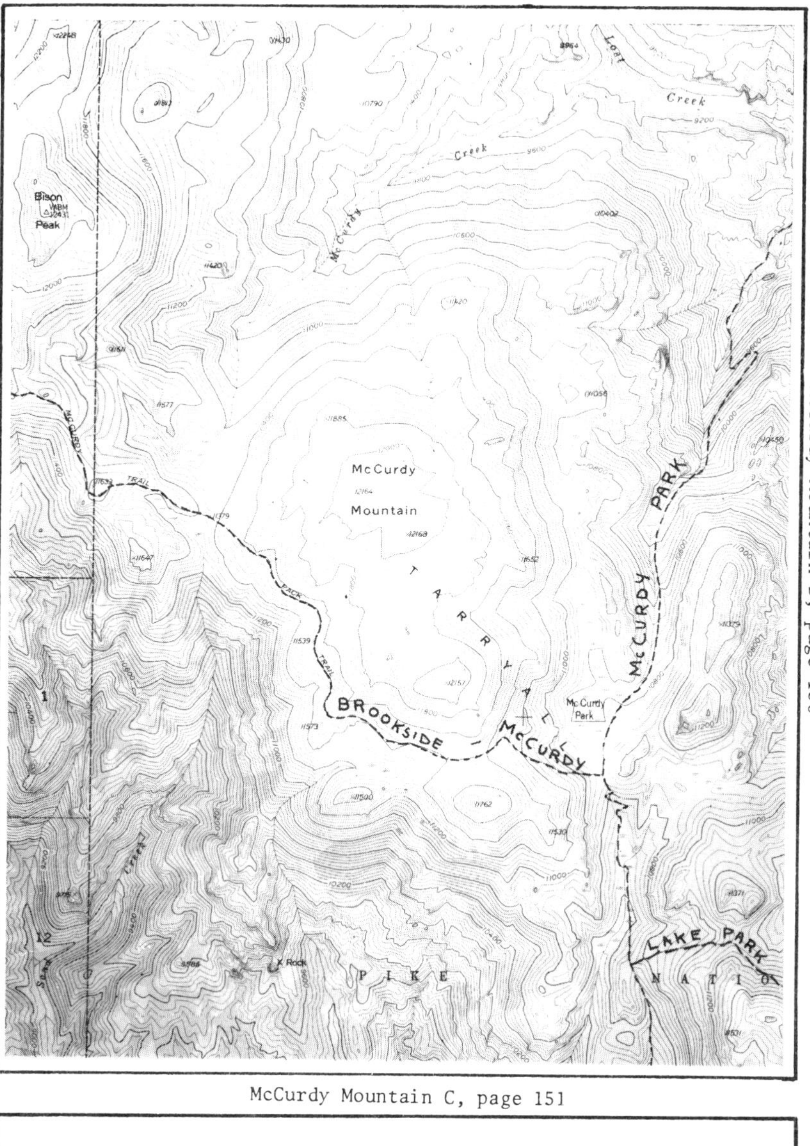

McCurdy Mountain B, page 150

McCurdy Mountain C, page 151

McCurdy Mountain A

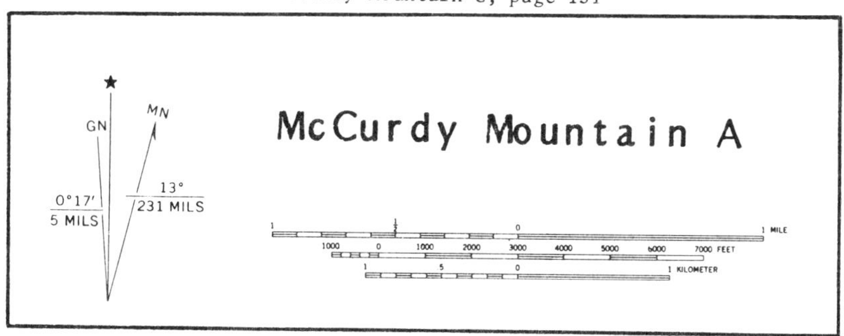

Windy Peak D, page 193

McCURDY PARK TRAIL

BOX CANYON USED BY TRAIL RIDERS

GOOSE CREEK

LAKE PARK TRAIL

McCurdy Mountain A, page 149

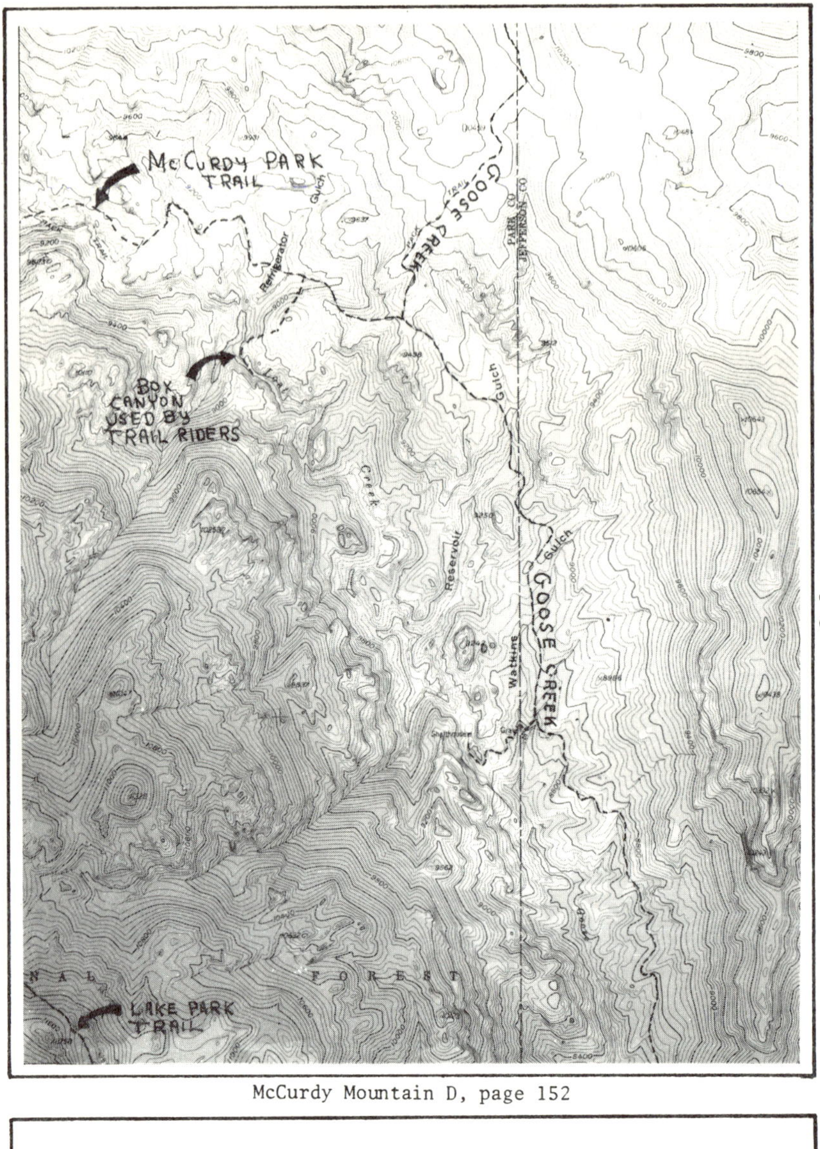

Cheesman Lake A, page 116

McCurdy Mountain D, page 152

McCurdy Mountain A, page 149

Farnum Peak D, page 131

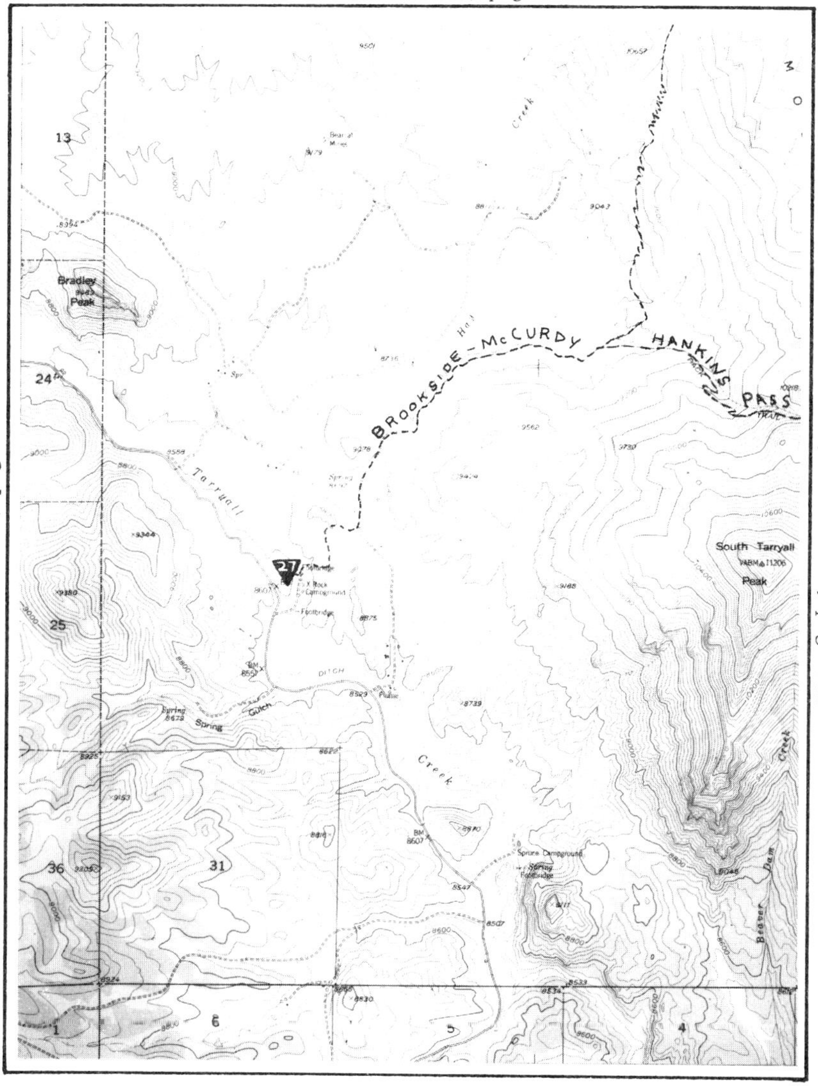

McCurdy Mountain D, page 152

McCurdy Mountain C

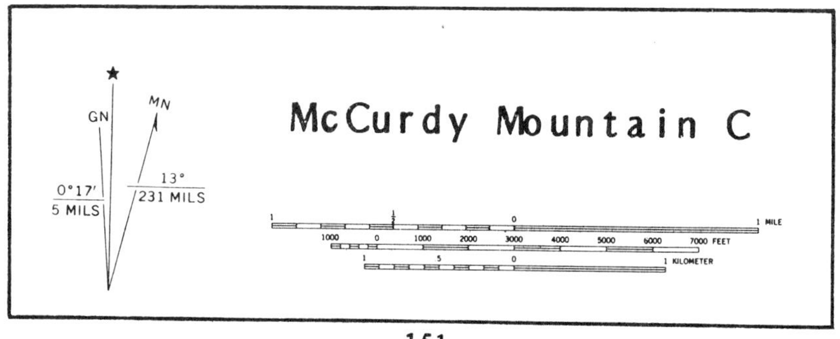

McCurdy Mountain B, page 150

McCurdy Mountain C, page 151

Lake Park
LAKE PARK
PACK TRAIL
Hankins Park
HANKINS
Hankins PASS
Gulch
APPROXIMATE BOUNDARY
GOOSE CREEK
Goose Creek Campground
30
JEFFERSON CO
PARK CO

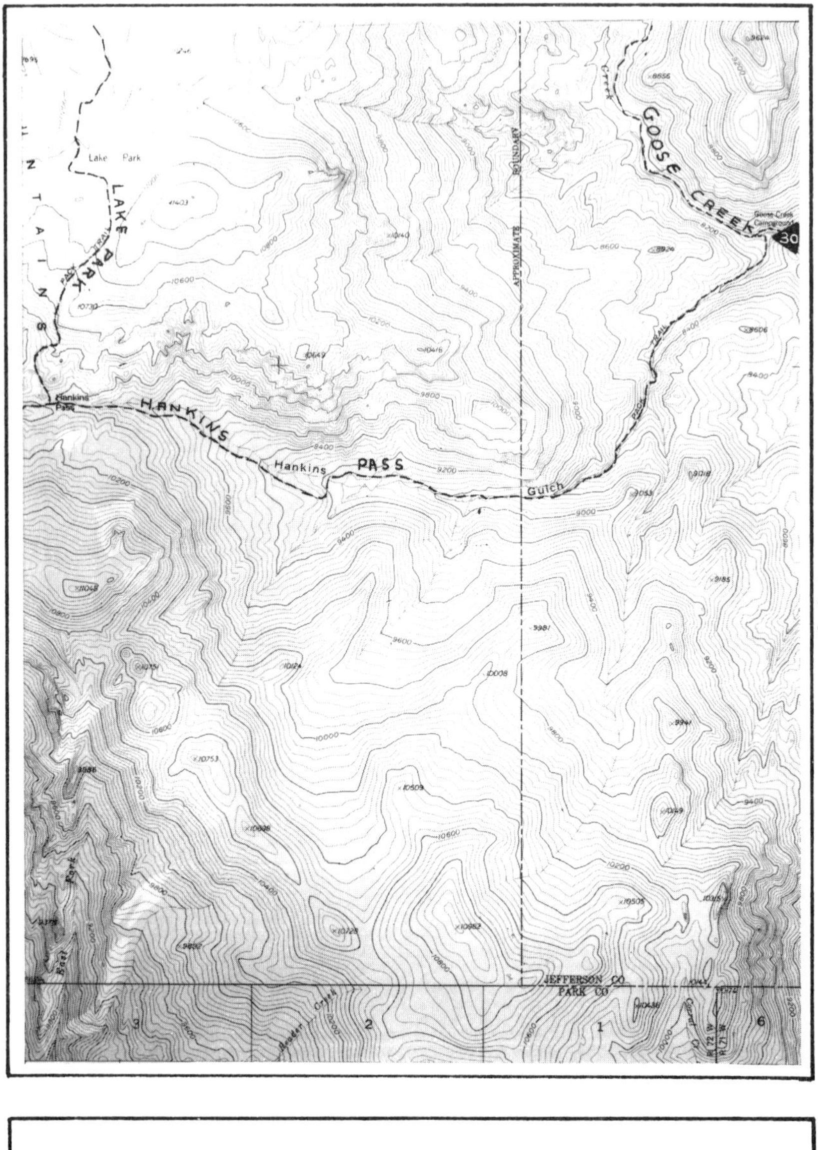

Cheesman Lake C, page 117

GN
MN
0°17′
5 MILS
13°
231 MILS

McCurdy Mountain D

1 MILE
7000 FEET
1 KILOMETER

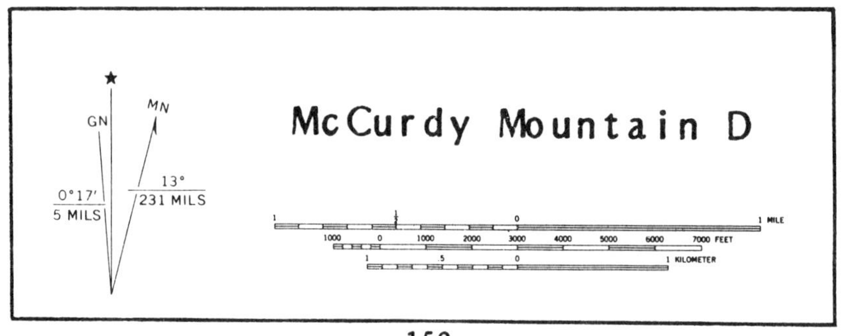

Palmer Lake B, page 172

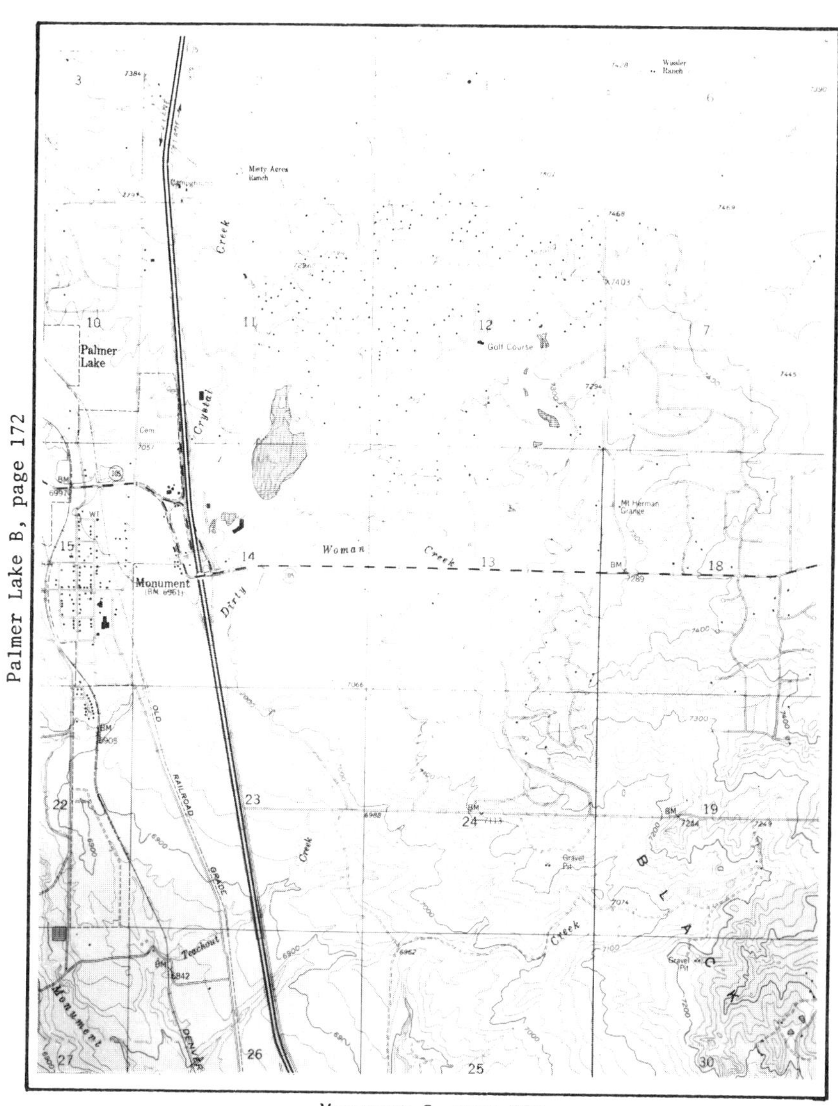

Monument C, page 154

Monument A

GN
MN
0°07'
2 MILS
12½°
222 MILS

1 ½ 0 1 MILE
1000 0 1000 2000 3000 4000 5000 6000 7000 FEET
1 .5 0 1 KILOMETER

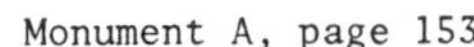

Monument A, page 153

Palmer Lake D, page 173

Pikeview A, page 178

Monument C

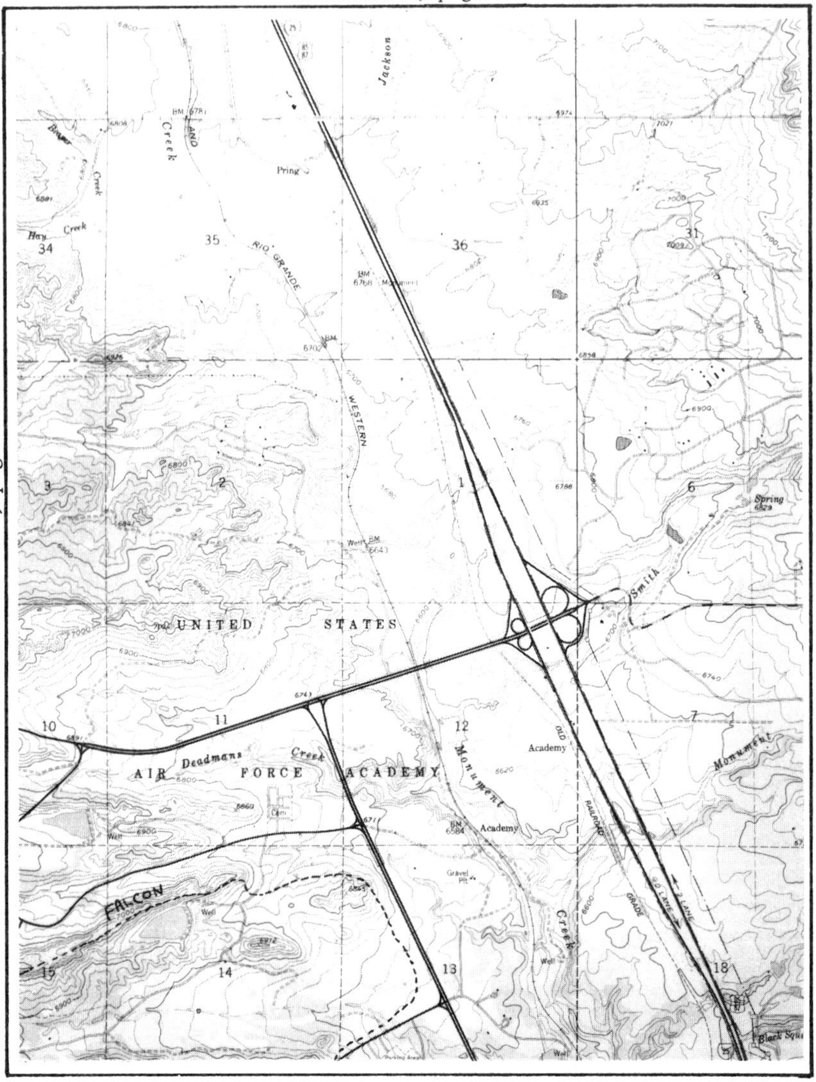

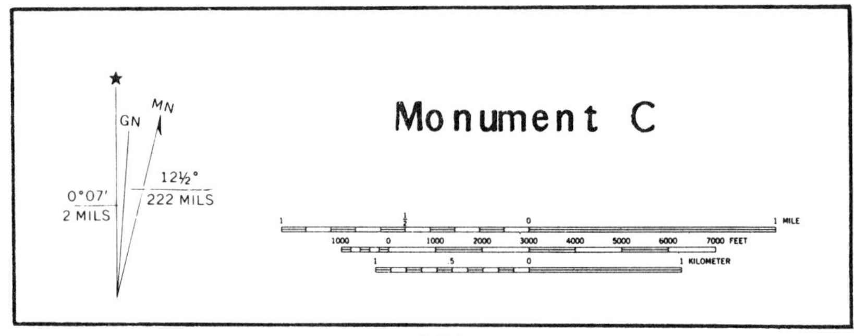

Mt. Evans A, page 159

Montezuma D, page 156

Montezuma B

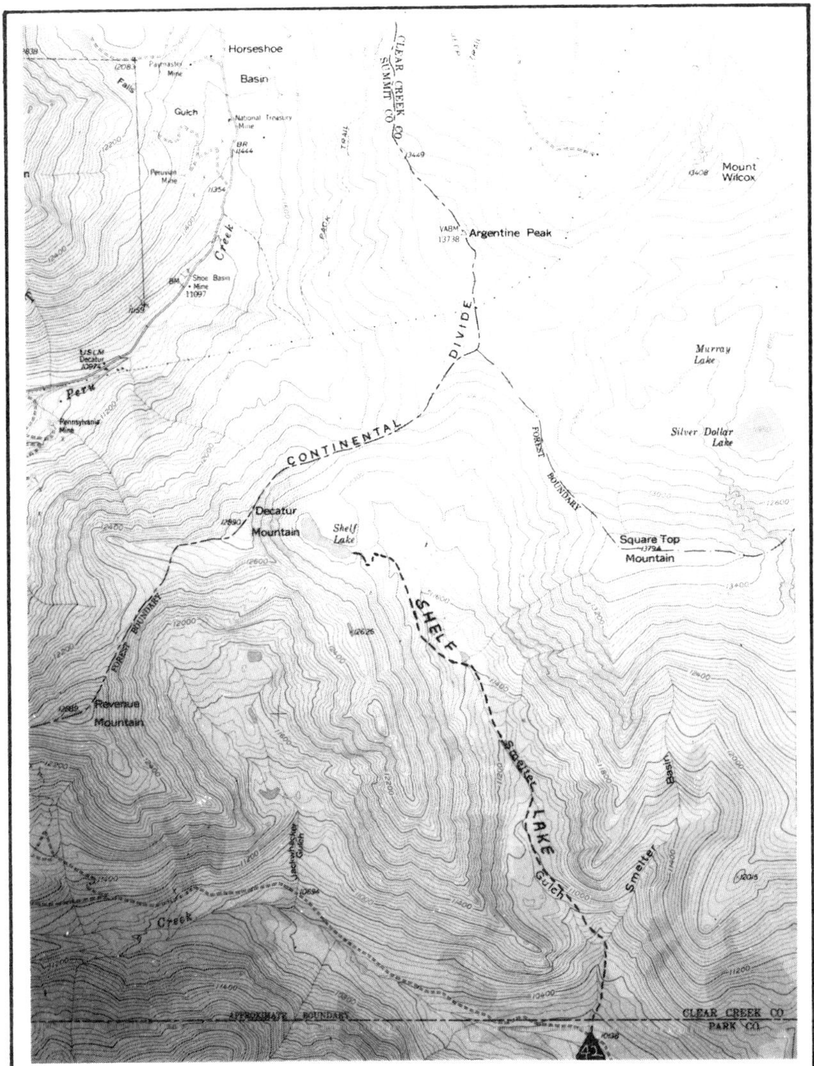

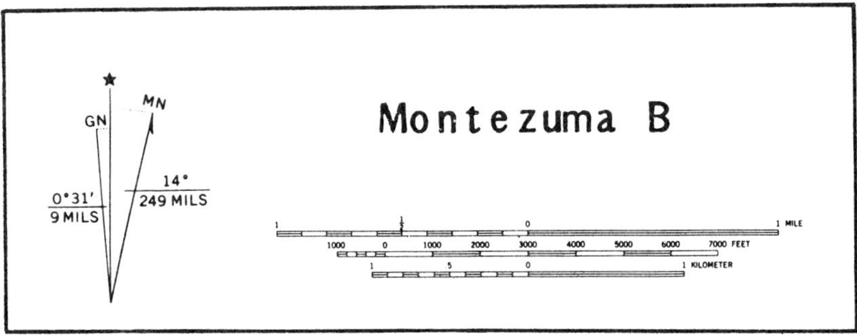

Montezuma B, page 155

Mt. Evans C, page 161

Jefferson B, page 137

Montezuma D

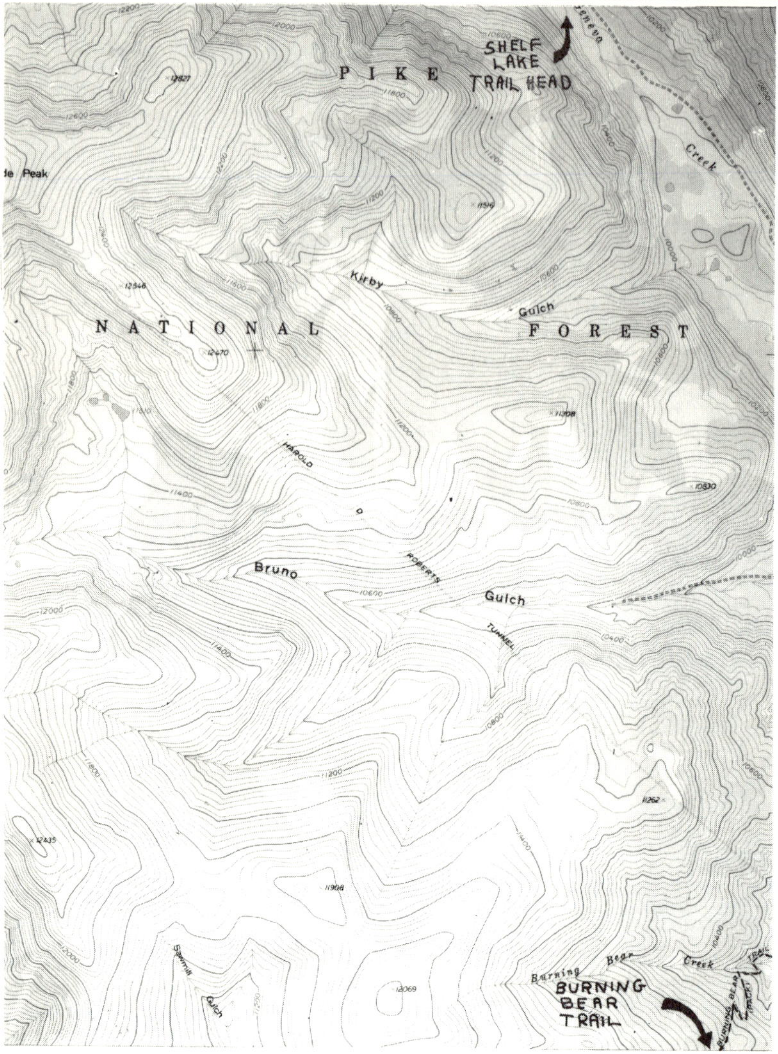

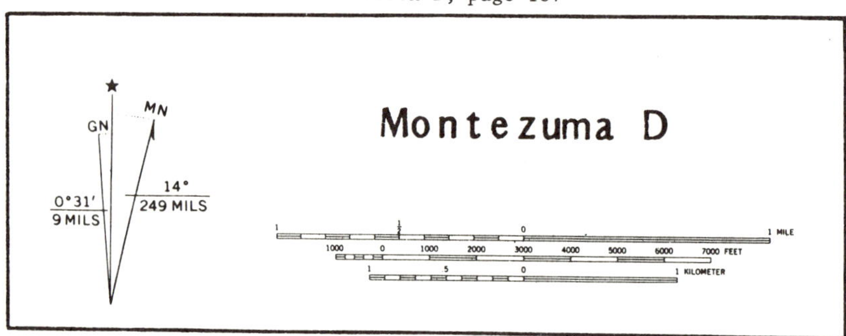

Manitou Springs C, page 147

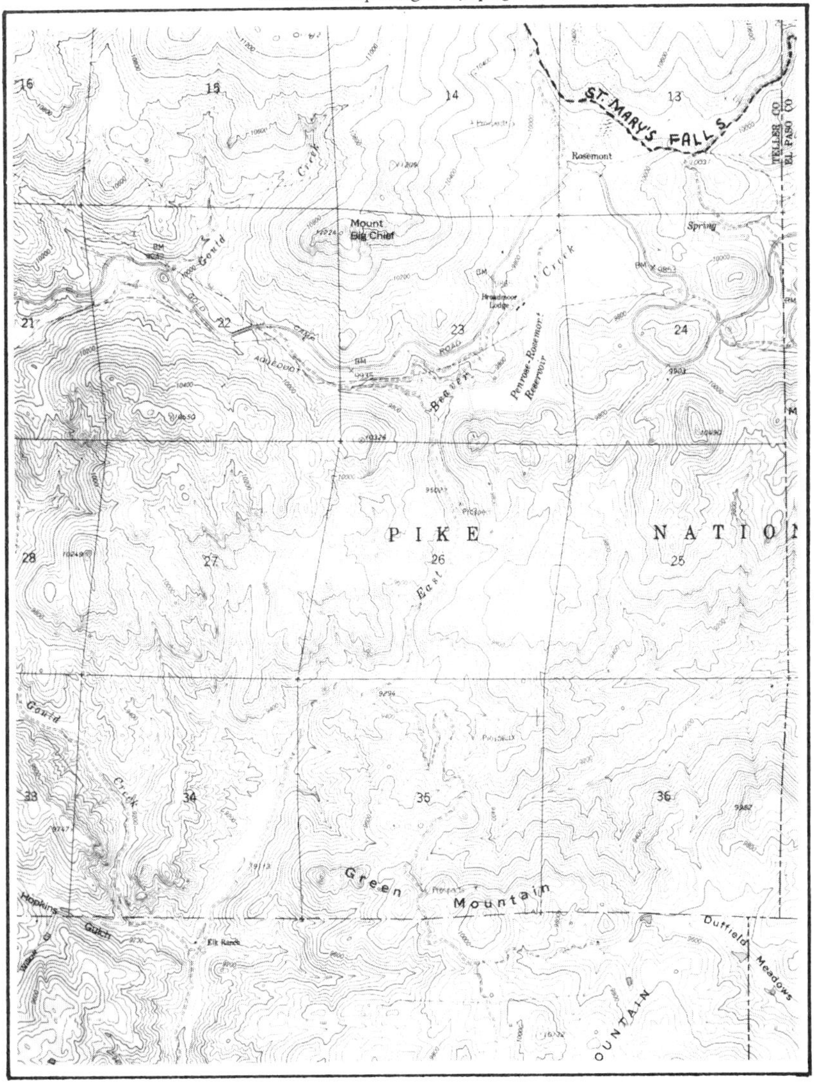

Mount Big Chief B, page 158

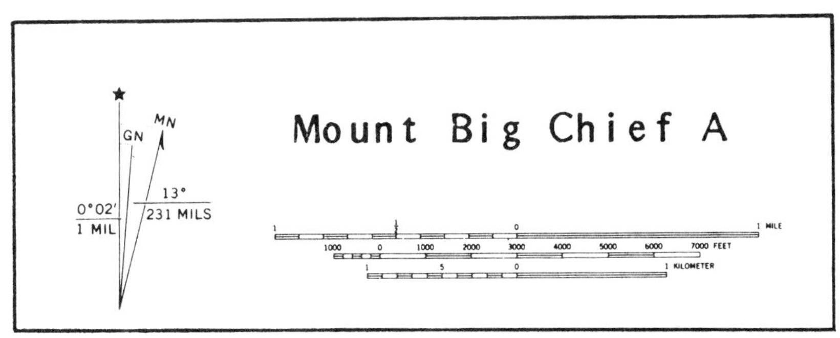

Mount Big Chief A

Manitou Springs D, page 148

Mount Big Chief A, page 157

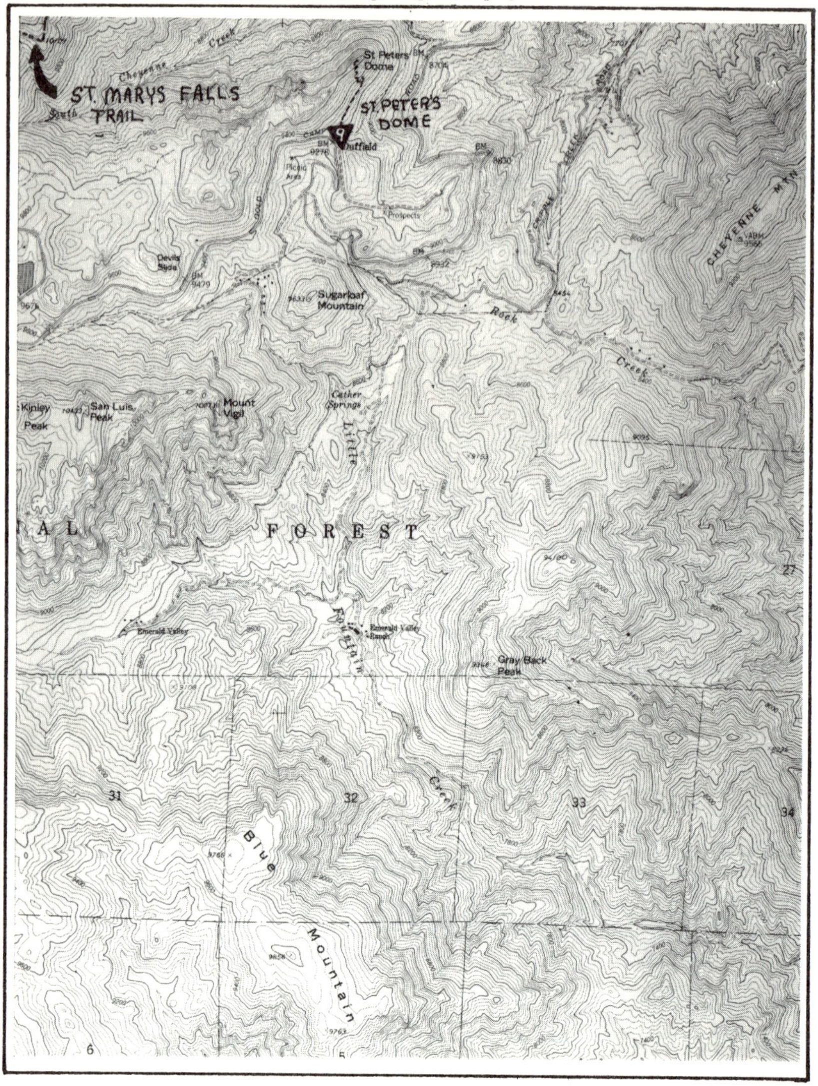

Mount Big Chief B

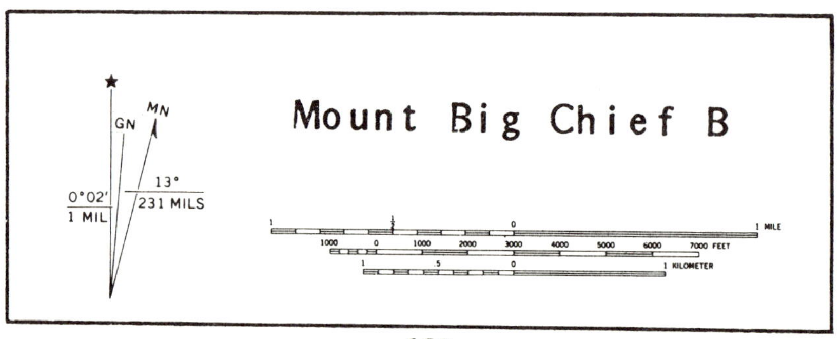

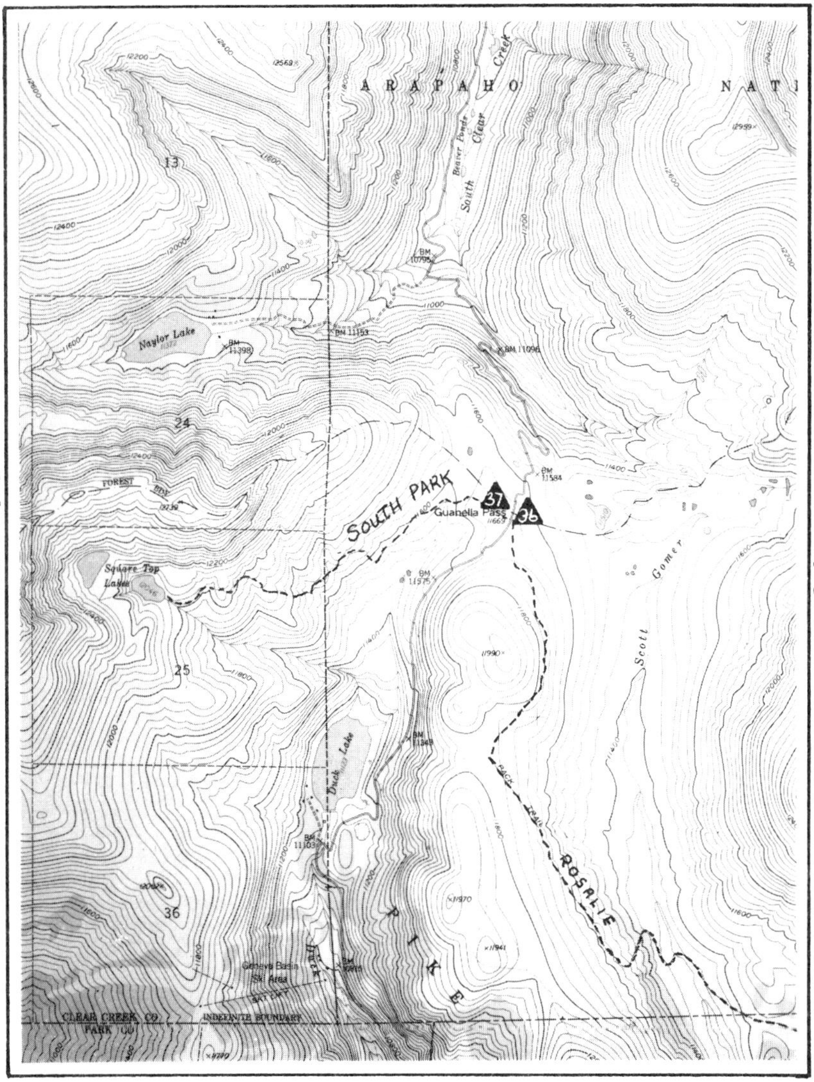

Montezuma B, page 155

Mt. Evans B, page 160

Mt. Evans C, page 161

Mt. Evans A

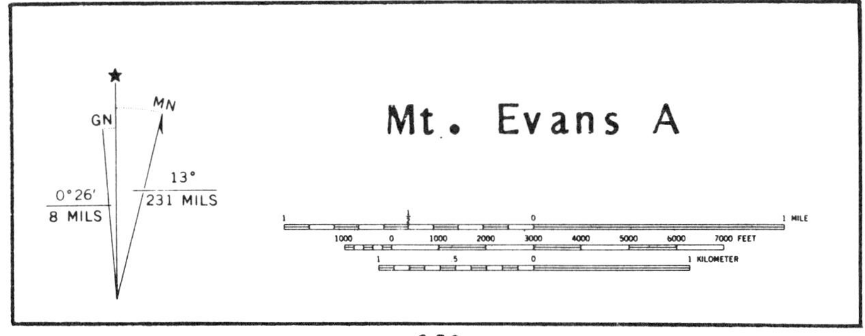

Mt. Evans A, page 159

Harris Park A, page 133

Mt. Evans D, page 162

Mt. Evans B

GN MN

0°26′
8 MILS

13°
231 MILS

1 0 1 MILE
1000 0 1000 2000 3000 4000 5000 6000 7000 FEET
1 .5 0 1 KILOMETER

Mt. Evans A, page 159

Montezuma D, page 156

Mt. Evans D, page 162

Mt. Logan A, page 163

Mt. Evans C

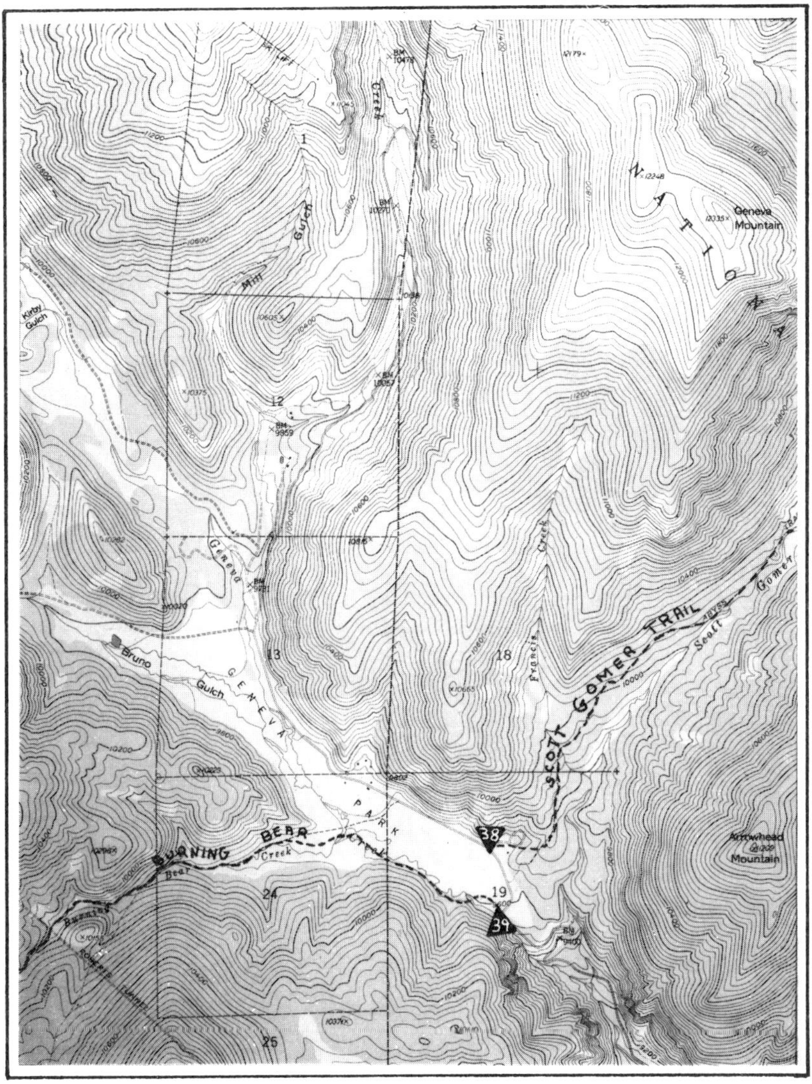

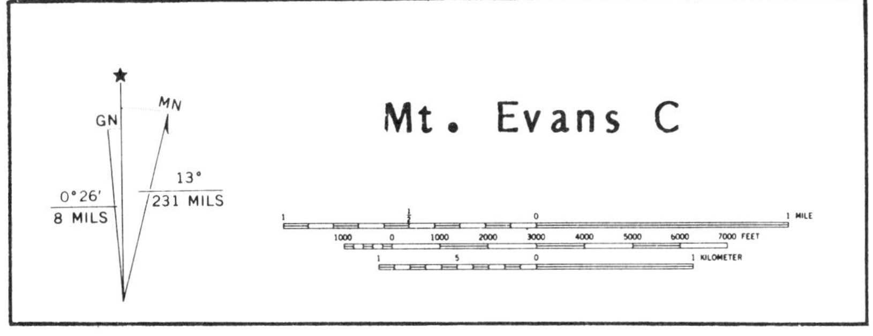

Mt. Evans B, page 160

Mt. Evans C, page 161

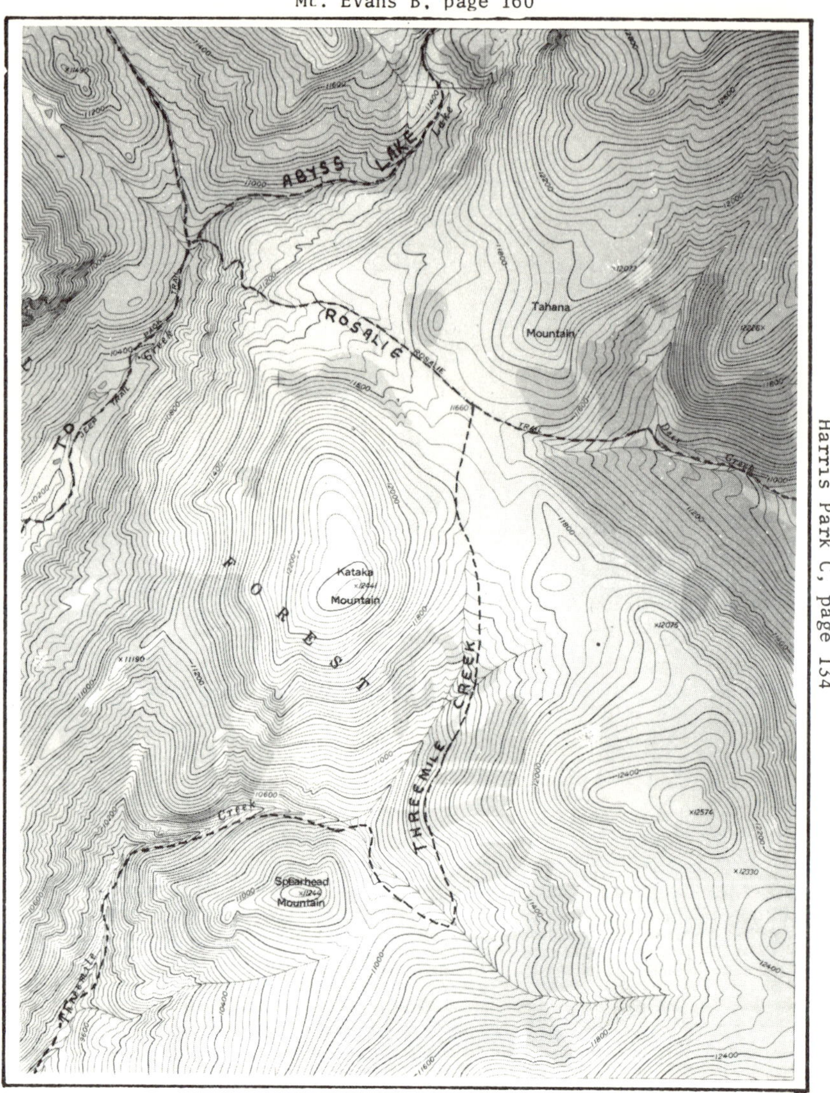

Harris Park C, page 134

Mt. Logan B, page 164

Mt. Evans D

GN

MN

0°26′
8 MILS

13°
231 MILS

1 ½ 0 1 MILE

1000 0 1000 2000 3000 4000 5000 6000 7000 FEET

1 .5 0 1 KILOMETER

Mt. Evans C, page 161

Jefferson B, page 137

Mt. Logan B, page 164

Mt. Logan C, page 165

Mt. Logan A

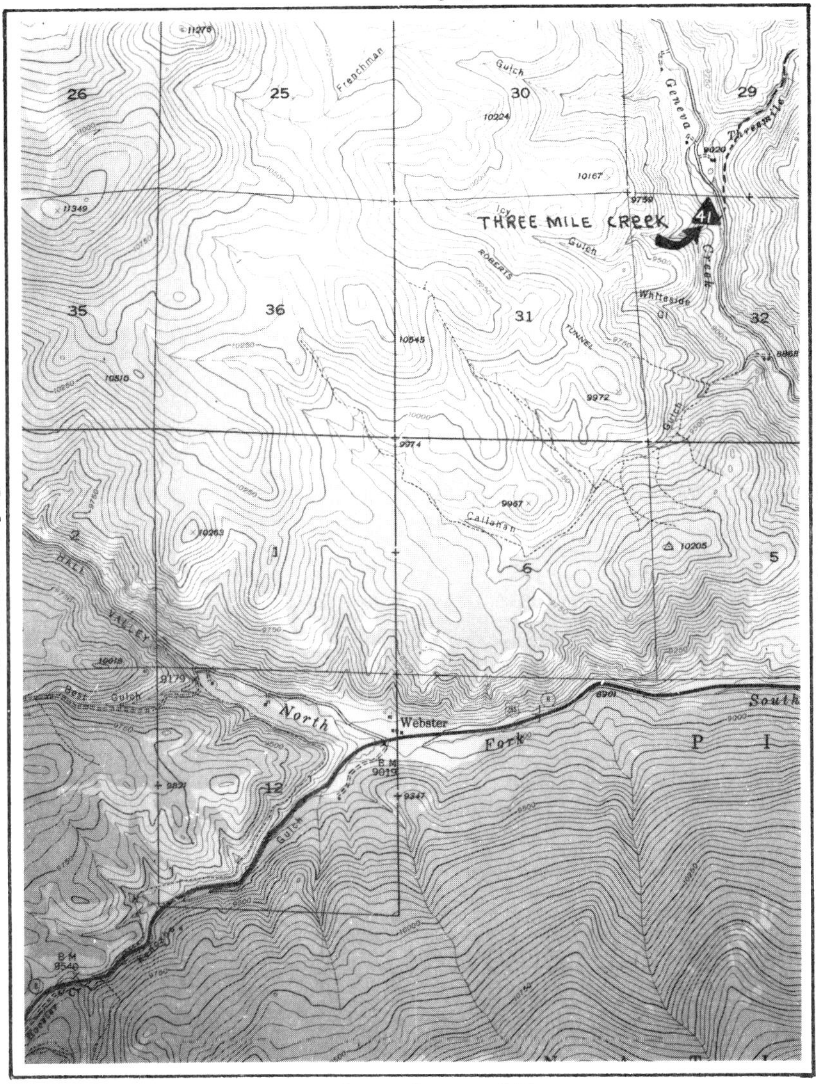

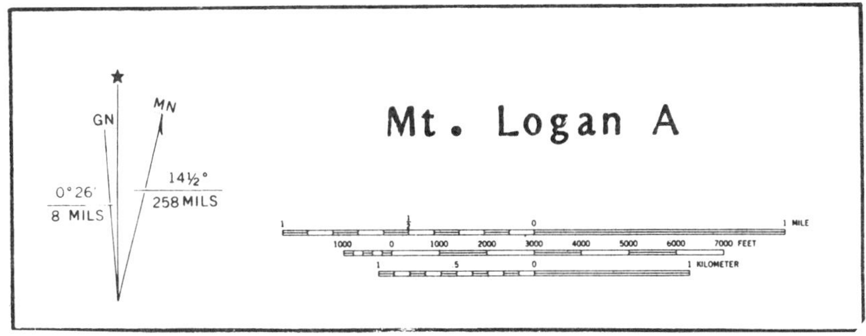

Mt. Evans D, page 162

Mt. Logan A, page 163

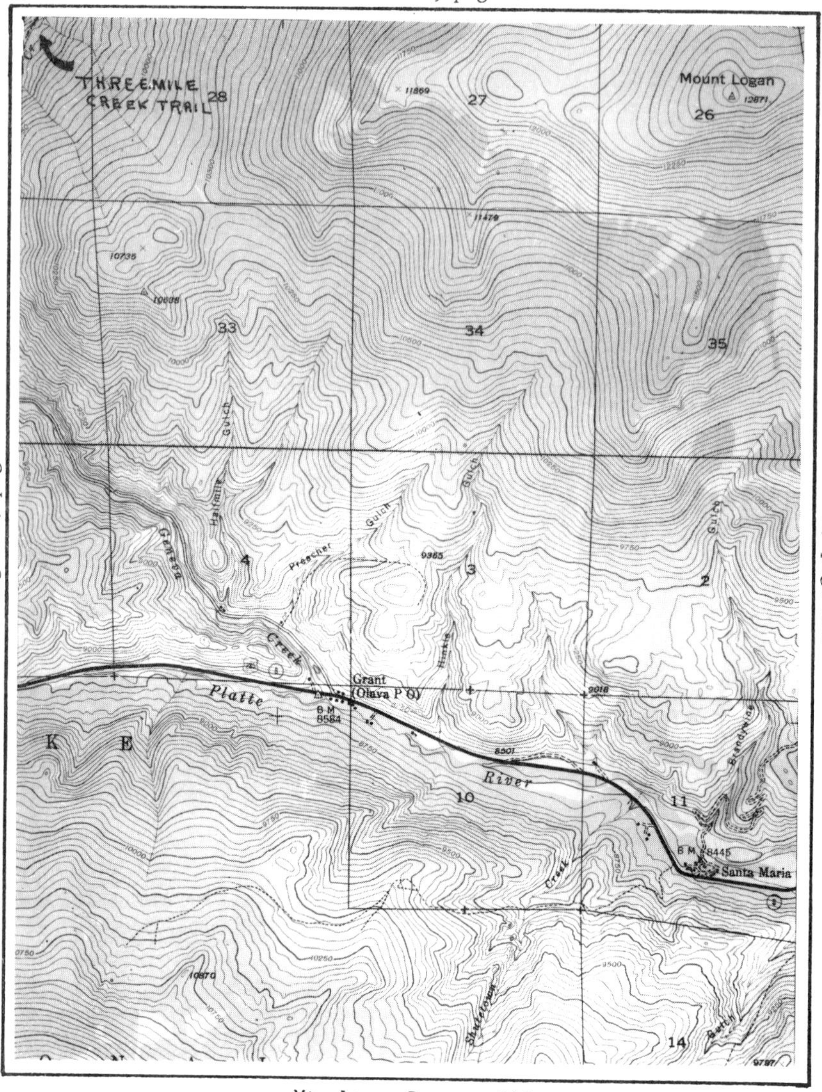

Shawnee A, page 182

Mt. Logan D, page 166

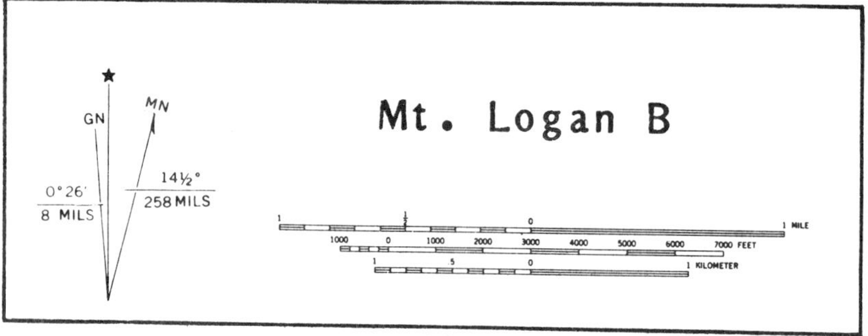

Mt. Logan A, page 163

Jefferson D, page 139

Mt. Logan D, page 166

Observatory Rock A, page 167

Mt. Logan C

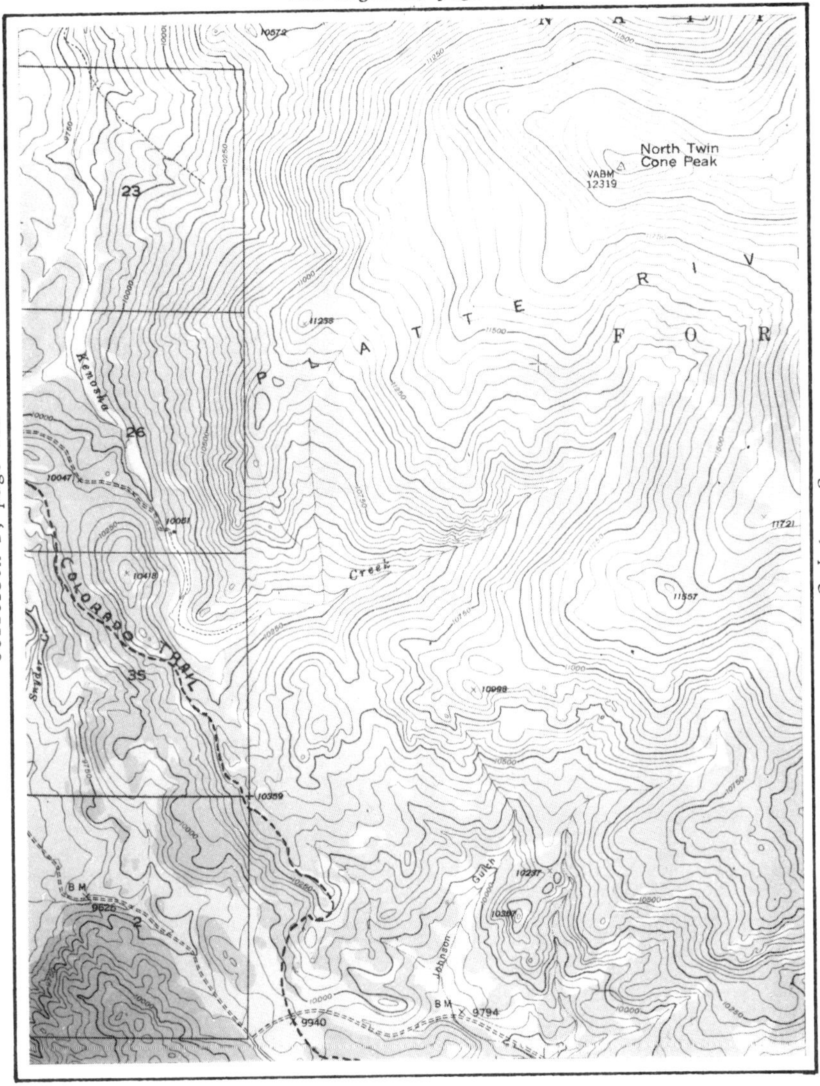

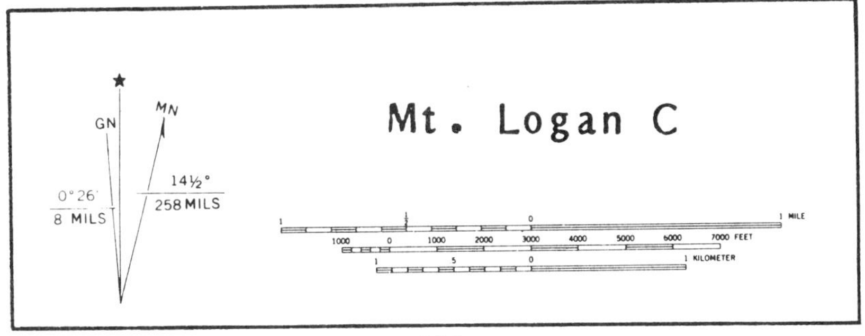

Mt. Logan B, page 164

Mt. Logan C page 165

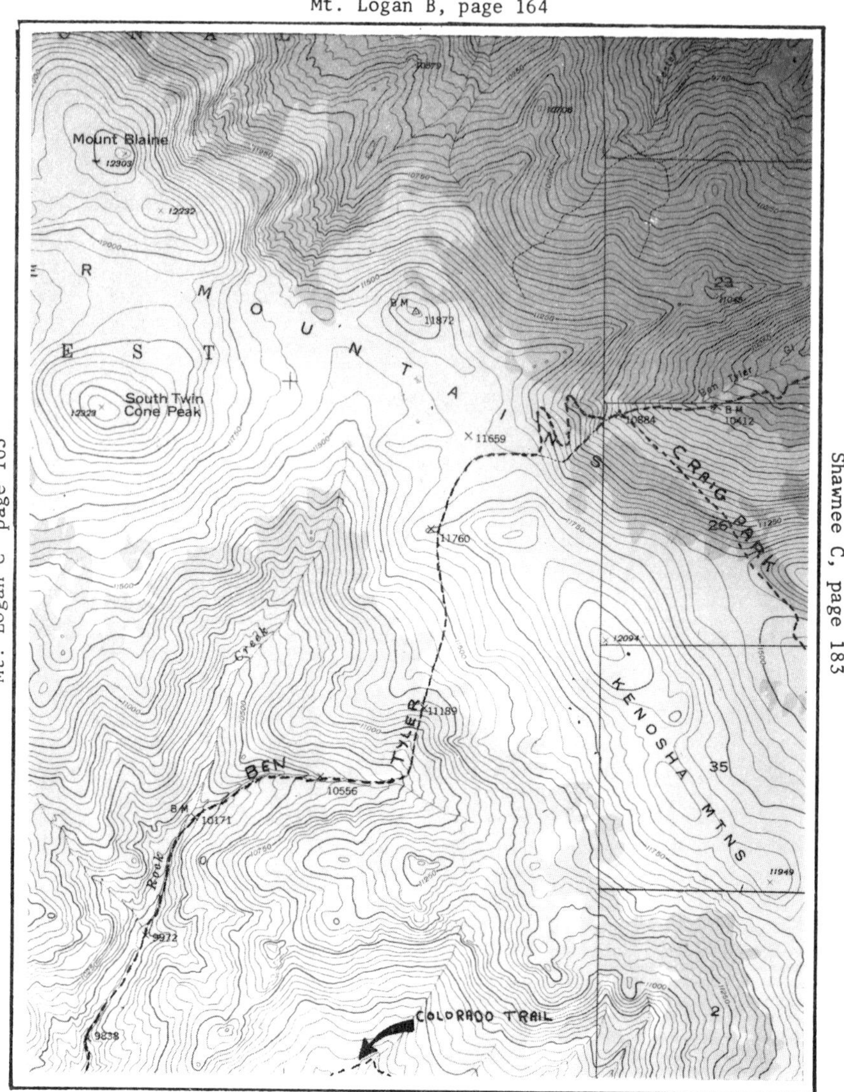

Shawnee C, page 183

Observatory Rock B, page 168

Mt. Logan D

GN MN
0°26′ / 8 MILS
14½° / 258 MILS

1 ½ 0 1 MILE
1000 0 1000 2000 3000 4000 5000 6000 7000 FEET
1 .5 0 1 KILOMETER

Mt. Logan C, page 165

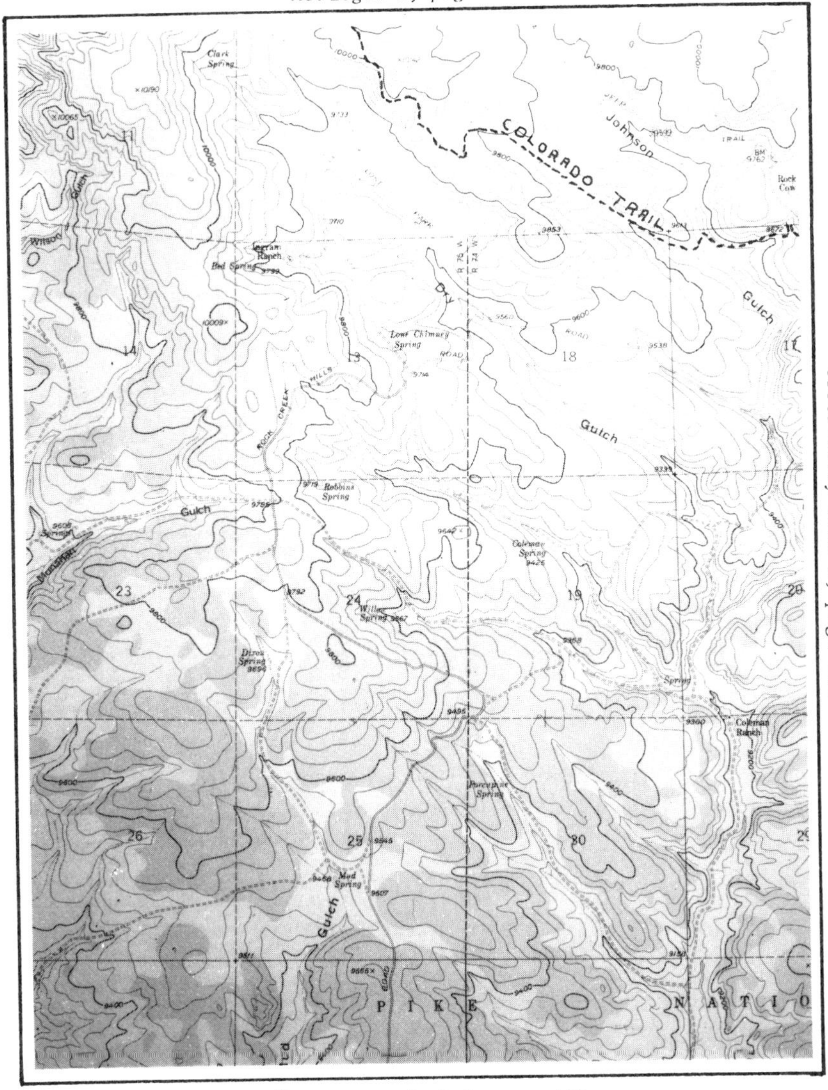

Observatory Rock B, page 168

Observatory Rock C, page 169

Observatory Rock A

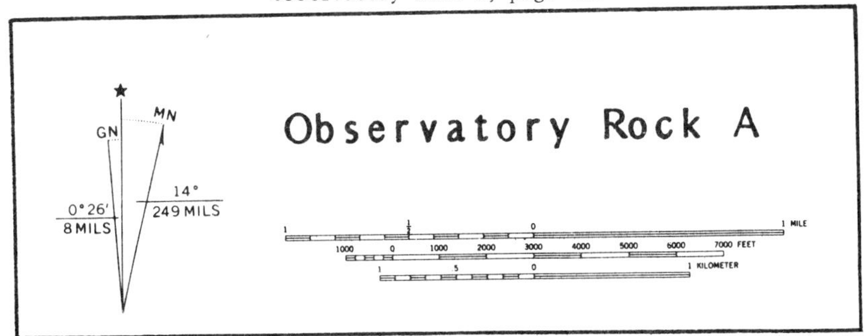

Mt. Logan D, page 166

Observatory Rock A, page 167

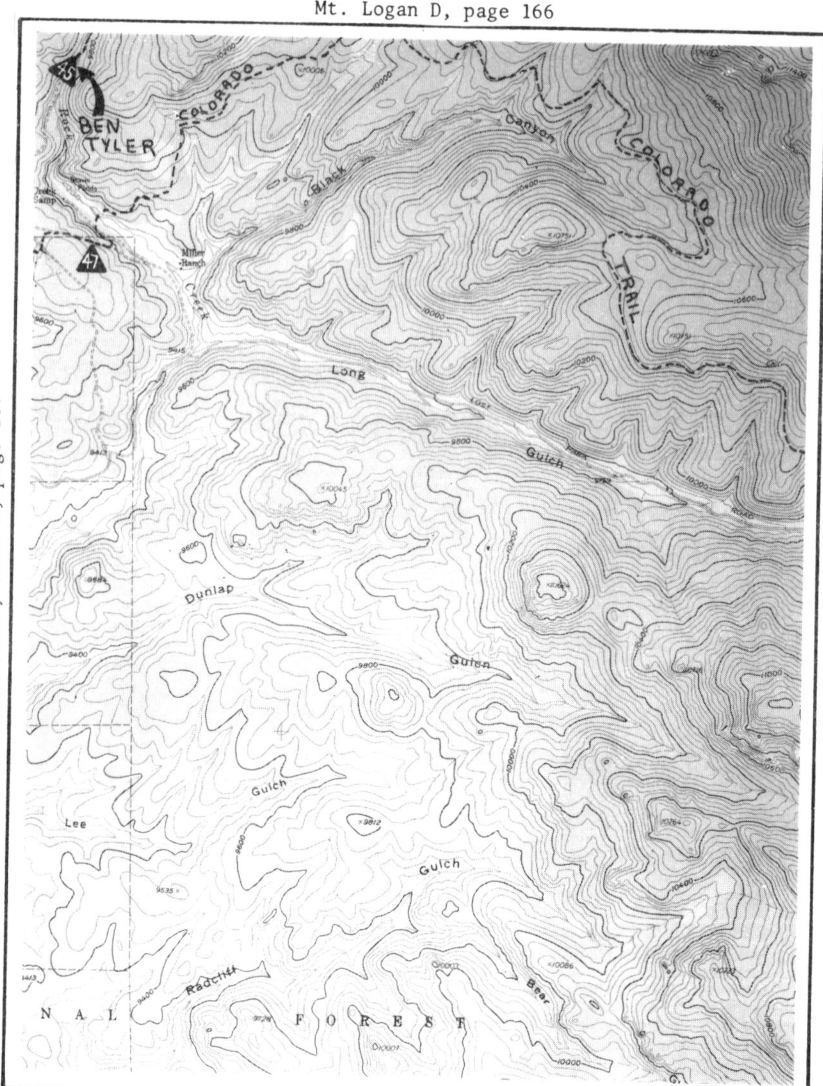

Topaz A, page 187

Observatory Rock D, page 170

GN MN

0°26′ 8 MILS

14° 249 MILS

Observatory Rock B

1 ½ 0 1 MILE

1000 0 1000 2000 3000 4000 5000 6000 7000 FEET

1 .5 0 1 KILOMETER

Observatory Rock A, page 167

Observatory Rock D, page 170

Observatory Rock C

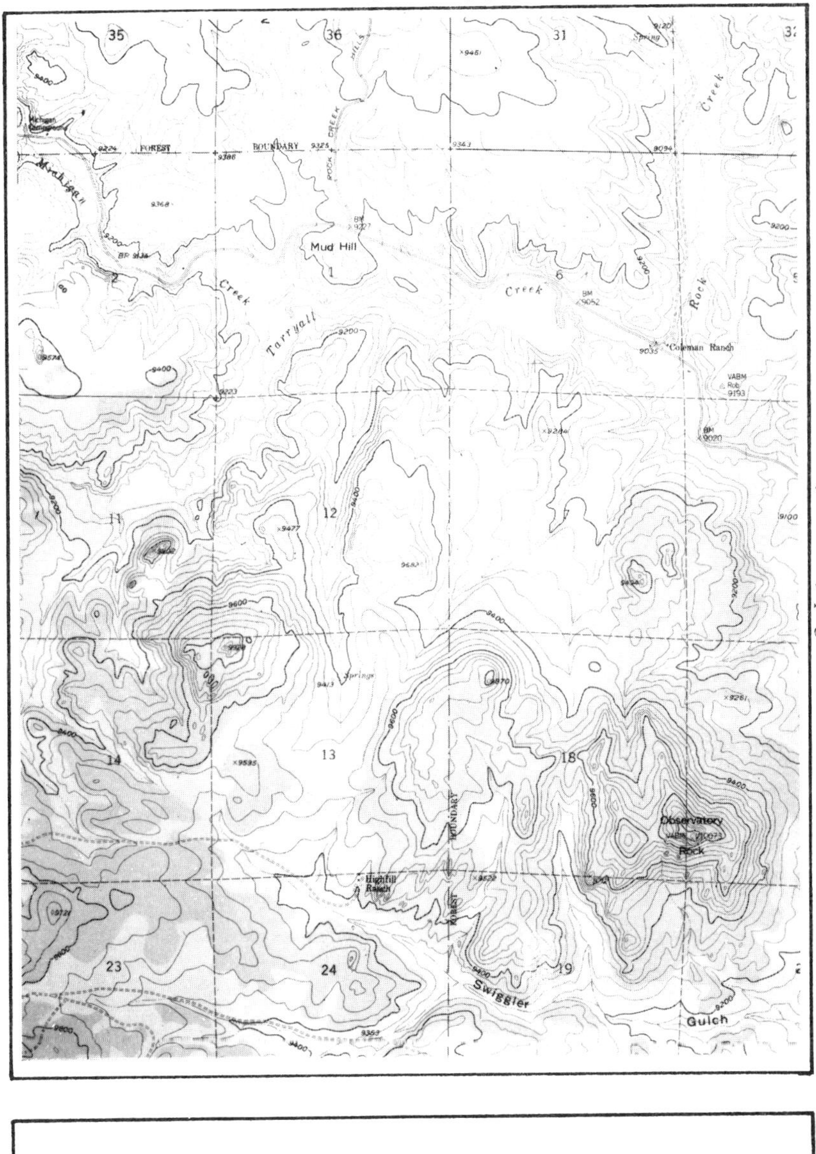

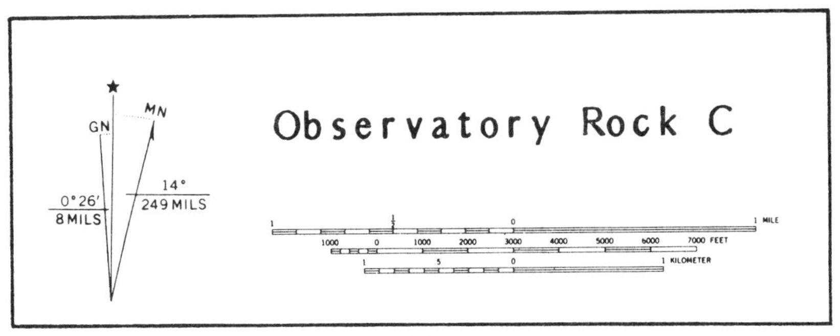

Observatory Rock B, page 168

Observatory Rock C, page 169

Observatory Rock D

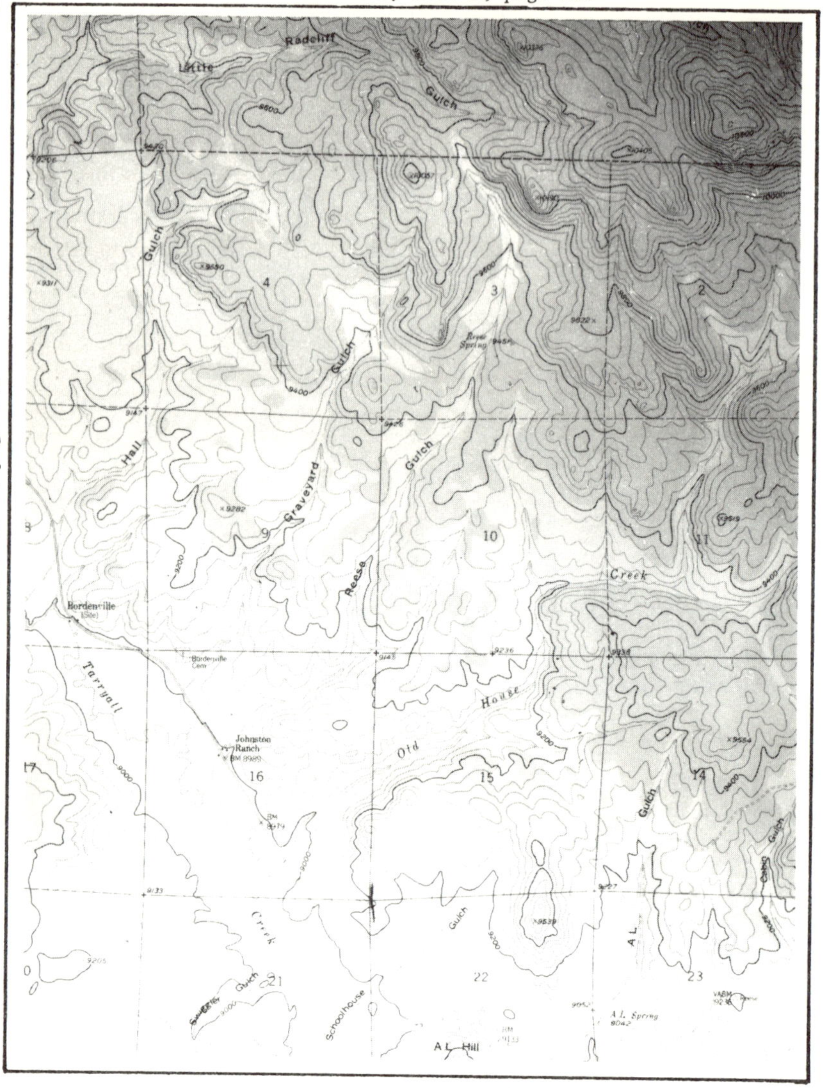

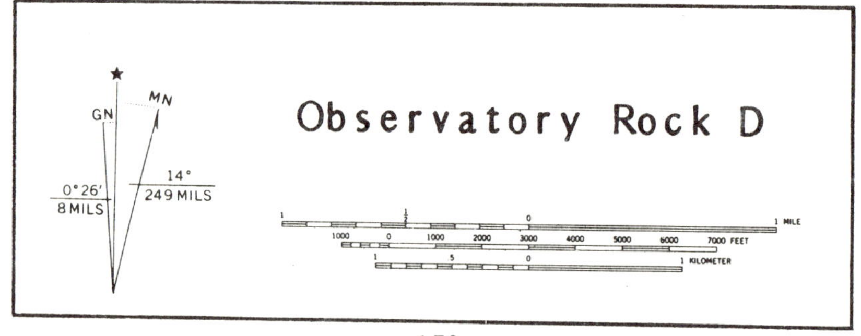

Palmer Lake B, Page 172

Palmer Lake A

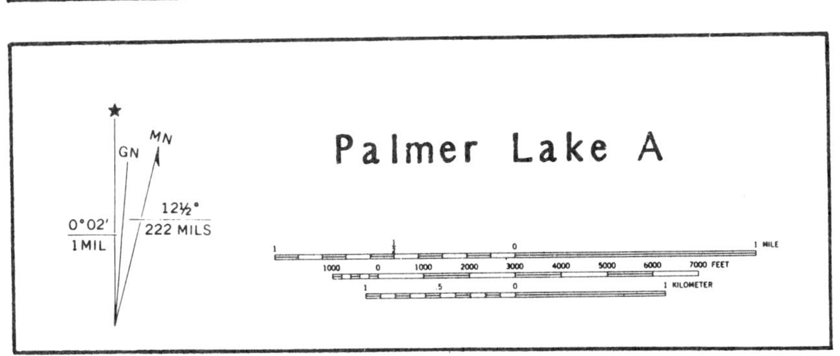

Palmer Lake A, page 171

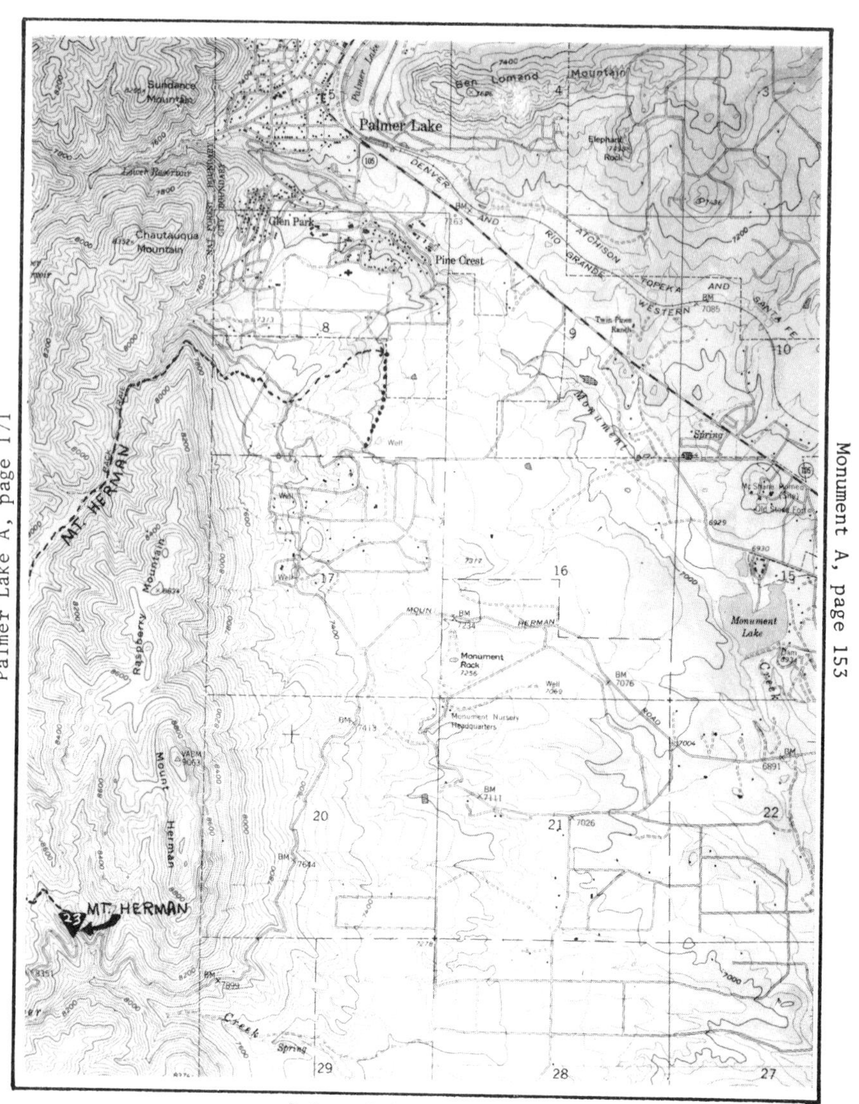

Monument A, page 153

Palmer Lake D, page 173

GN

MN

12½°

222 MILS

0°02'

1 MIL

Palmer Lake B

1 MILE

1000 0 1000 2000 3000 4000 5000 6000 7000 FEET

1 KILOMETER

Palmer Lake B, page 172

Monument C, page 154

Cascade B, page 113

Palmer Lake D

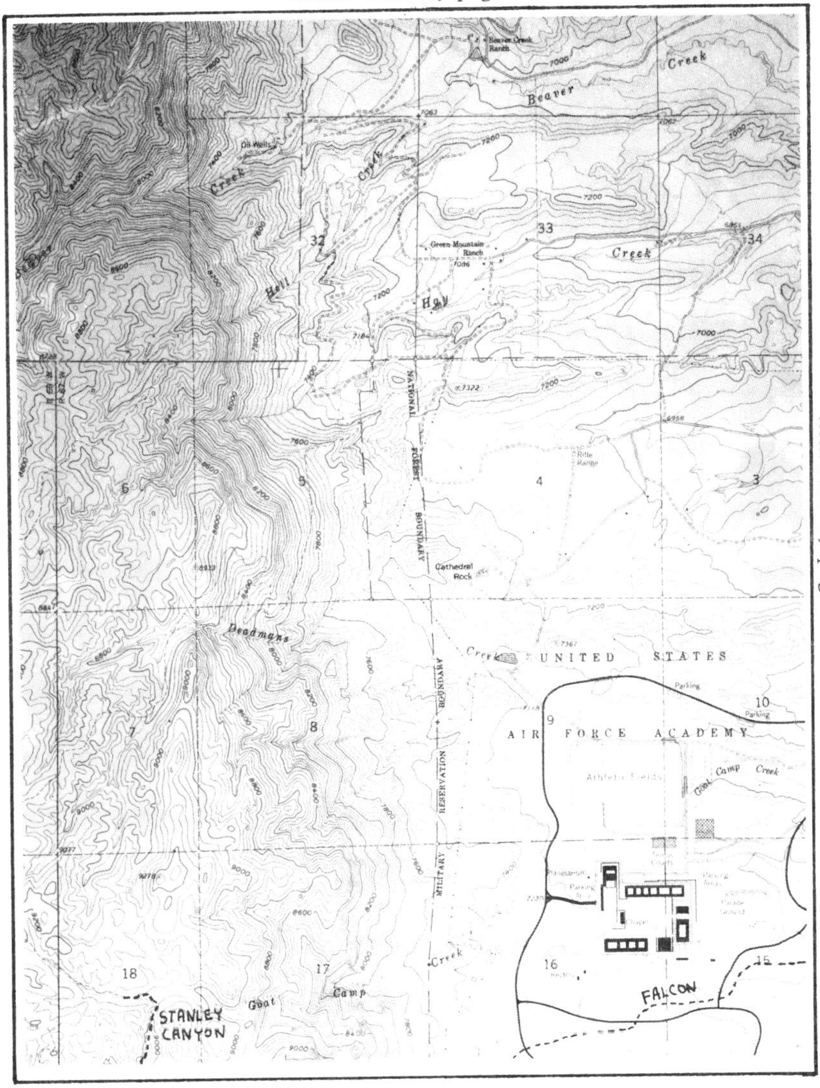

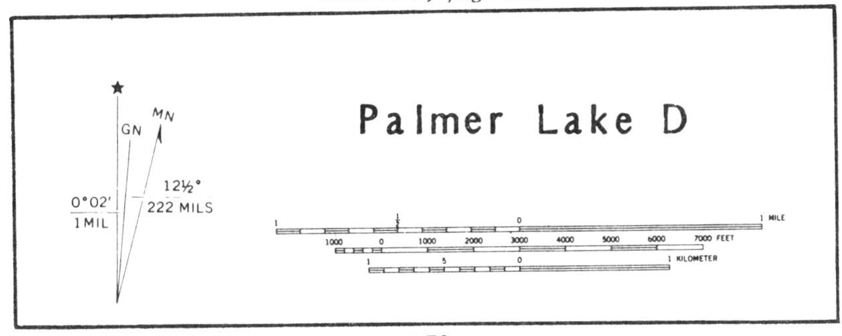

Woodland Park C, page 196

Cripple Creek North B, page 122

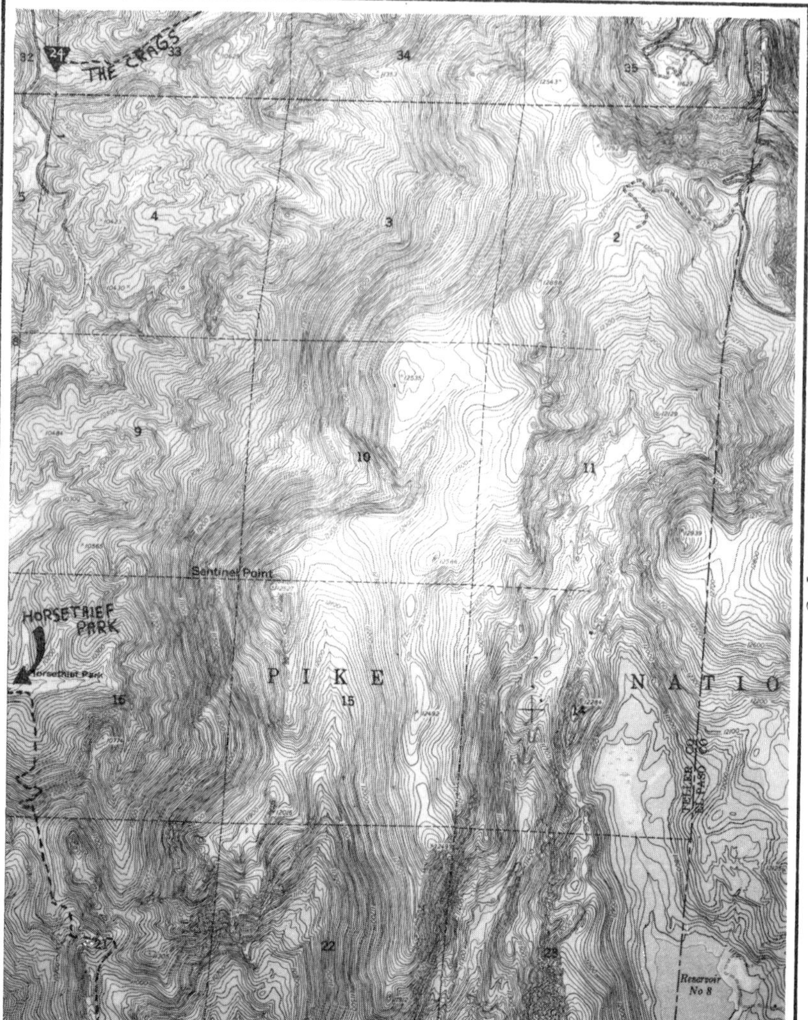

Pikes Peak B, page 175

Pikes Peak C, page 176

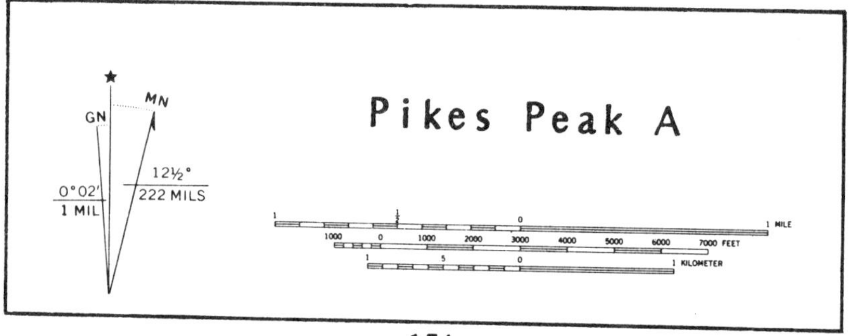

Woodland Park D, page 197

Pikes Peak A, page 174

Manitou Springs A, page 145

Pikes Peak D, page 177

Pikes Peak B

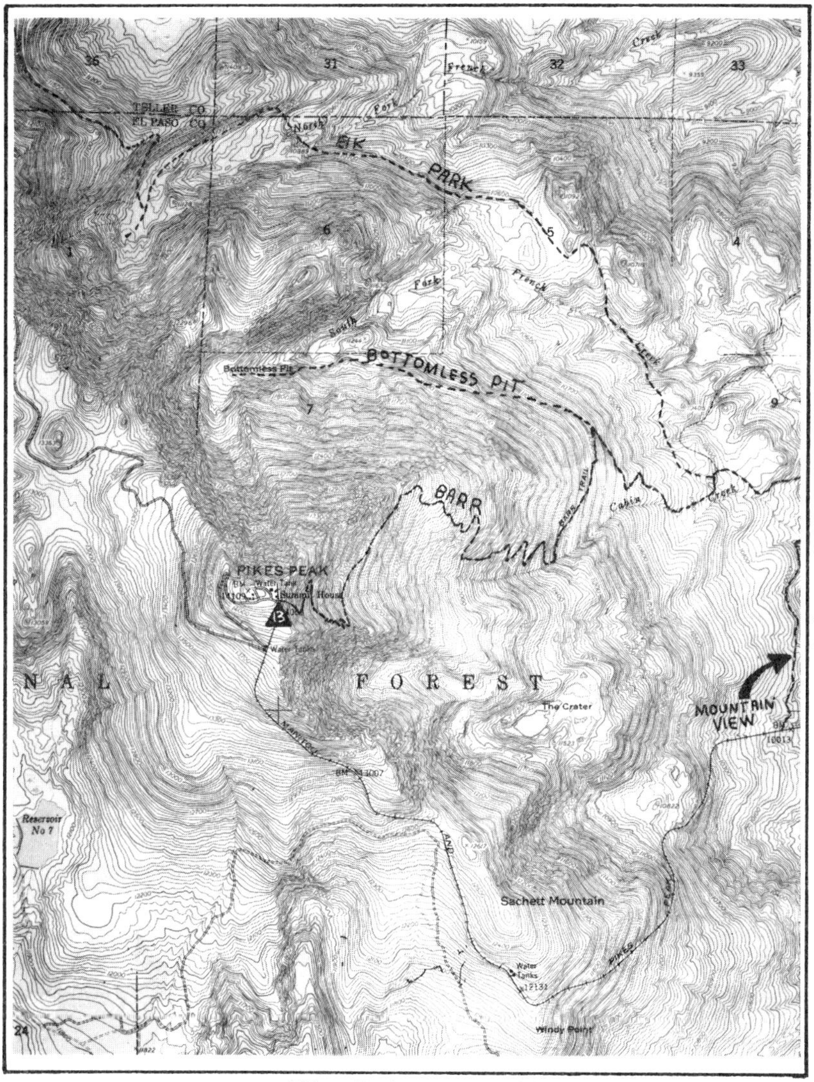

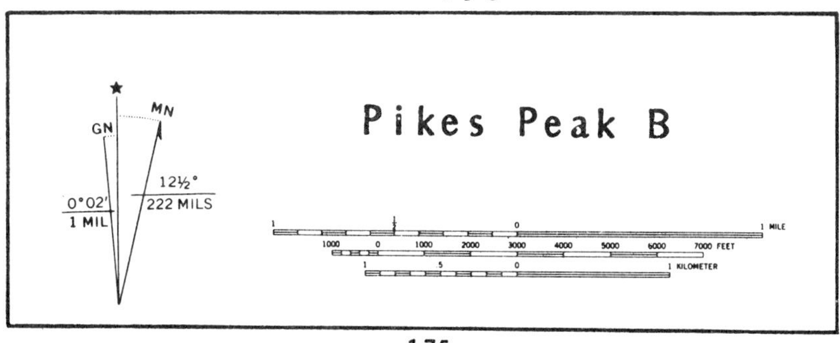

Pikes Peak A, page 174

Cripple Creek North D, 123

Pikes Peak D, page 177

Pikes Peak C

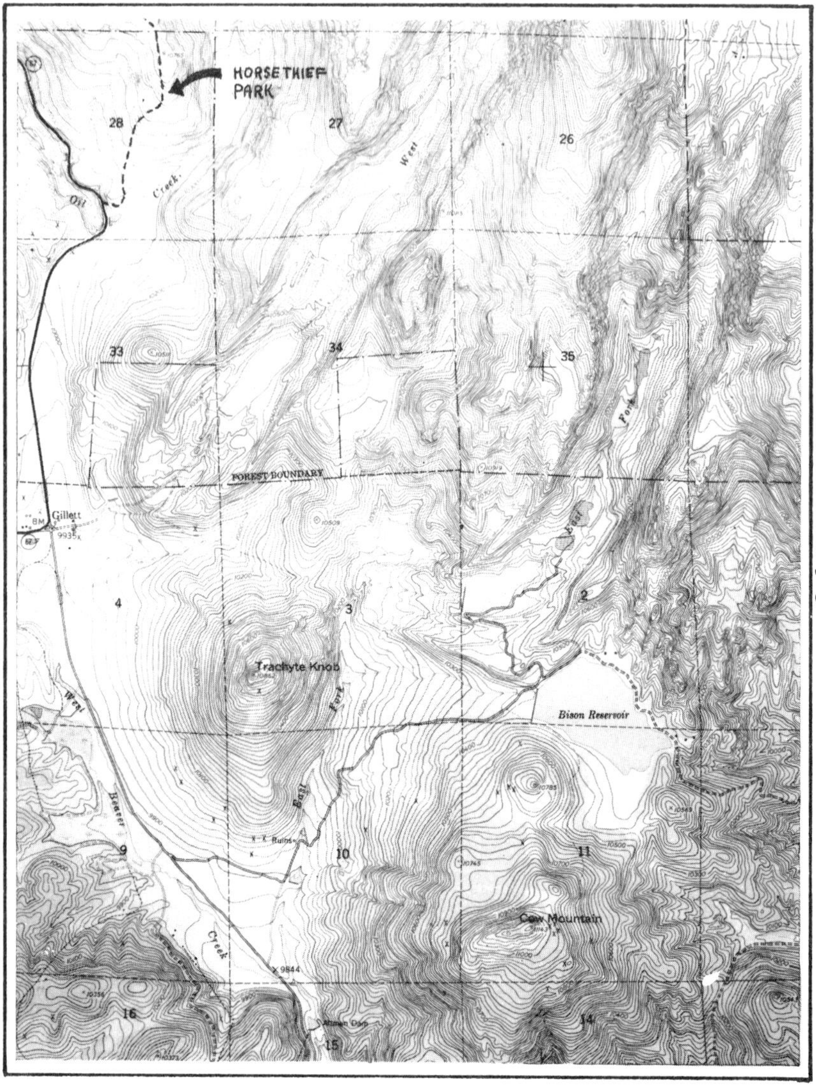

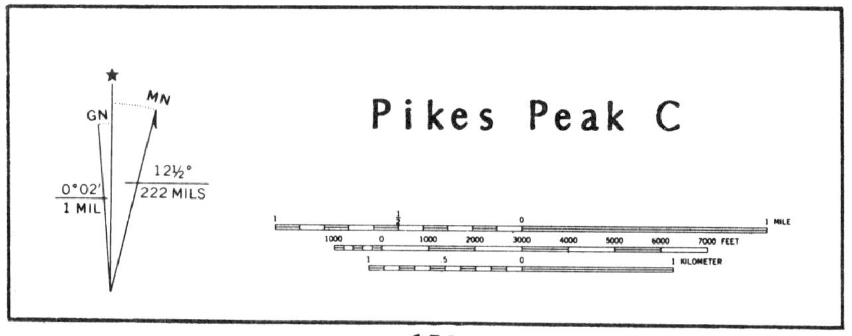

Pikes Peak B, page 175

Pikes Peak C, page 176

Reservoir No 2
25
30
29
28
EL PASO CO
TELLER CO
Boehmer
Creek
Sheep Mountain
36
31
32
33
Dead Lake
Reservoir No 4
Seven Lakes
Reservoir No. 5
6
5
4
Bull Park
Middle
Beaver
Bison
PIKE NATIONAL FOREST
2
7
8
9
Creek
Creek
13
18
17
16

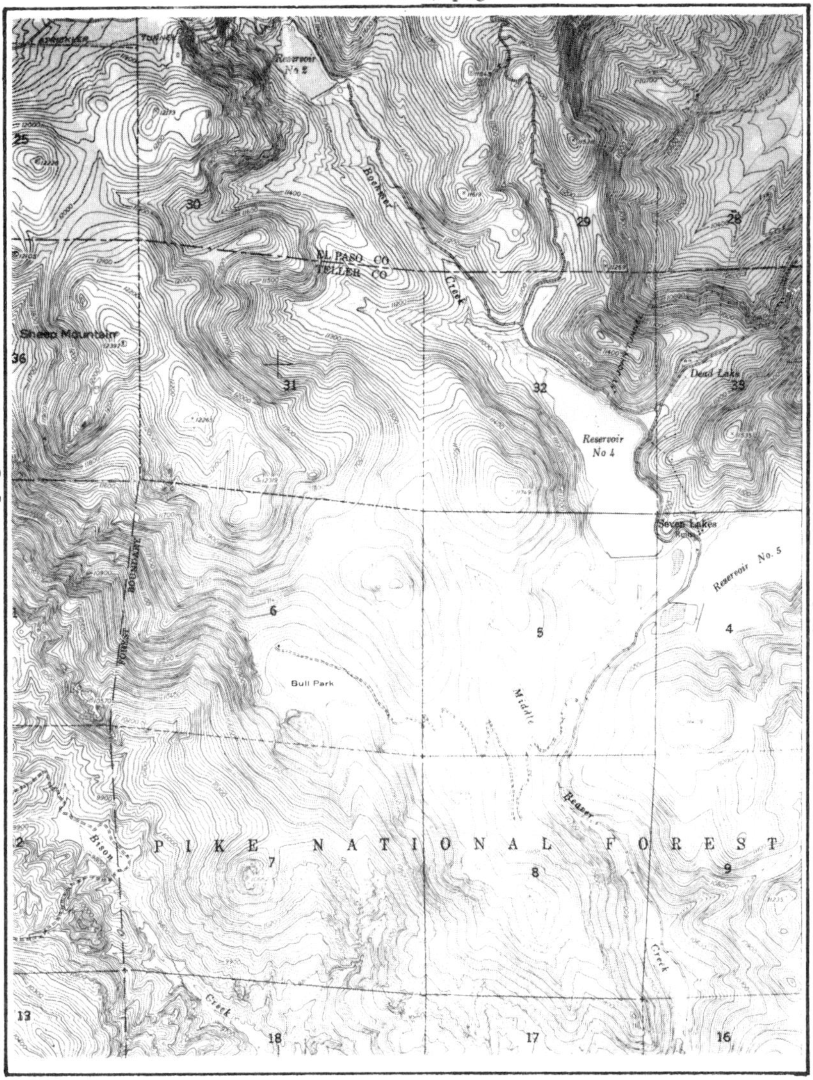

Manitou Springs C, page 147

GN
MN
0°02′
1 MIL
12½°
222 MILS

Pikes Peak D

1 MILE
1000 0 1000 2000 3000 4000 5000 6000 7000 FEET
1 KILOMETER

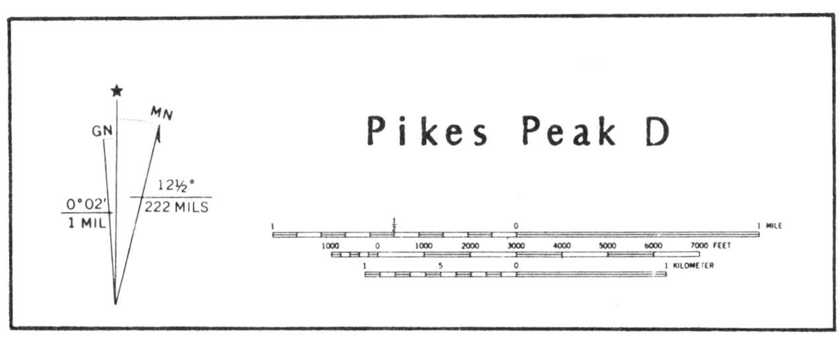

Monument C, page 154

Cascade B, page 113

Pikeview B, page 179

Pikeview C, page 180

Pikeview A

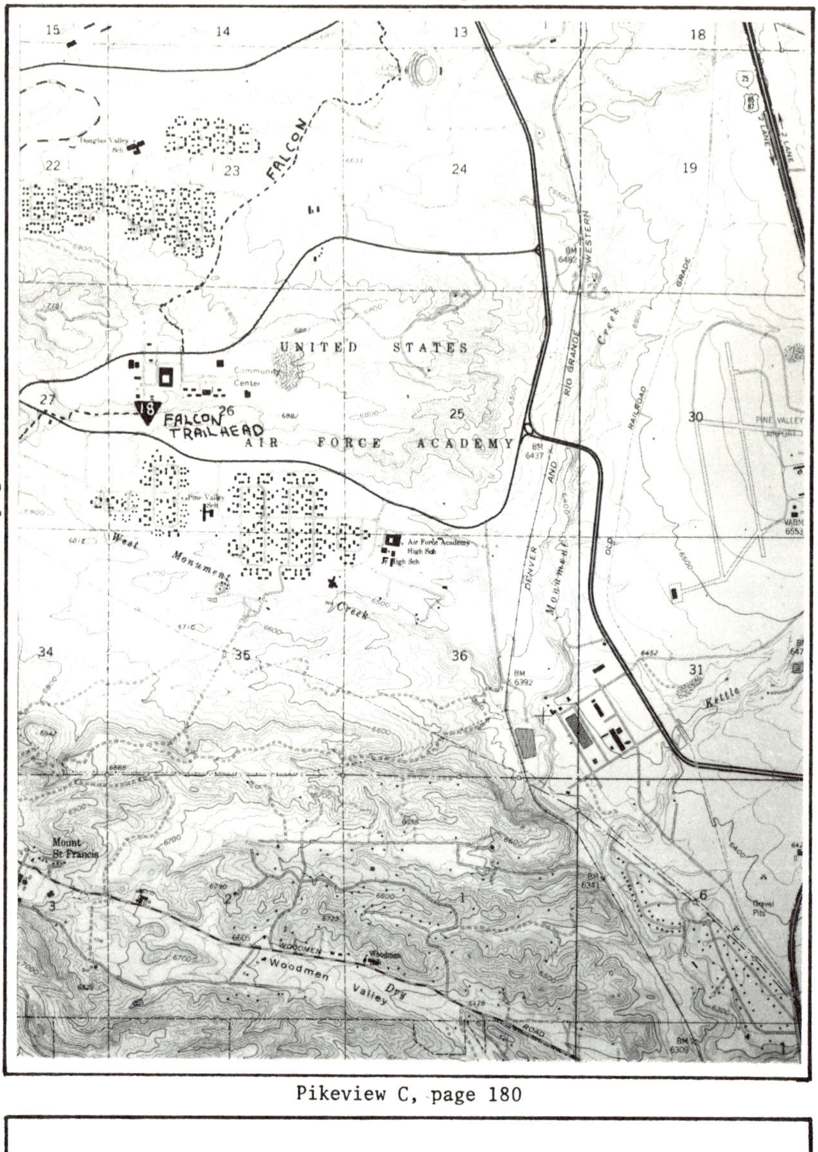

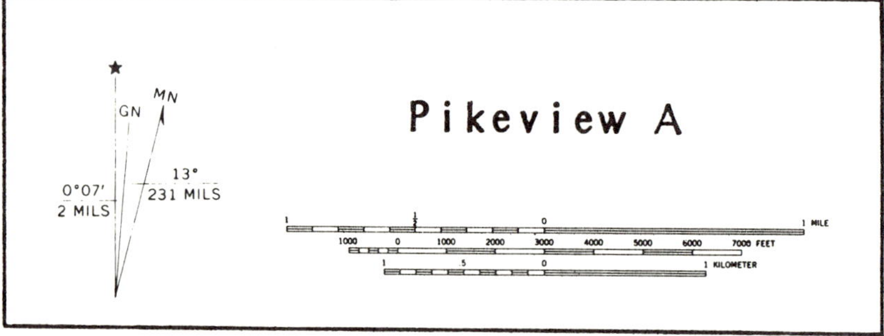

Pikeview A, page 178

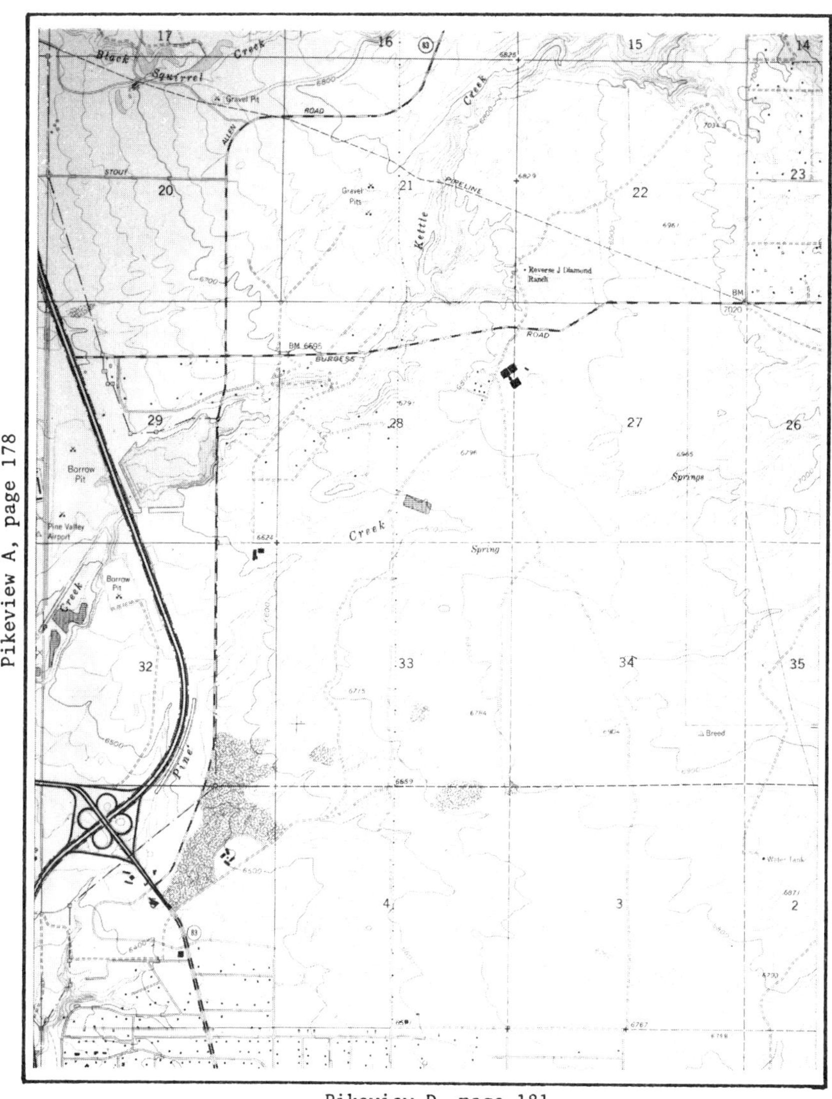

Pikeview D, page 181

GN

MN

0°07'
2 MILS

13°
231 MILS

Pikeview B

1 ½ 0 1 MILE

1000 0 1000 2000 3000 4000 5000 6000 7000 FEET

1 .5 0 1 KILOMETER

Pikeview A, page 178

Cascade D, page 115

Pikeview D, page 181

Colorado Springs A, page 118

Pikeview C

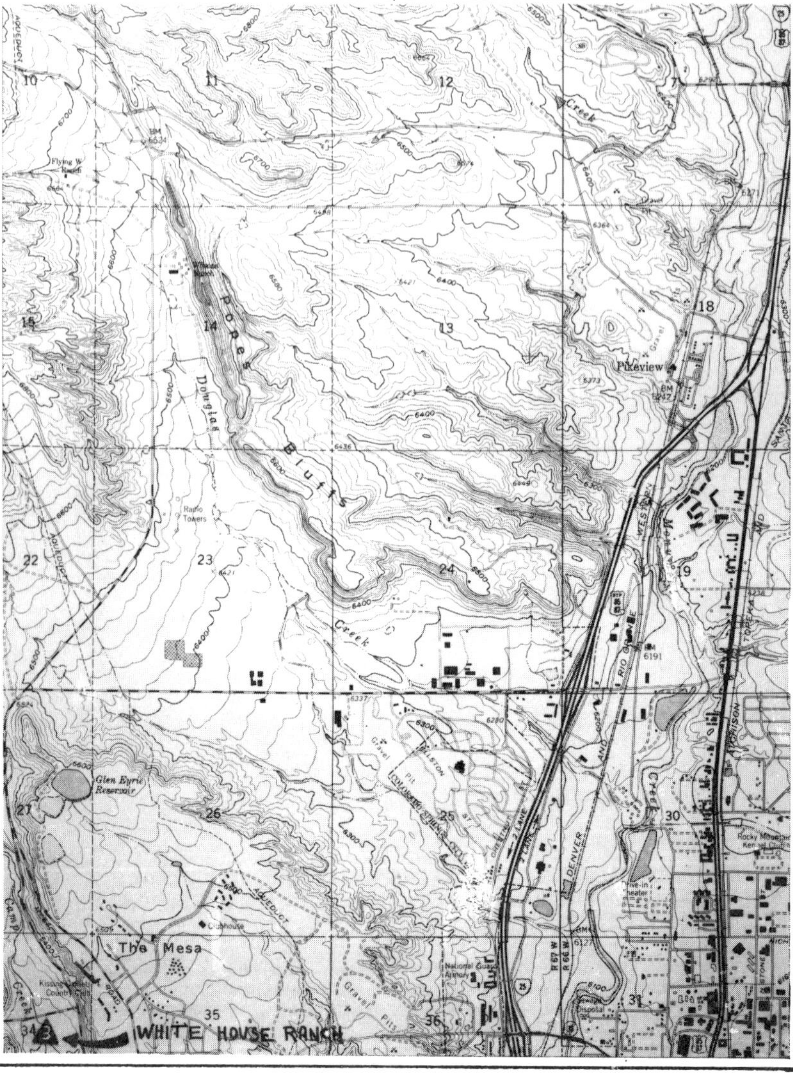

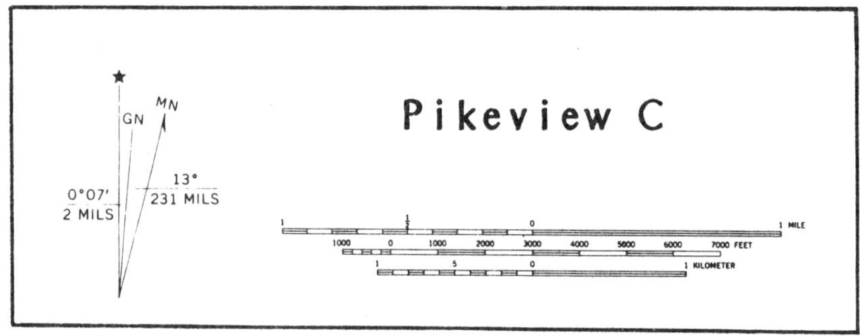

Pikeview B, page 179

Pikeview C, page 180

Colorado Springs B, page 119

Pikeview D

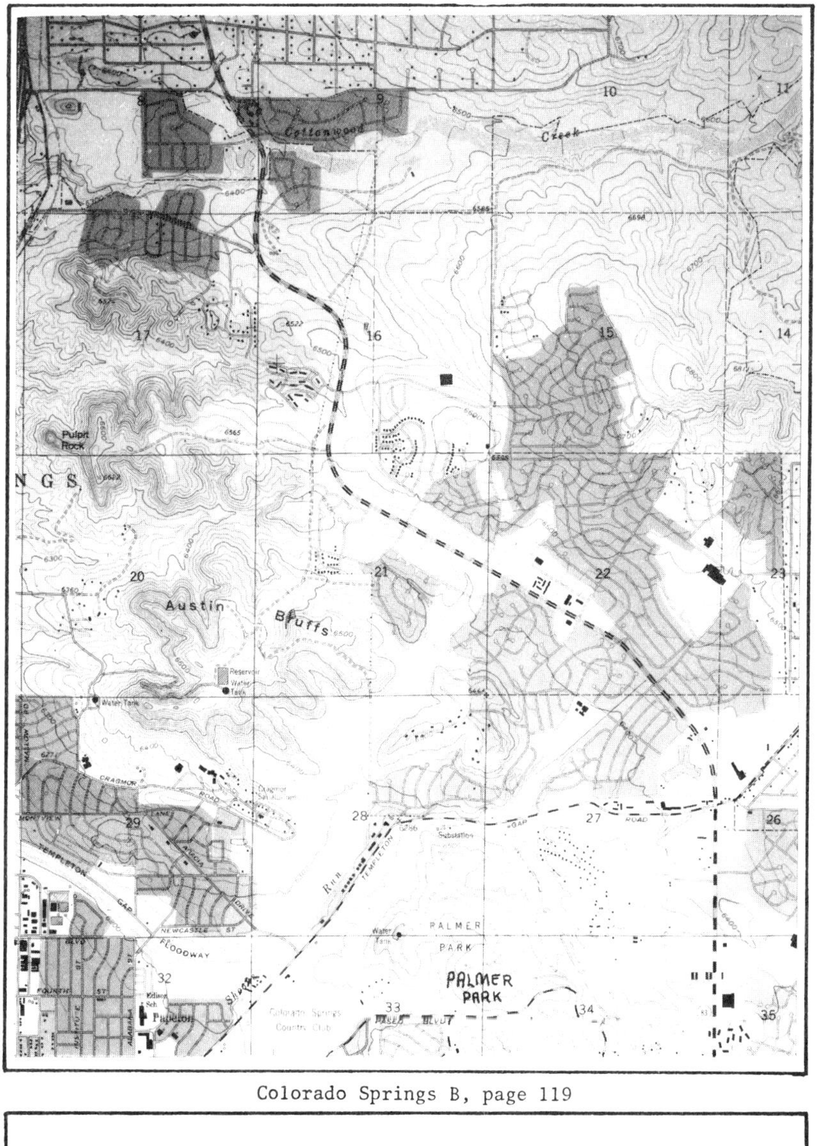

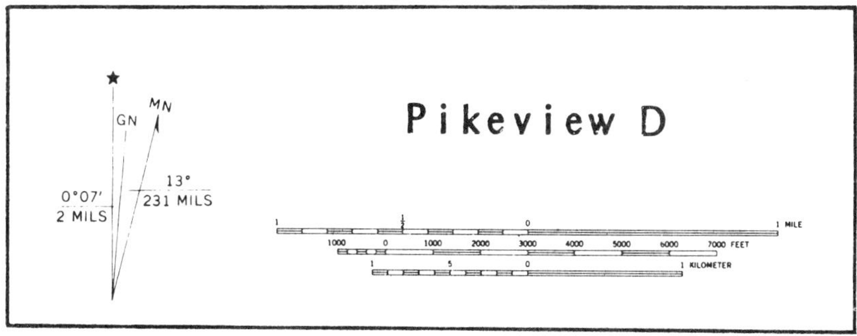

Harris Park C, page 134

Mt. Logan B, page 164

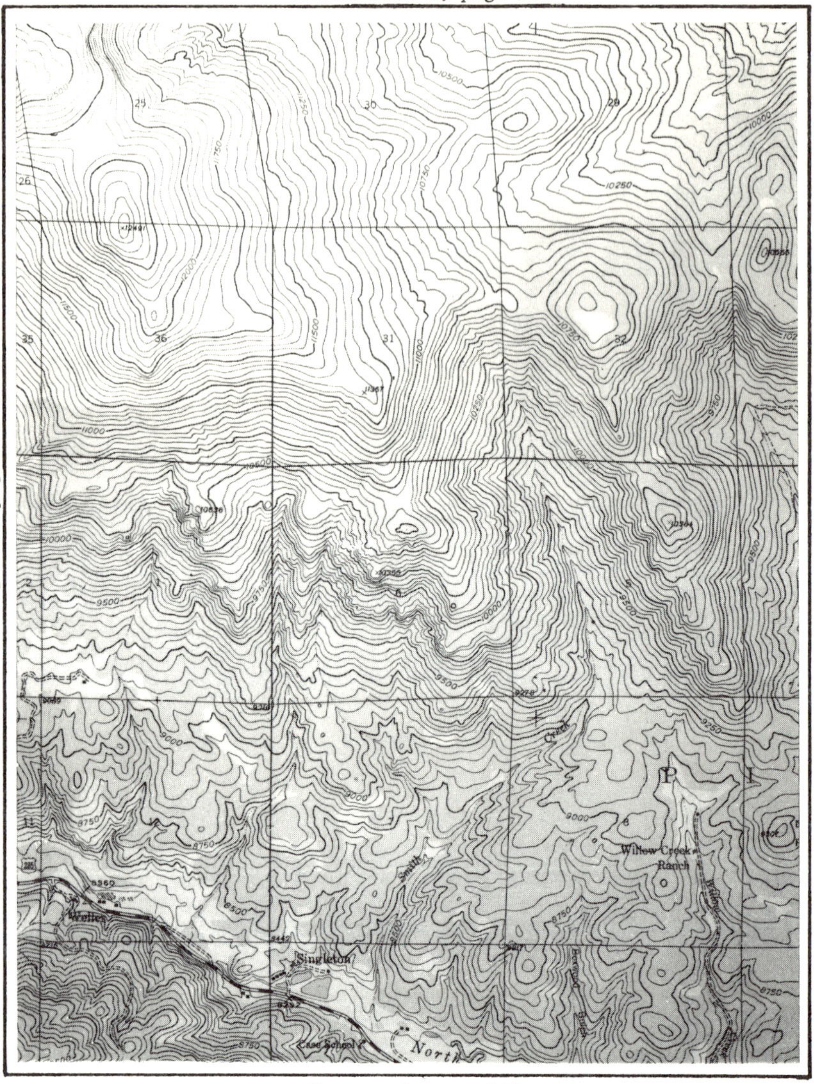

Shawnee C, page 183

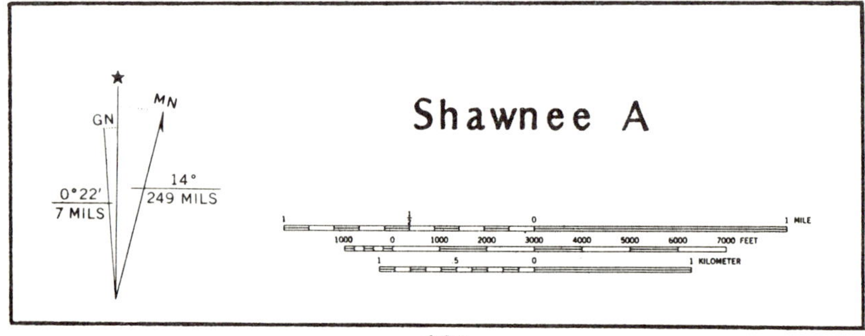

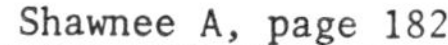

Shawnee A, page 182

Mt. Logan D, page 166

Shawnee D, page 184

Topaz A, page 187

Shawnee C

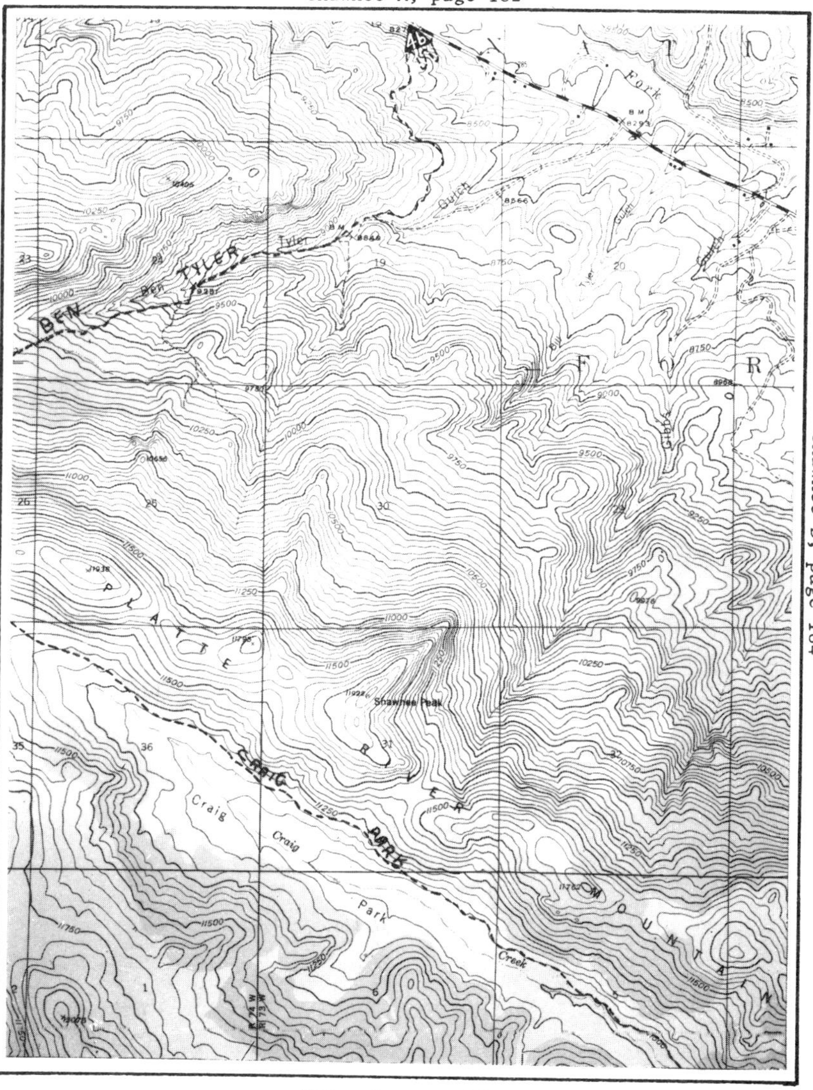

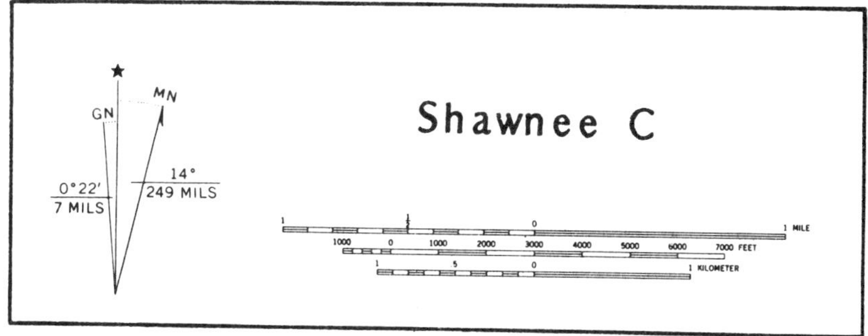

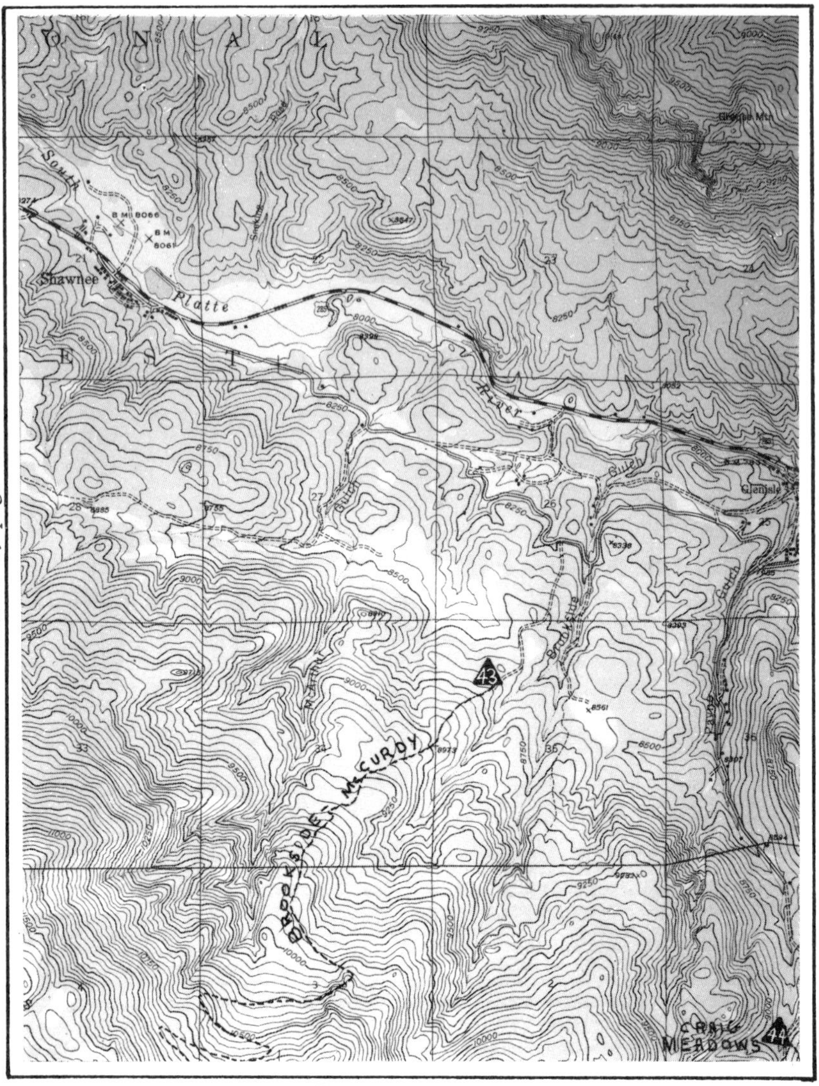

Shawnee C, page 183

Bailey C, page 109

Topaz B, page 188

Shawnee D

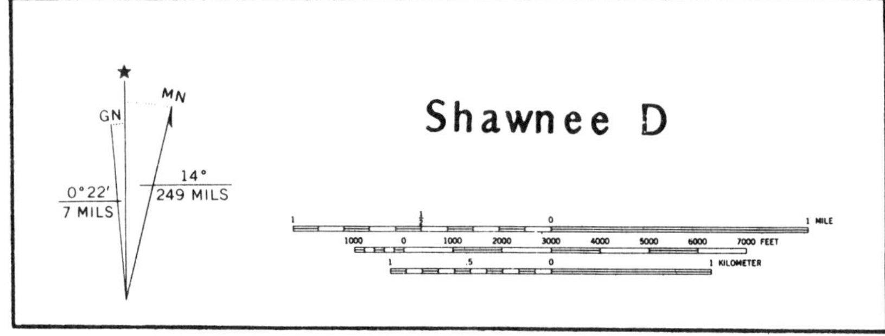

Jones Hill A, page 140

South Peak D, page 186

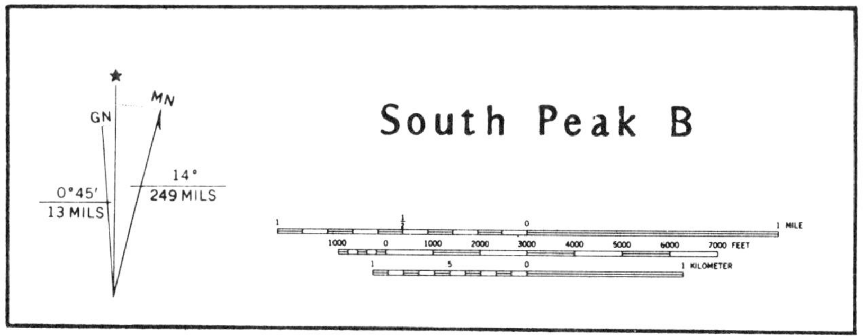

South Peak B, page 185

Jones Hill C, page 142

South Peak D

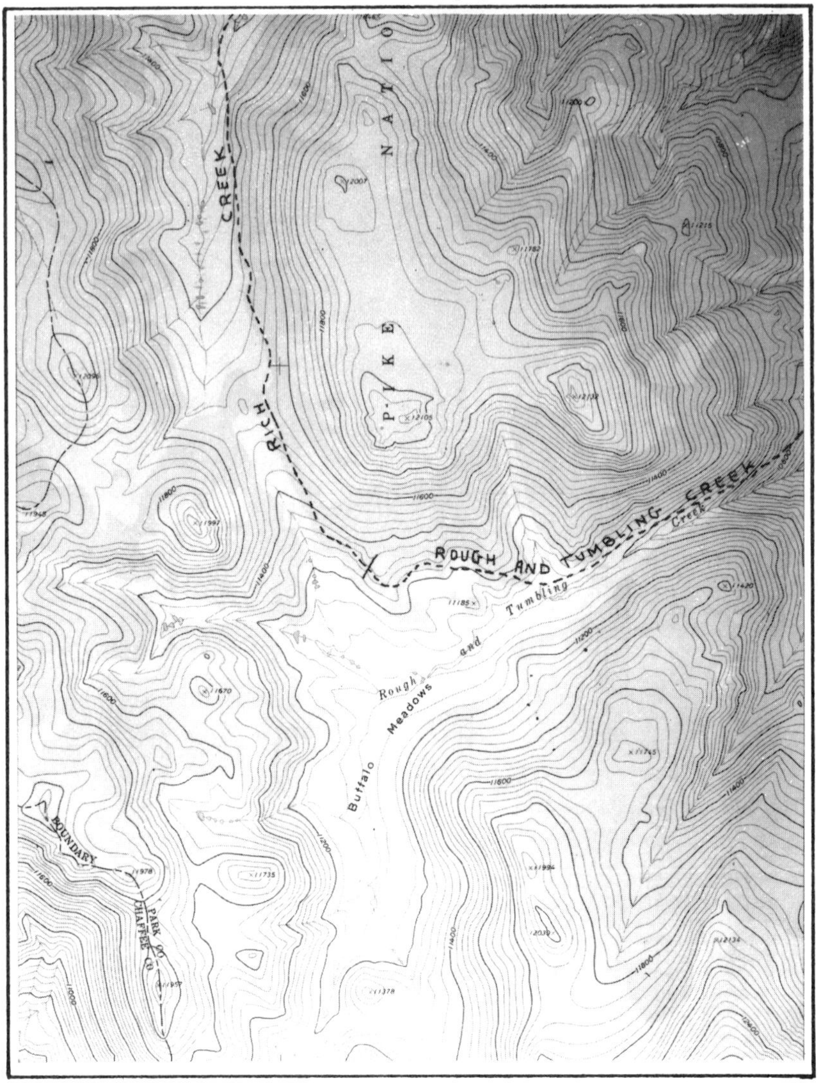

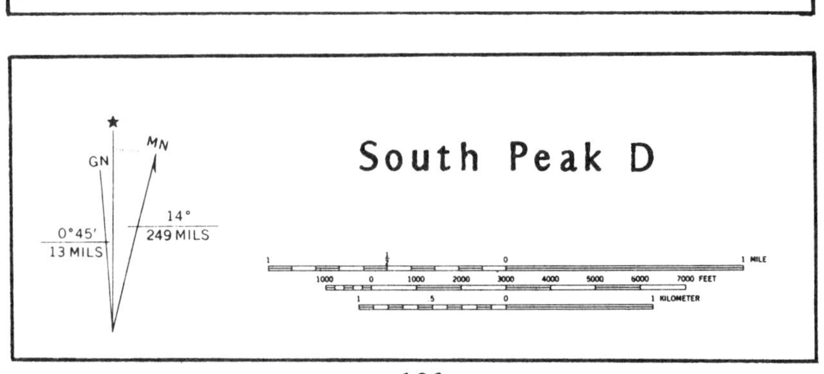

Shawnee C, page 183

Observatory Rock B, page 168

Topaz B, page 188

Topaz A

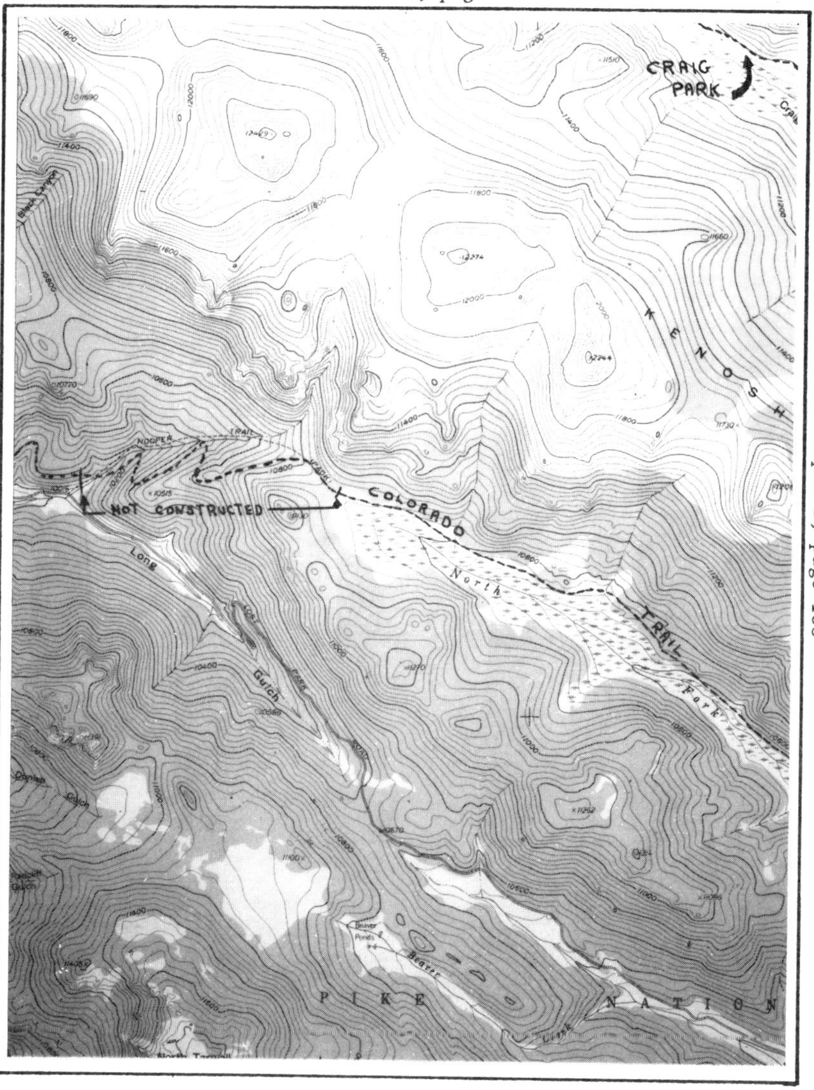

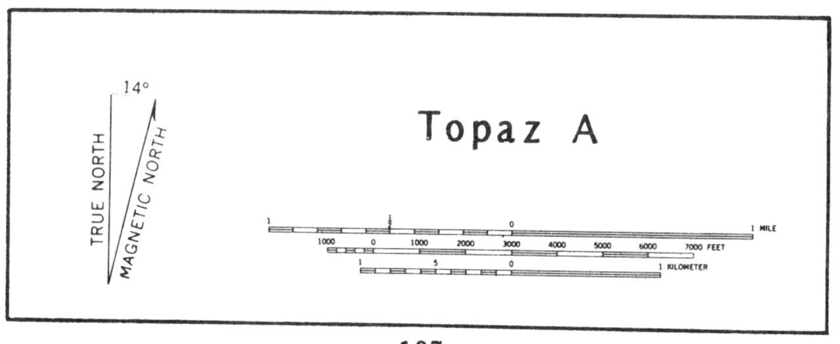

Shawnee D, page 184

Topaz A, page 187

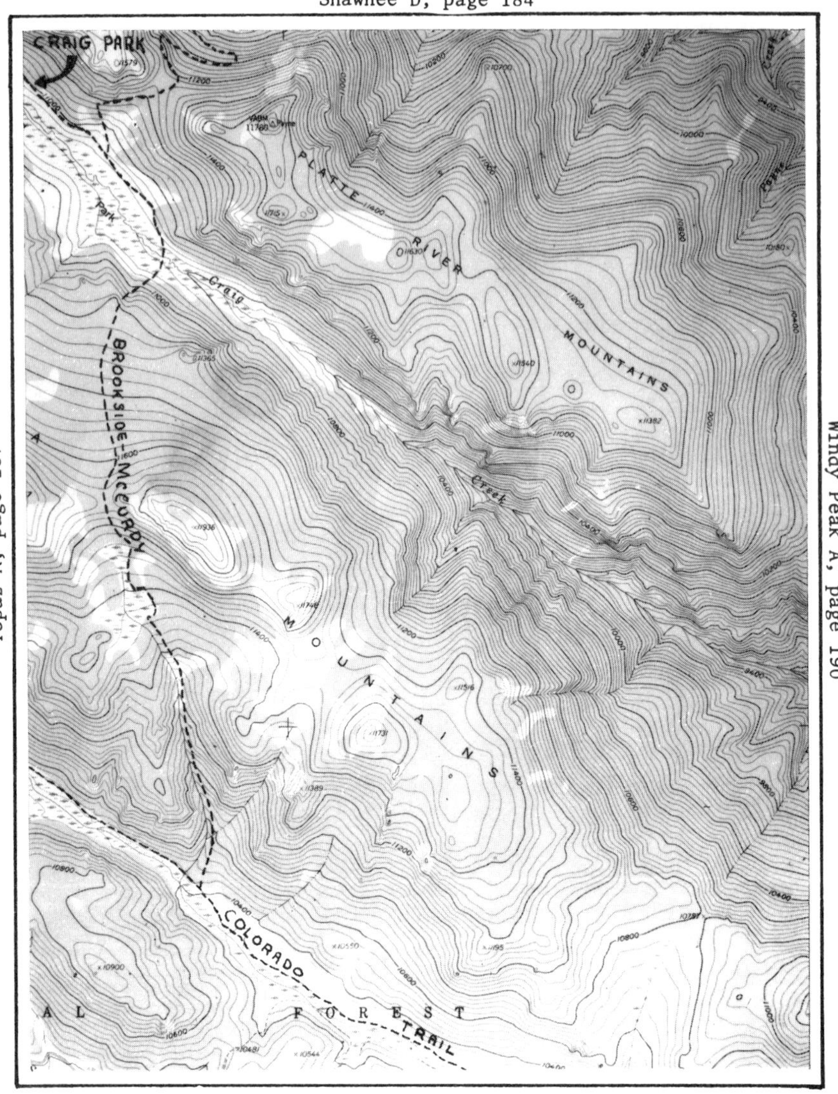

Windy Peak A, page 190

Topaz D, page 189

14°

TRUE NORTH

MAGNETIC NORTH

Topaz B

1 ½ 0 1 MILE

1000 0 1000 2000 3000 4000 5000 6000 7000 FEET

1 .5 0 1 KILOMETER

Topaz B, page 188

Windy Peak C, page 192

Farnum Peak B, page 130

Topaz D

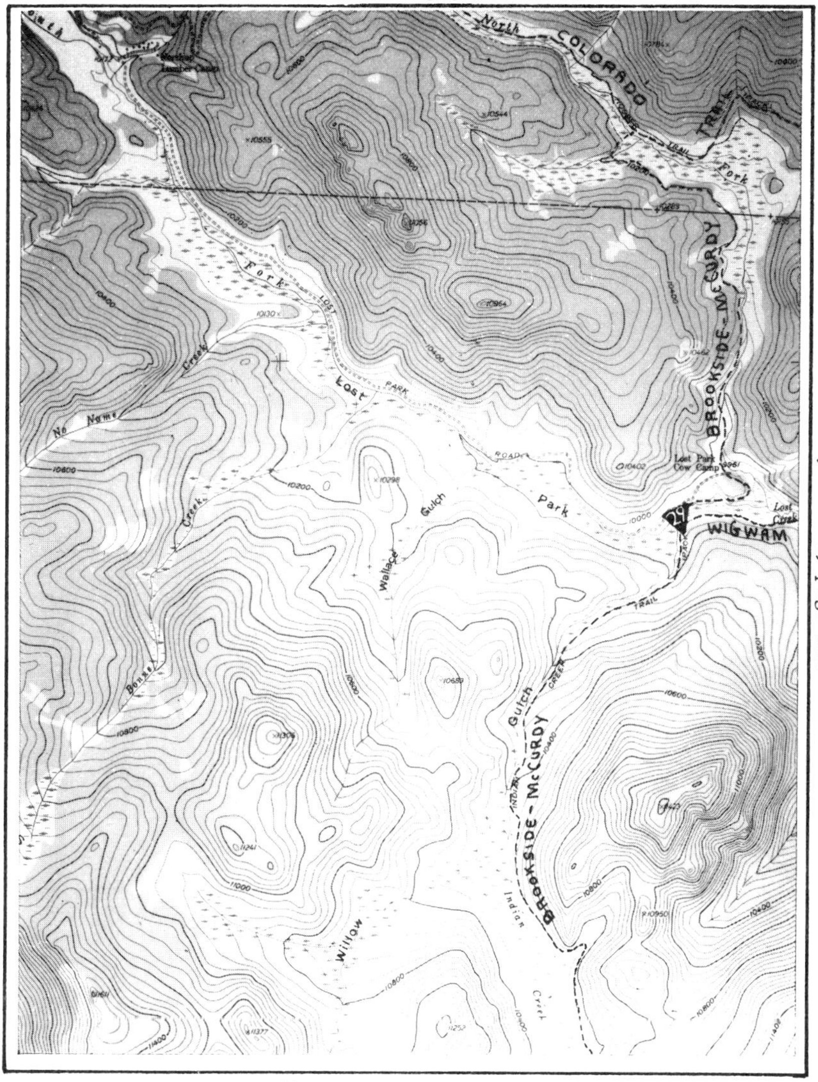

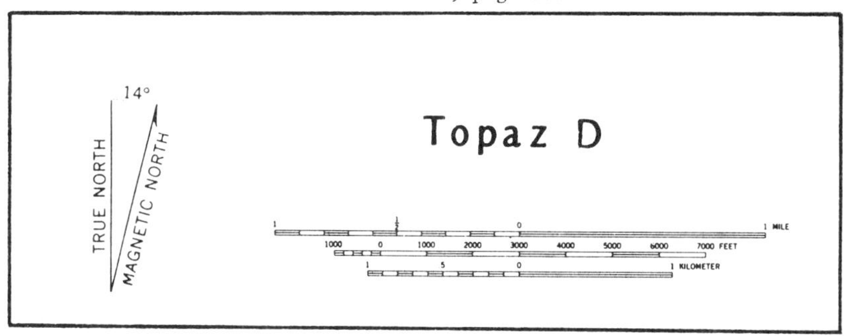

Bailey C, page 109

Topaz B, page 188

Windy Peak B, page 191

Windy Peak C, page 192

Windy Peak A

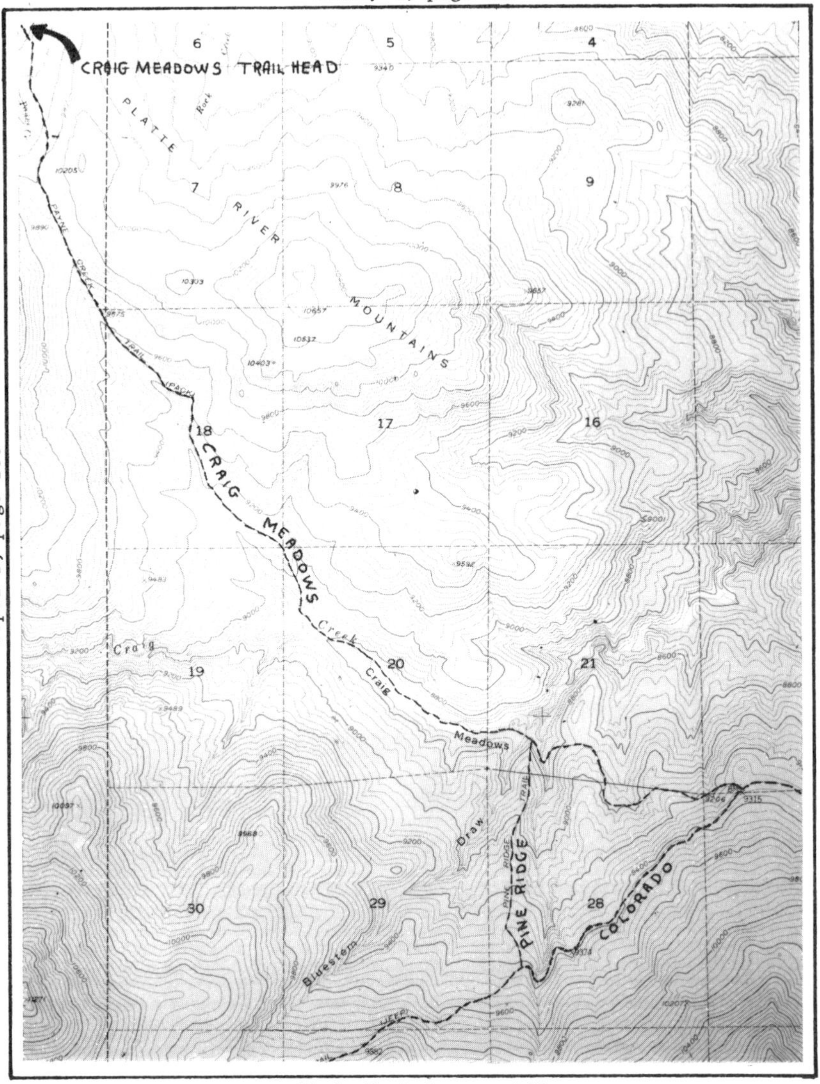

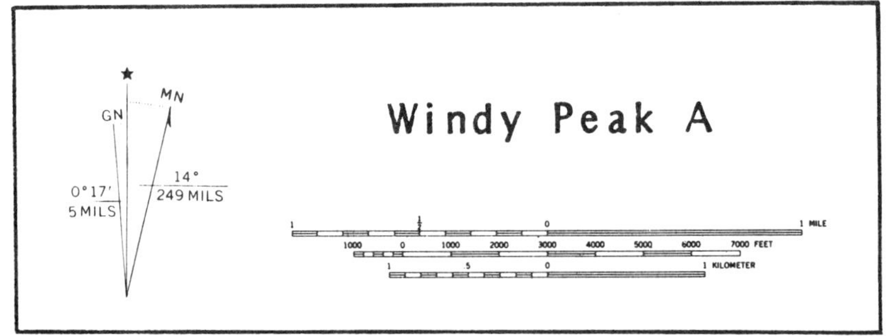

Windy Peak A, page 190

Windy Peak D, page 193

Windy Peak B

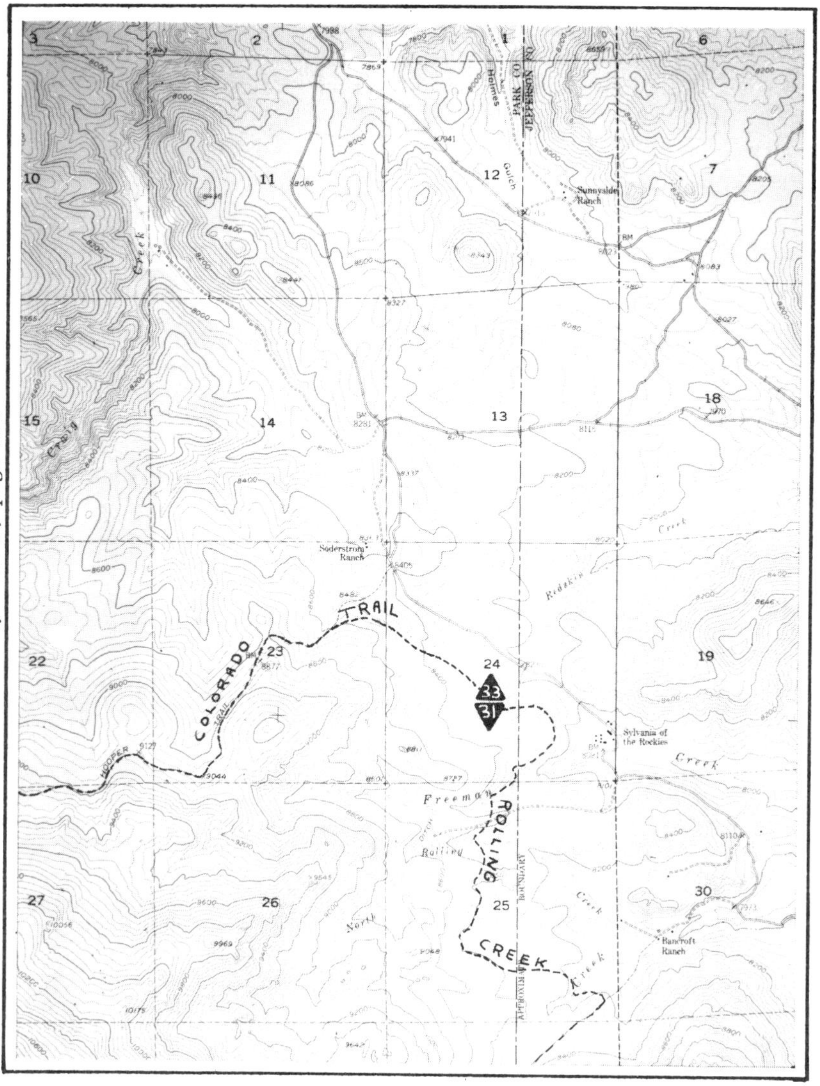

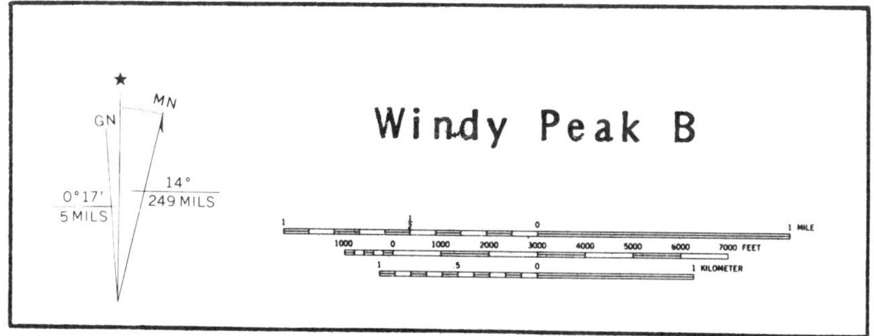

Windy Peak A, page 190

Topaz D, page 189

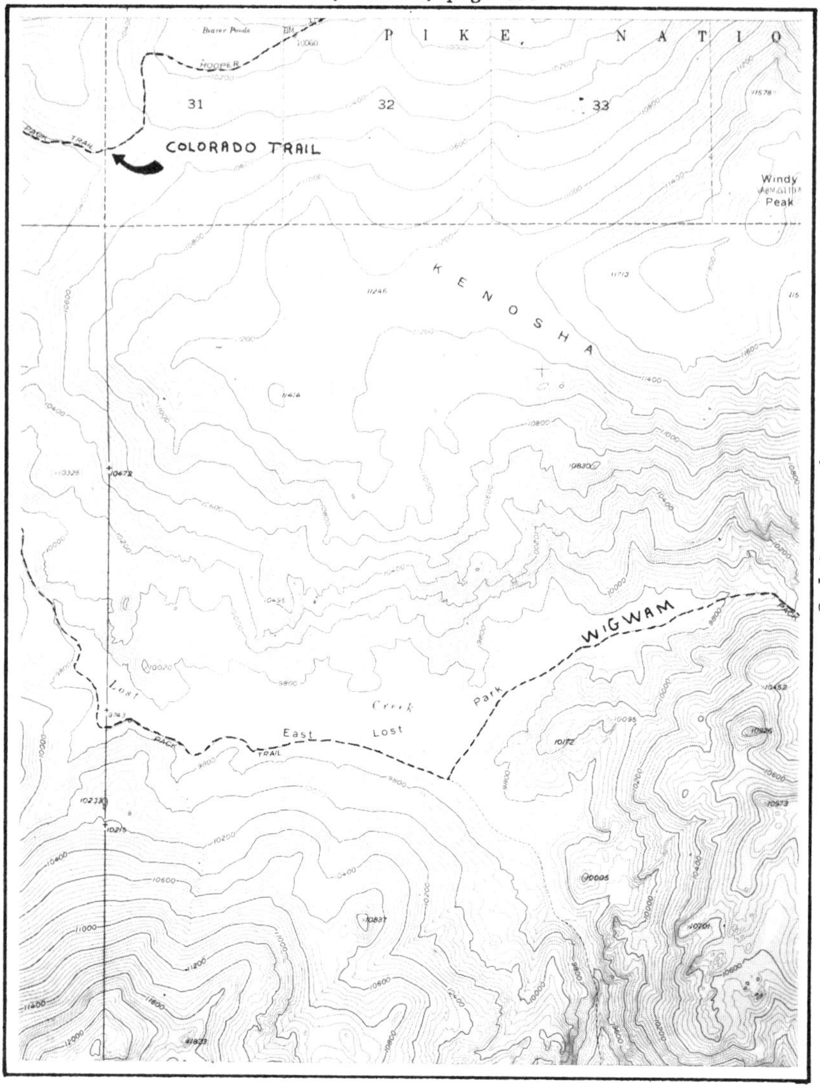

PIKE NATIO
31
32
33
COLORADO TRAIL
Windy Peak
KENOSHA
WIGWAM
Lost
East Lost Creek Park
PARK TRAIL

Windy Peak D, page 193

McCurdy Mountain A, page 149

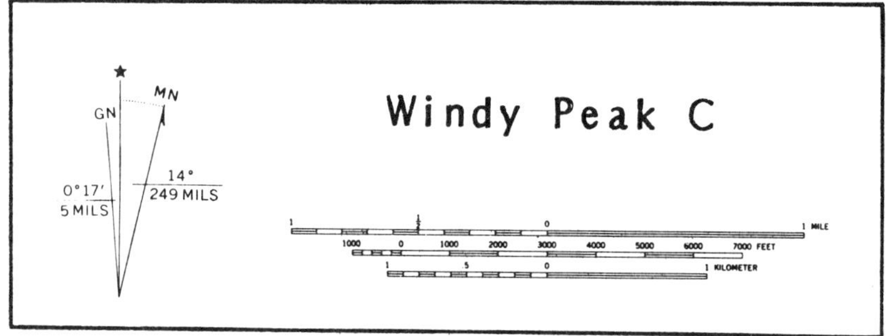

Windy Peak B, page 191

Windy Peak C, page 192

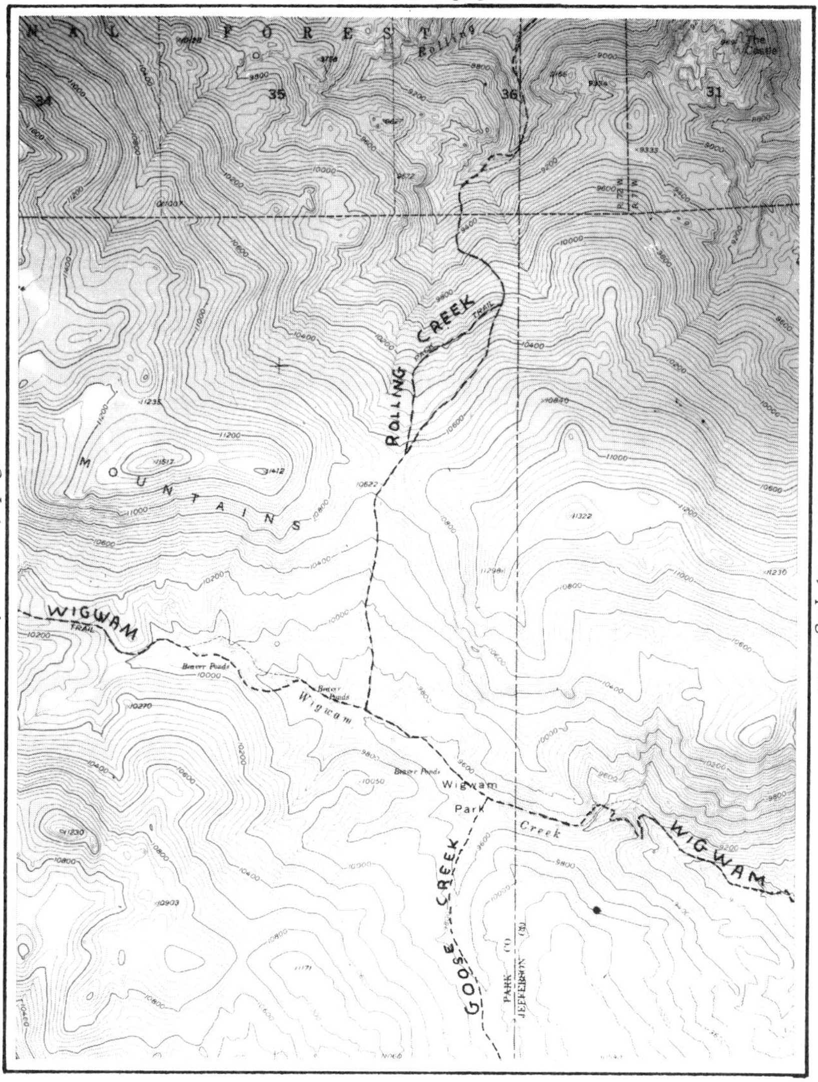

Green Mountain C, page 132

McCurdy Mountain B, page 150

Windy Peak D

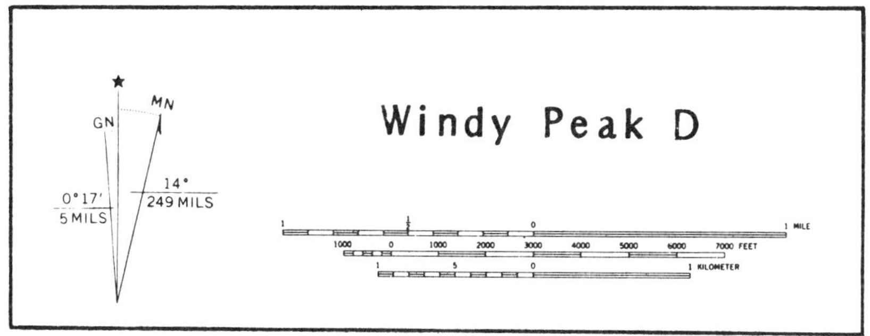

Divide B, page 126

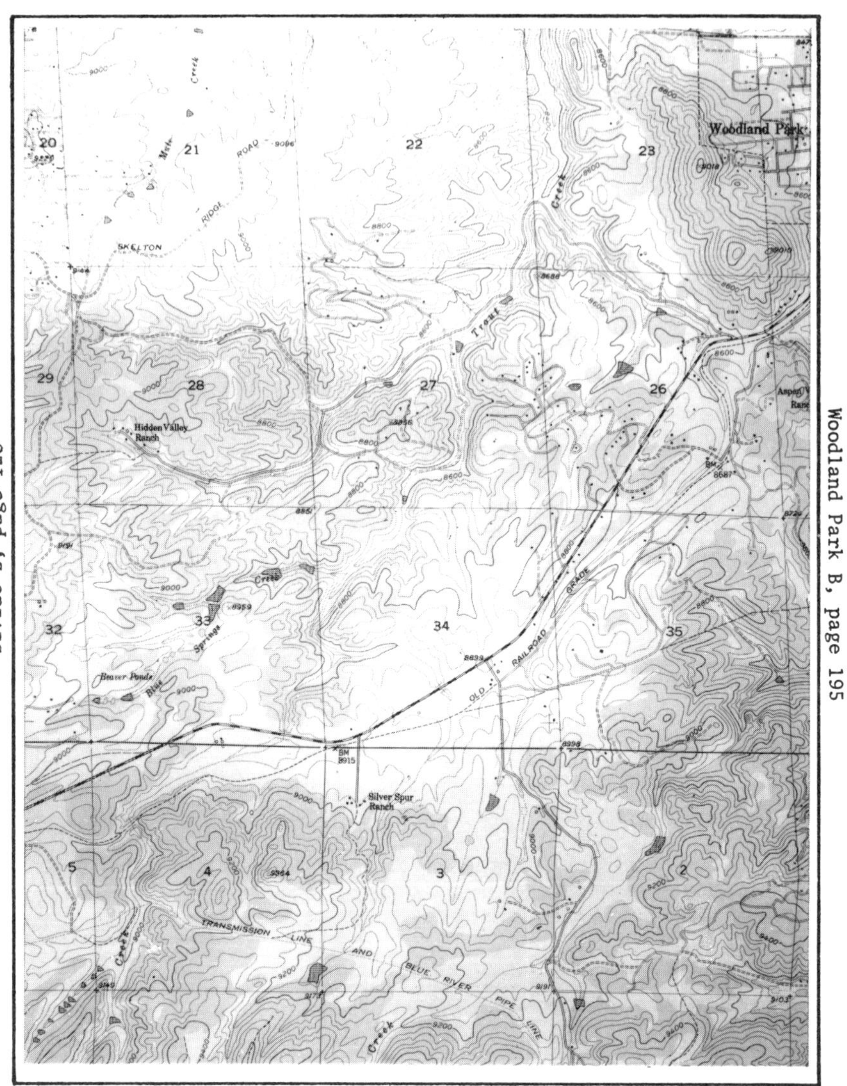

Woodland Park B, page 195

Woodland Park C, page 196

Woodland Park A

GN
MN
0°20′
1 MILS
12½°
222 MILS

1 ½ 0 1 MILE
1000 0 1000 2000 3000 4000 5000 6000 7000 FEET
1 .5 0 1 KILOMETER

Woodland Park A, page 194

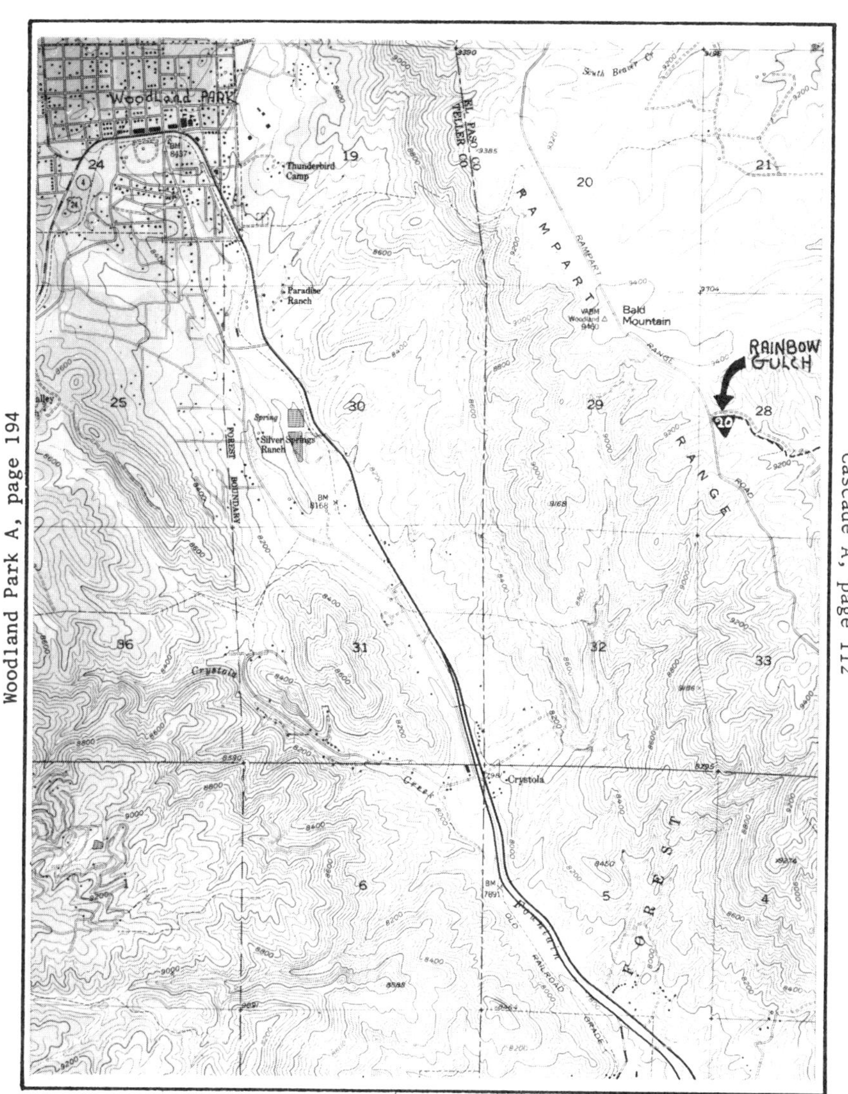

Cascade A, page 112

Woodland Park D, page 197

GN
MN
0°20′
1 MILS
12½°
222 MILS

Woodland Park B

1 ½ 0 1 MILE
1000 0 1000 2000 3000 4000 5000 6000 7000 FEET
1 .5 0 1 KILOMETER

Woodland Park A, page 194

Divide D, page 128

Woodland Park D, page 197

Pikes Peak A, page 174

Woodland Park C

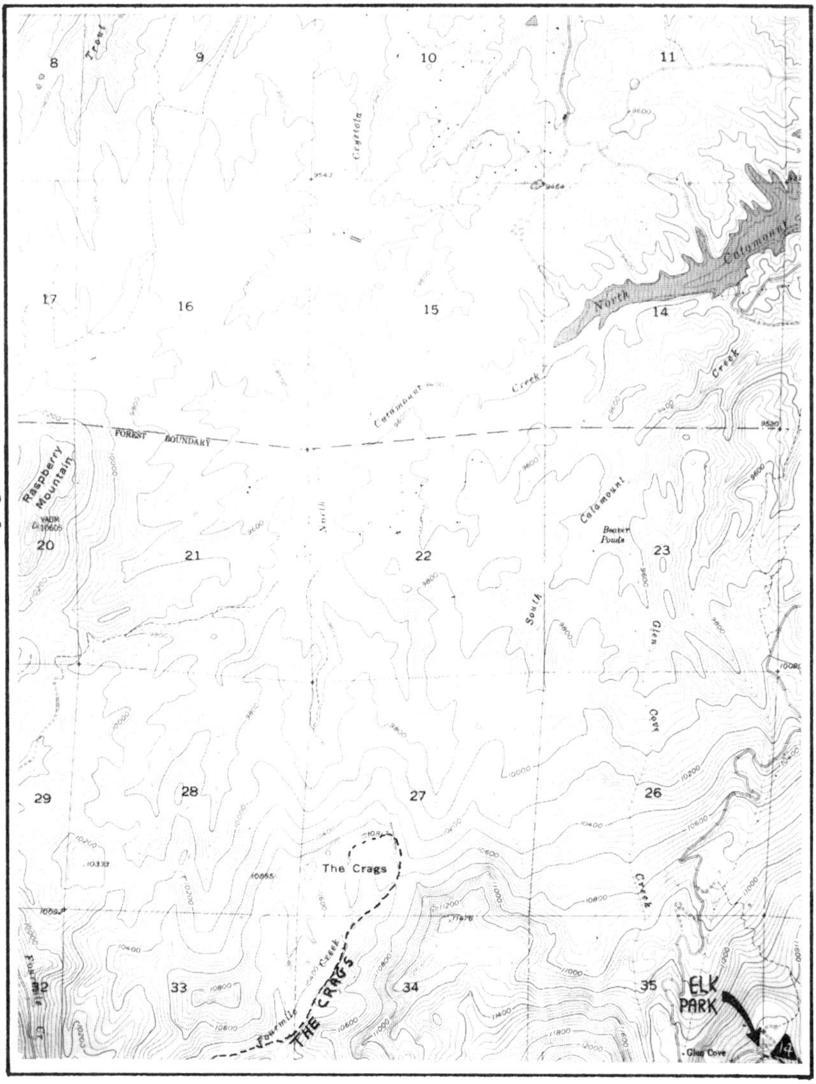

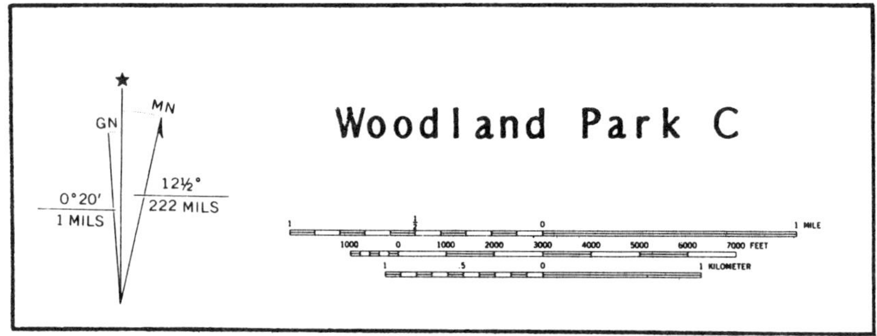

Woodland Park B, page 195

Woodland Park C, page 196

Cascade C, page 114

Pikes Peak B, page 175

Woodland Park D

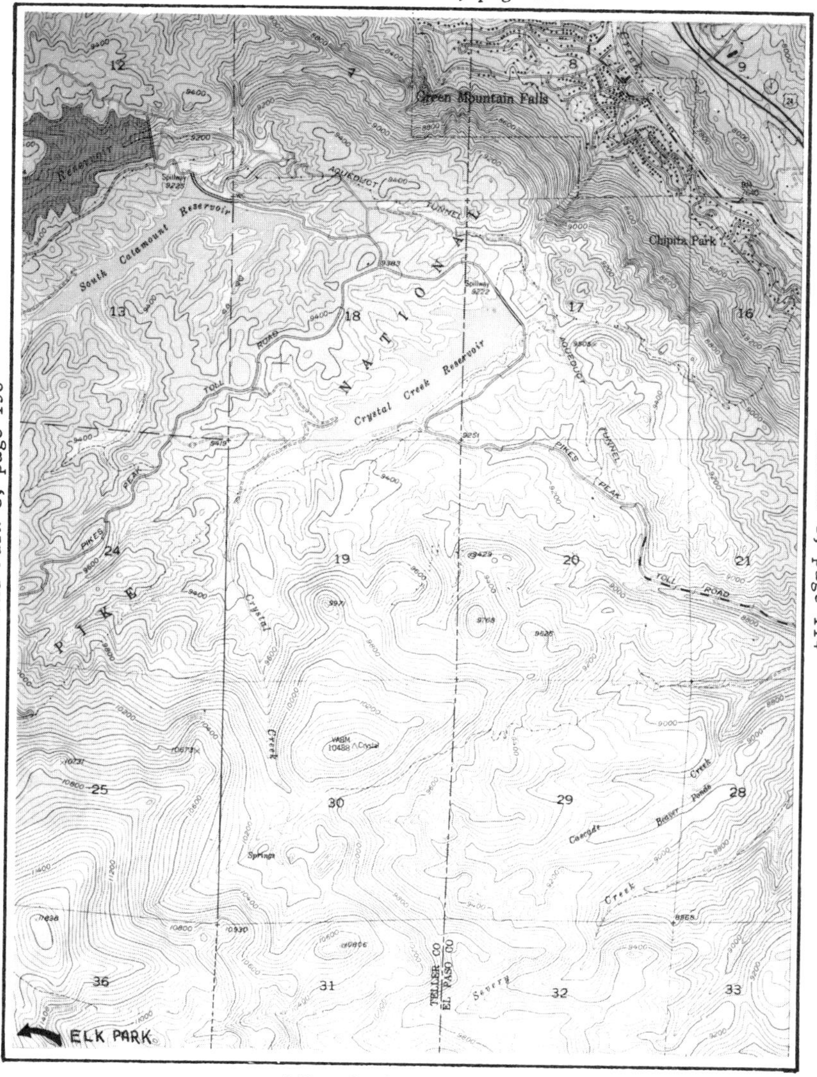

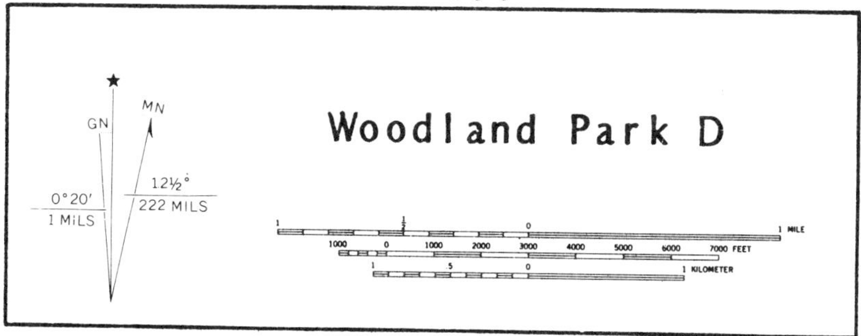